RECOMBINANT URBANISM

Conceptual Modeling in Architecture, Urban Design, and City Theory

David Grahame Shane

Published in Great Britain in 2005 by Wiley-Academy, a division of John Wiley & Sons Ltd

Copyright © 2005 John Wiley & Sons Ltd,
The Atrium, Southern Gate, Chichester, West Sussex PO19 8SQ, England
Telephone (+44) 1243 779777

Email (for orders and customer service enquiries): cs-books@wiley.co.uk
Visit our Home Page on www.wileyeurope.com or www.wiley.com

Other Wiley Editorial Offices
John Wiley & Sons Inc., 111 River Street, Hoboken, NJ 07030, USA
Jossey-Bass, 989 Market Street, San Francisco, CA 94103-1741, USA
Wiley-VCH Verlag GmbH, Boschstr. 12, D-69469 Weinheim, Germany
John Wiley & Sons Australia Ltd, 33 Park Road, Milton, Queensland 4064, Australia
John Wiley & Sons (Asia) Pte Ltd, 2 Clementi Loop #02-01, Jin Xing Distripark, Singapore 129809
John Wiley & Sons Canada Ltd, 22 Worcester Road, Etobicoke, Ontario, Canada M9W 1L1

ISBN 0470093293 (Cloth)
ISBN 0470093315 (Paperback)
UPC 723812768172 (Cloth)
UPC 723812768189 (Paperback)

Cover and book design by Artmediapress Ltd, London
Cover image – Collage by Ward Verbakel 2005
Printed and bound in Italy by Conti Tipocolor

RECOMBINANT URBANISM

I dedicate this book to my wife, Regina Wickham, and to our children Ben, Rachael, and Michael; to my mother, Irene Shane Diederichsen, and to Jurgen Diederichsen; and to my late father, Asher Lewis Shane, who taught me to love books.

Preface

Any discussion of "recombinant" systems must begin with Francis Crick and James Watson, who first popularized the concept in their descriptions of DNA in the 1960s. I was a student in London when Crick, Watson, and Maurice Wilkins received a Nobel Prize in 1962 and was struck by the power of their discovery. There were clearly many potential applications to architecture and urbanism.

The discovery of DNA's structure by Crick and Watson in 1953 revealed the mechanism underlying mutation: a coded, heritable, alterable sequence of amino acids. If you change the sequence, you change the structure of the organism. I was haunted by the idea that there might be an urban sequencing apparatus analogous to biology's DNA spiral code. How urban actors related to this mechanism, however, was a mystery. Even apart from the difference of sheer scale, there are limits to the analogies that can be drawn between the two fields; the deliberate design of cities is clearly different from biological processes of change, and the flow of energy through a biological cell is clearly different from the flow of energy through a city. Nonetheless, the idea that urban actors shared some sort of urban DNA provided an inspiration—and lingering question—through many years of research. What were these shared patterns and how were they communicated from one generation to another?

Merriam-Webster's Online Dictionary defines *recombinant* first as "relating to or exhibiting genetic recombination," second as "relating to or containing recombinant DNA; also: produced by recombinant DNA technology." Recombinant DNA is "genetically engineered DNA prepared *in vitro* by cutting up DNA molecules and splicing together specific DNA fragments usually from more than one species of organism." Recombination itself is the process of "crossing-over and independent assortment of new combinations of genes in progeny that did not appear in the parents." The process of recombination allows for change in actors and their responses to altered circumstances, explaining the mutation of traits from one generation to another and Darwin's natural selection process.

Similar processes of mutation can be seen in patterns of development that we recognize as urban. Seeking increased efficiency, profit, or pleasure, urban actors splice together urban structures that handle urban flows, producing new settings for their activities or reusing old ones for altered circumstances. Urban splicing, analogously to genetic recombination, involves the sorting, layering, overlapping, and combining of disparate elements to create new combinations. Mutant or hybrid forms are produced that give the city its edge, allowing actors to grow and change without a prescribed future. Urban actors engaged in these processes create spaces for their activities in the layered spatial matrix of the city. Further, I believe that the terms of this activity have been fundamentally altered by the acceleration of communication networks and the feedback of information to citizens, governments, and corporations on a global scale. I am interested in theories that help us operate in a complex and recombinant world where nobody is in charge of the overall system. Feedback inside informational systems provides checks and balances without preordaining every interaction.

Urban theorist Kevin Lynch has provided us with a language to discuss urban recombination through his techniques of city-modeling. Lynch creates a language to describe the systems of the city with clarity, analyzing dynamics at every scale from the pedestrian to the automotive and beyond. His research on urban and conceptual models remains a valuable tool for studying our contemporary, global, sprawling megacities, whose patterns we can best name using his terminology: galaxies, polycentric nets, lacework nets, alternating nets. In this book I attempt to interpret his work afresh as a quasi-genetic recombinant system. I link his three great normative models—the City of Faith, the City as a Machine, and the Ecological City—into an overall transformative, recombinant system of urban elements activated by urban actors. In this recombinant system, no one actor dominates.

Sorting, sequencing, splicing, and recombining urban elements has a long history. I, too, have worked as a recombinant agent. In searching out ways to handle the city's intricacies, I have leaned heavily on the shoulders of many earlier urban writers in addition to Lynch, especially Spiro Kostof, Françoise Choay, Michel Foucault, Colin Rowe, and Alvin Boyarsky. I try to convey these great authors' original insights, yet also bend them to my own purposes. The result is necessarily a book that seems immersed in other people's voices at times, half sunk in other authors' theories. Yet readers will see that while I attempt to be true to my sources, I also have my own agenda, my own reasons for selecting these authors in the first place. And finally, I am not a Lynch, Kostof, Choay, or Foucault specialist and so have had to draw on close readings by those who are. I owe many debts, and try to acknowledge them in the body of my text.

My treatment of Lynch is a good example of my approach to creative appropriation and recombination. I never studied with Lynch nor met him; it is quite possible that I misunderstand him. But while using his work for my own argument about urban morphogenesis and recombination, I try to state his goals and methods clearly. Similarly, I reinterpret the teachers of my youth in the Archigram Group in London and Colin Rowe at Cornell to support my own ideas about the breakdown of the Modernist ideal of the machine city and its fragmentation into special enclaves.

Thus, like all urban actors I have collaged together fragments to achieve my goals, piecing together diverse examples to illustrate my arguments and point toward what I believe is the future. Lynch gives us a vocabulary with which to discuss the postmodern city-territory at large; Colin Rowe and Fred Koetter give us a vocabulary for describing cities constructed of urban fragments, each under the control of a dominant actor or group of actors. From these two disparate languages, working at different scales, I concoct a third, a hybrid that uses elements from both as well as Foucault's concept of the heterotopia as a place that facilitates urban change.

As an aid to focusing on important design issues I next offer seven points or benchmark concepts as a guide to the first four chapters. These claims about the present and predictions about the future are intended to help readers (and especially designers) not only to move through the subsequent text but to reconceptualize their urban situation and adapt to their new urban environment.

1. *The disappearance of the master plan.* There is no one person in charge of the postmodern city; the age of the single authority in absolute charge of a vast city is over. There is no longer one logic, voice, or time-clock that can decree or coordinate comprehensive changes. Designers must work with multiple actors and multiple clocks. Change occurs piecemeal, in incremental fragments ranging in scale from the minute to the partial.

2. *The incorporation of the irrational in the postmodern city.* Given the absence of a single center of control, the old codes of single-function zoning will inevitably give place to a heterogeneous and flexible system that accommodates multiple actors more easily. There will be in the city strange juxtapositions of wealth and poverty, efficiency and waste, industry and commerce, residential life and work, pleasure and pain. Rather than suppressing the irrational in a collective unconscious as in the past, urban actors are articulating their desires without guilt, allowing the uncanny to appear in everyday urban situations and juxtapositions. Designers will therefore have to work in an increasingly "irrational" situation and incorporate the irrational into their work. Actors will still seek social justice, but without the effective help (or hindrance) of a central controller or censor. This absence of central control allows leisure activities and previously illicit pleasures to surface throughout the city. But the absence of a central total authority does not mean that there will not be new repressive responses from conservative forces. These forces, too, will be part of the new urban situation. They will use it for *their* purposes.

3. *The city is a chaotic feedback system.* As net importers of energy and people, cities have always existed in a state of imbalance and disequilibrium. To propose a city that exists in a state of perfect equilibrium, ecologically or socially, is to propose an impossible utopia. Jane Jacobs highlighted the dynamic nature of cities in her work from the 1960s onwards, showing that it is based on urban actors' need to measure and mediate differences in contested spaces. For Jacobs this is a good thing: insofar as cities become uniform and homogenous they become stagnant, fixed, inflexible, incapable of change, dead. Through conflict, contestation, and the negotiation of differences, urban actors create new knowledge and new products, which aids human survival.

4. *The city is composed of heterogeneous flow systems.* Kevin Lynch invented a terminology of heterogeneous urban systems to deal with the new urban

situation, providing tools for the discussion of what later critics termed the "reverse city" (Viganò) or "net city" (Oswald), which are ultimately descended from Frank Lloyd Wright's Broadacre City, the city claiming vast landscapes. To enable us to track this new, decentralized reality Lynch shifted the focus of observation to large-scale systems. Here he found new urban patterns—stars, nets, constellations, and so forth—held together by modern communication and transportation systems as essential armatures. He contrasted this multiform city with the traditional small-scale city enclaves of the old Euro-Asian urban order, which, he argued, remain embedded in the larger city. He examined the lived reality of the small-scale city through psychological interviews and mapping projects to find, in his words, the "image of the city" alive in the minds of its inhabitants. Unlike the Modernists, who simply condemned the sprawling megalopolis or the historic enclaves at its center, Lynch sought to uncover their inward logics as a matter of pragmatic concern.

5. *The city is a patchwork of heterogeneous fragments.* Lynch gives little guidance for understanding how the rational and irrational desires of urban actors are accommodated in particular locations or enclaves. In creating these patterns or "patches" of urban order, actors exclude elements and actors who do not easily fit. In considering this problem I turn to collage as an inclusive strategy, working from Rowe and Koetter's *Collage City* (1978). This was an early attempt to understand the city as a multiscalar system bound together by disparate urban actors and elements, a system of fragments. Rowe's expertise on Palladio, Cubism, layering, and transparency lent the work depth while Koetter focused on the multiscalar urban elements composing the postmodern city-territory. Collage techniques analogous to those developed by Dada and the Surrealists in the 1920s and 1930s, wielded by actors operating without an overall restraining system, can be seen as generating many of the combinations and surprising juxtapositions of postmodern urbanity. The Urban Design Group in New York City in the 1960s applied similar theories after the demise of Robert Moses and his previously all-powerful highway master-planning techniques. *Collage City* provides strategic *method* without giving a complex universe of *models* (these are provided by Lynch) or examining the many ways in which elements can combine and recombine across a *broad city-territory.*

6. *Urban heterotopias are specialized patches, acting as testbeds of change.* I use Michel Foucault's theory of heterotopias to articulate how urban systems and fragments change in modern and postmodern urban systems as actors slice and recombine urban elements. Foucault's concept of the heterotopia enriches Rowe and Koetter's complex and "ambiguous" building typologies as urban instruments on a medium scale that can accommodate diverse urban actors over time. In the 1970s, Foucault identified particular places in the city where processes of change and hybridization are facilitated, dubbing them

heterotopias. Actors' utopian aspirations are at work inside the heterotopia as rules and goals, yet heterotopias are delimited, time-bound places, not actual utopias. Foucault instanced clinics, hospitals, schools, and prisons as heterotopic enclaves where professionals seek to cure the sick, educate students, and reform criminals. This heterotopic system is crucial to modernity, its goal being to rationalize society and to create a more open and equitable system *through architectural means*. In order to facilitate this process, urban actors build miniature cities, with multiple cells and codes that differ from those of the host city in ways that allow internal controls and interactions forbidden outside.

By bottling up change in heterotopic spatial pockets or patches, urban actors can conduct concrete utopian experiments without endangering the established disequilibrium of the larger system. If an experiment is successful, actors can export the new model, copying (and altering) it so that it becomes, over time, a new norm. What were once surprising and surreal juxtapositions can—and have—become integrated slowly into the social practices of the host city. Foucault distinguished many types of heterotopia; I concentrate on only three, heterotopias of crisis, deviance, and illusion, linking each to associated urban actors and models.

7. *The city is a layered structure of heterotopic nodes and networks*. Urban actors use collage and various bonding systems to form patches of order in the city; they also create heterotopias with multicellular internal structures to facilitate change. Urban actors can arrange such patches or cells horizontally across the landscape in the "reverse city" configuration or concentrate them in nodes, in which case the vertical section becomes all-important. Or they can do both at once. Understanding this allowed designers in the 1980s and 1990s to develop heterotopic strategies for integrating the most diverse actors and activities. Landscape Urbanists could accommodate both growth and shrinkage across a city-territory in their view of urban systems, giving their work particular relevance to shrinking postindustrial cities like Detroit.

The disequilibrium of the dynamic city was mirrored in the 1980s in the sectional configurations and recombinant poetry of the Deconstructivists' imagined city sections. They and other designers incorporated the irrational, the lack of a central reference point, and the "subconscious" in their invention of new, highly mediated (media-rich) public spaces in the hyperdense nodes of the global network city. The layering of elements in space became especially important, and a new poetry emerged from the ambiguity of potentially contradictory readings made possible by the abandonment of single-point perspective. Systems of collage, bricolage, decoupage, montage, assemblage, and rhizomic assemblage (all discussed in later chapters) described different bonding techniques in this new, hypermediated environment. These bonding techniques reflect the relationships between urban actors and the dynamics of flows between each patch or urban fragment.

These seven points underline my belief that the postmodern city is in a qualitatively new urban condition. Urban actors and designers now deal inevitably and everywhere with urban situations that are heterogenous and mixed, not simple and pure. I believe also that the role played by media and communications systems in the dispersed reverse city has altered the way we see and use cities. Information is available to citizens as they move through the city in ways that did not exist before, and the mass-marketing of place extends beyond the previous pilgrimage sites of the great religions to Disney World and its like.

These seven points also reveal my perspective as a European now resident in America. Despite my wide network of information and sources, as a writer, urbanist, and urban actor I have distinct limitations based on my own interests and experiences. One of these limitations is my Eurocentrism. This is a product of limited travel—mostly to Europe (including Istanbul), the United States, and Japan—rather than of a bias against global developments. I try to write about places that I have visited personally and so have some hands-on sense of, though I break this rule sometimes for the sake of exceptionally illuminating examples. This self-imposed rule limits my scope to cities I know well or have at least visited, such as Hong Kong, Caracas, and Melbourne. The result is that this book omits the massive urbanization taking place in Africa, for example, and on the Indian subcontinent. My hope is that by limiting this book's scope I can keep its feet on the ground. Despite its wide range of examples, it is not intended as an all-embracing text: it is focused on specific problems of urban design.

In *Recombinant Urbanism* I attempt to splice together many strands of urban design in order to strengthen urban design as an emerging field of inquiry. I have sought to provide designers and students of urbanism with a working approach to cross-fertilization and interchange between disparate urban actors. I hope readers will be patient; my own choices and preferences will emerge toward the end of the book. On the way there I have tried to give some idea of the rich ground out of which my opinions emerge. My goal is to outline useful strategies for designers and urban actors who must work in the "expanded field" of the twenty-first-century network city, a wired and mediated environment that comprises sparsely populated landscapes as well as hyperdense, global city nodes. We need new strategies and tactics to deal with this hybrid patchwork of past environmental traditions and cybernetic, informational environments.

Introduction

This book reexamines the way in which urban actors recombine elements in order to create conceptual models of the city at various scales. Urban actors work as catalysts in the city and depend on conceptual models to guide them, whether they act as architect, urban designer, or landscape or city designer. A city model enables a designer to construct an understanding of the city and its component elements, facilitating design decisions. It orients urban actors in complex situations and at multiple scales.

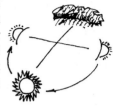

Kevin Lynch: City of Faith diagram detail, A Theory of Good City Form, 1981

Urban theorists have identified various normative city models (almost always in threes) that act as stabilizing patterns for large urban systems over time. The advantage of these models is that they combine a system of normative ideals—notions of what the city *should* be like—with simple organizational structures and clear methods of implementation. Further, each model tends to represent a stage of urban development. The three stages associated with the three models are often termed the *preindustrial*, *industrial*, and *postindustrial*.

In *A Theory of Good City Form* (1981), Kevin Lynch described his own influential triad of models, the City of Faith, the City as a Machine, and the City as an Organism (a.k.a. the Ecological City). Standard urban-history texts such as Spiro Kostof's The City Shaped (1991) cite these three models, but without describing how each might transition to another. I will argue that all three are built from three basic urban elements—namely, the armature, a linear organizing device; the enclave, a self-centering device; and the heterotopia, a type of hybrid space embedded within the larger system—and that the heterotopia, in particular, plays a key role both in stabilizing city models and in catalyzing transitions from one city model to another. The armature, the enclave, and the heterotopia are the basic components of any city, constantly combined and recombined in different cultures, places, and periods.

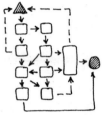

Lynch: City as a Machine diagram detail, Good City Form, 1981

In Chapter 1, I focus on the "city theory" of Kevin Lynch, outlining his attempt to provide a trio of city models that would take into account not only the static structure of the city but also its transient and utopian aspects. Lynch criticized his contemporaries for their shortsighted attention to city fragments, total control, and the urban design of local settings based on functional and economic considerations rather than on higher aspirations. I end the chapter by tracing Lynch's influence on various contemporary designers who emphasize "city design" as a large-scale, systemic process, such as the Landscape Urbanist movement.

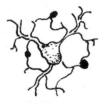

Lynch: City as an Organism diagram, Good City Form, 1981

In Chapter 2, I outline the object of Lynch's unflattering remarks, the theory of "urban design." This theory was linked, in his mind, largely to the design of shopping malls. While there is some truth to his accusations about the origins of urban design, Lynch himself studied malls and participated in major changes that were taking place in the adaptive reuse of traditional city centers (e.g., the creative use of old city codes and regulations). His own *The Image of the City*

Opposite Portrait of the mathematician Lucas Pacioli and an unknown young man, *Jacopo de'Barbari, 1440–1515 (© Photo SCALA, Florence)*

Left *Istanbul bazaar, 1464*
Right *Giuseppe Mengoni: Galleria Vittorio Emanuele, Milan, 1877*

(1960) and work on downtown Boston (1958–59), which preceded I. M. Pei's urban-design Boston master plan of 1961, contributed to these changes. Such interventions accelerated beyond his control and his taste, however, in the commodification of downtown real estate in the 1970s and 1980s. I also look at the work of Jonathan Barnett and the Urban Design Group in New York in the 1960s and at the emergence of a competing theory of urban fragmentation in Rowe and Koetter's *Collage City* (1978). The European tradition of urban design (exemplified by the Enlightenment extensions to Munich, Germany, in the 1820s) was poorly prepared for the advent of Modernism and the sprawling city-region, originating as it did in the closed perspectives of the Renaissance. Rowe and Koetter sought to bring this tradition up to date, allowing practitioners to recombine traditional elements in carefully controlled suburban enclaves of stasis (as also later advocated by members of the American New Urbanist movement). I also show how the Deconstructivist designers of the 1980s and 1990s altered city-design codes to produce their novel recombinations, learning from *Collage City*'s analysis of the layering of the city section and plan. Here I emphasize the armature's role as a linear organizing device in urban design (organizing the vertical section of the city or skyscraper) and the role of the heterotopia in enabling experimentation.

In Chapter 3, I examine the armature and enclave in detail, describing their combinatorial operation in different city models and urban-design fragments. I conclude the chapter by giving examples of various combinations of armatures and enclaves, ancient, modern, and contemporary.

In Chapter 4, I examine heterotopias as places of change in more detail, looking at different strategies for combining and recombining urban elements in plan or section at various scales. I stress the altered situation of the postmodern city and the role of heterotopias in accommodating accelerated change brought about by faster communication and transportation systems. I also review the role of heterotopias in stabilizing the three great normative city models that constitute Lynch's great gift to city designers and urban designers alike.

It is the argument of this book that cities are necessarily built around a variety of patches or enclaves that are interconnected by an ecology of armatures—transportation and communication networks—set in the landscape and crucially complicated by a wide variety of embedded heterotopias. Heterotopias are primary places of urban change, accommodating exceptional activities and persons. I distinguish three types of heterotopia, selected from Michel Foucault's larger list. I believe that the emergence of enclaves, armatures, and heterotopic, hybrid spaces is fundamental to the urbanization process.

The first type, the heterotopia of crisis, hides agents of change within the standard building types of the city, masking their catalytic activity. The second, Foucault's heterotopia of deviance, comprises institutions that foster change in highly controlled environments. In these small pockets of highly disciplined order, relationships between members of society are organizationally restructured to facilitate the emergence of a new order that may transform society. Examples include universities, clinics, hospitals, courthouses, prisons, barracks, boarding schools, colonial towns, and factories. Here people are gathered, sorted, manipulated, and eventually exported by stable public organizations that provide institutional and cultural continuity—and novelty. In the case of the factory, for instance, goods are produced in an ordered environment that introduces people to the discipline of industrial work, implying a new normative model for society. The urban actors in charge of the larger urban scene, whoever they might be, act to enforce the new codes.

The third category of heterotopic change-fostering place comprises realms of apparent chaos and creative, imaginative freedom. In the heterotopia of illusion change is concentrated and accelerated. The rules governing the local system's organization can change quickly and arbitrarily. Such places include formal and informal institutional markets, bazaars, shopping arcades, department stores, atria, malls, megamalls, stock exchanges, casinos, hotels, motels, cinemas, theaters, museums (including museums of contemporary art), fairgrounds, universal exhibitions, theme parks, spas, gyms, bordellos, and more. Here the primary values are pleasure and leisure, consumption and display, not work.

Clearly, cities change. The question is: how? This book's view of the urbanization process is that the novel, unstable, shifting processes developed in heterotopic places of change can transform each of the three dominant, normative city models from one to another. Such transformations have occurred throughout history and continue to occur all around us as actors search for fresh recombinations of existing elements that will better house their activities.

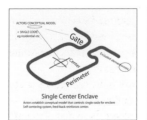
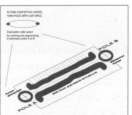
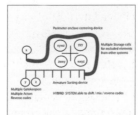

Left *Enclave diagram*
Centre *Armature diagram*
Right *Heterotopia diagram*

a

b

c

a, **c)** *Armature; rooftop view. The Fremont Street Experience, Las Vegas, NV, Jon Jerde Partnership, 1995*
b) *Armature plan and section, Fremont Street Experience*
Opposite *Enclave. Multilayered analysis of Munich, drawn by Rodrigo Gardia Dall'Orso, 2004*

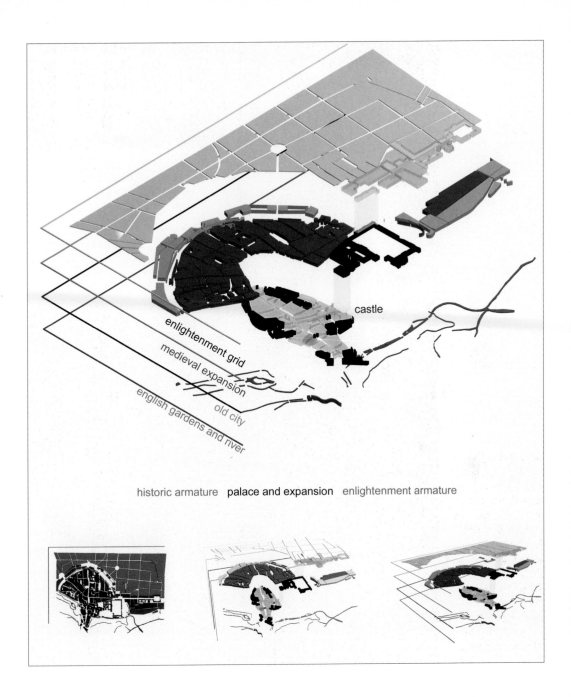

castle

enlightenment grid

medieval expansion

old city

english gardens and river

historic armature   **palace and expansion**   enlightenment armature

Chapter 1

What Is City Theory?

1.1 WHAT IS A CITY?

> A city is a relatively large, dense, and permanent settlement of socially
> heterogeneous individuals.
> —L. Wirth, "Urbanism as a Way of Life"[1]

> Cities are places where a certain energized crowding of people takes
> place. This is nothing to do with absolute size or with absolute numbers:
> it has to do with settlement density.
> —Spiro Kostof, *The City Shaped* [2]

At first sight, it seems easy to define a "city." In the Eurocentric tradition, as in many other cultures, a city is a dense settlement distinct from the countryside, with *city* and *country* forming one of the basic cultural polarities. For many centuries, an actual wall separated the city from the country. This separation was reinforced on occasion by regulations that provided for a defensive glacis or no-build zone around the wall, forcing the development of sub-urbs (less-than-cities) at some distance from the city gate. This separation, primarily a military and defensive strategy, entailed a system of enforcement: taboos, gates, and walls to keep the worlds of country and city distinct. Movement from one to the other was controlled, as was the incorporation of agricultural land into the city (the latter required expansion of the walls). The city was a specialized enclave accumulating wealth within the context of a largely agrarian, rural, feudal society organized around farms and villages and powered by animals and serfs working the land. In the feudal system, people were tied to the land and were inherited with it as tenants and laborers; city inhabitants were "free" in the sense that they were released from this form of bondage.

This system of walls and taboos is built into the structure of the English language. The word *city* denotes one point on a descending urban scale recognized by Anglo-American dictionaries and defining a network of relationships. At the top of this traditional hierarchy is the *metropolis*, defined by Webster as "the chief city of a country, the capital" and derived from the Greek *metropolis*, meaning "parent state" (*metro* = mother, *polis* = city-state).[3] A "city" Webster defines as "an inhabited place with a greater size population than a town or a village." The Oxford English Dictionary defines a "city" as an *important* town, a "town created by city charter, especially as containing a cathedral (but not all cathedral towns are cities, and vice versa)." The *town*, the next rung down on the urban ladder, is "a collection of houses enclosed by a wall or hedge: a considerable collection of dwellings etc. (larger than a village and often opposed

Opposite Effects of Good Government in the City *(detail)*, Ambrogio Lorenzetti, 1285–c. 1348. (© Photo SCALA, Florence)

to the country)." Below this is the *village*, "an assemblage of houses, larger than a hamlet and smaller than a town," and at the bottom is the *hamlet*, "a small village, especially one without a church."[4]

Sebastian Serlio, in his *Five Books of Architecture* (c. 1537), gives visual analogies for the levels of this traditional European urban hierarchy. He recognizes three basic urban settings for theatrical productions, envisioning each within the representational framework of the newly discovered "science" of single-point perspective: the Noble (or Tragic), the Comic, and the Satyric. Serlio bases his three settings or scenes on Vitruvius's descriptions of Roman theater sets in the first century BC, but they also mirror the emerging Renaissance city and its specializations. To present them he exploits the newly developed medium of the printed book. All three of his stage-set woodcuts depict streets and are clearly "urban" in terms of the dictionary-defined urban spectrum, even if the hamlet, the lowest rung of the urban ladder, is half sunk in the natural environment.

Each of Serlio's urban settings constitutes a distinct visual order and is conceived by him as the life-world setting for the activities of a specialized urban actor in the Renaissance city network. Each such actor requires a particular environment and a particular set of props or symbols. For example, ancient Roman monuments are the thematic signature of the Noble scene, where all transpires amid a fixed, hierarchical social order; the corner merchant's shop is the thematic signature of the Comic scene, which is completed by a brothel and disorderly layout.[5] Each scene thus represents a different urban system; each has its specific actors and attractors, activities and settings, performance spaces and props.

In the Tragic or Noble scene, the street is ordered, classical, dignified. This is the symbolic setting for the activities of princes and courtiers acting in the public interest of the state. Their street of classical palaces leads from the city center to the city gate. Beyond the city gate, ancient Roman funeral monuments—obelisks and pyramids—are scattered around the approach to the city, which is glimpsed through the gate's arched opening. At the midpoint of the street, dwarfed by the Renaissance palaces of the princes, crouches an ancient Roman temple modeled on an actual one beside the Tiber in Rome. Here, too, are the ancient Roman Tower of the Winds (from the Forum), a corner of the Colosseum, and the dome of the Pantheon. There can be no doubt about Serlio's identification of this city-scene with ancient Rome, the imperial capital (largest city of the ancient world at one time, with over one million inhabitants)—if not the *real* ancient Rome, at least the ancient Rome of his imagination.[6]

Serlio's second image of the city, the Comic scene, is far less orderly. The dynamic give-and-take of the marketplace creates a chaotic setting in which each individual expresses himself or herself from the bottom up, disrupting the overall order. The Comic scene displays diverse building alignments, heights, and styles. The street is a dead-end, a cul-de-sac blocked by a half-ruined church or chapel with a tower. Here Serlio represents the commercial city of the medieval trading network that stretched from northern Europe (Bruges and Antwerp) to

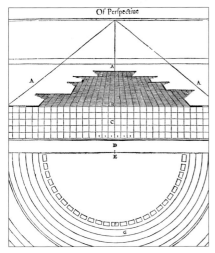

Left *Sebastian Serlio: perspective construction for stage sets,* The Five Books of Architecture, *ca.1537*
Right *Serlio: the Tragic scene,* Five Books of Architecture

Istanbul and beyond. Each merchant inside the city walls strove for maximum self-expression; each house differed from its neighbors, announcing itself as loudly as possible by its signage. Row houses served both as dwellings and as places of trade where apprentices from the countryside were trained. In a Gothic corner store in Serlio's woodcut of the Comic scene, the trading floor and counter open out onto the street while the rooftop bears fabrics drying on lines, fresh from weaving and dyeing in the factory below. Another corner building, closer to the front of the set, houses an inn with a projecting, wood-framed upper story that is labeled as a brothel. The church at the end of the street suffers from obvious neglect, with a small tree sprouting from its fortified bell tower. This image refers to the clan enclaves called *castellare* that formed in medieval Italian hill towns such as Siena or San Giminiano. Each clan enclave had its own fortified church-cum-citadel within the city walls, often in a cul-de-sac. Shakespeare's *Romeo and Juliet* (c. 1592) references a similar urban mythology (and grimly balkanized reality).[7]

At first glance, Serlio's third point on the urban spectrum does not appear to be urban at all. The city has sunk in the landscape. An avenue of large trees dominates the scene, forming the setting for a series of small, isolated cottages. This avenue terminates at an inn, the focus of village life. This Satyric scene represents the hamlet, the rural terminus of the urban hierarchy. It is in deliberate contrast to the densely urban scenography of the two previous stage sets. Here the urban actor is at a disadvantage and must work within the fluidity of weather, crops, farming techniques, and necessarily dispersed settlement patterns. The name *Satyric* is significant, for classical satyrs were half-human, half-animal hybrids. (Recall Shakespeare's use of a donkey's head in *A Midsummer Night's Dream*, c. 1595, to transform a man into a creature half human, half ass.) The geometric formality of the Satyric scene's tree-lined village street is the last trace

of a perspectival street structure that is merging with nature. Serlio belonged to a generation of Mannerist designers who specialized in strange hybrids that disturbed the perfect, smooth symmetries of the early Renaissance, such as Bramante's Tempietto at the Vatican, Rome (San Pietro in Montorio, 1502). Similarly, Serlio's designs for city gates offered disturbing hybrids, merging rough-cut stonework with finely cut, classical masonry.

The Satyric scene is intended to mock both the pretensions of the city's classical princes and the bourgeois shambles of the mercantile enclave. Like Shakespeare's country bumpkins in *A Midsummer Night's Dream*, Serlio's villagers stand outside the folly of the urban court and mercantile bourgeoisie in a parallel universe. This strange, hybrid order indulges a folly of its own that merges into the agricultural landscape, undermining the finer points of the higher rungs of the Renaissance city ladder.

Real cities of Serlio's time combined all three of his stage settings in a hybrid of governmental control, dynamic market and trading forces, and the long cycles of agricultural production, marketing, and storage. These distinct elements of the city were well known to Renaissance artists such as Serlio and Shakespeare, as was the energy produced by their interaction. It is no accident, then, that Serlio's three scenes are linear and street-centered. The linear organization of the street-and-square sequence ordered the clustering and congestion of crowds, and this compression created a density of action and of human diversity that were essential to a successful city.

The city was above all *different* from the country. Yet it remained in close relationship with the country through a network of food supply, defense, services, and manpower. Urban historian Spiro Kostof defines this relationship in *The City Shaped* (1991) by offering a series of points. He begins with the quotation from Wirth cited at the head of this section and continues with Lewis Mumford's statement that a city is "the point of maximum concentration for the power and culture of a community."[8] He then goes on to stress that the city acts as a focus of energies, a regional economic "motor" or pump. Cities generate profits from multiple, interlinked, specialized activities or resources. As examples he lists "trade, intensive agriculture, . . . the possibility of surplus food, a physical resource, a geomorphic resource like a natural harbor, or a human resource like a king."[9] Interested citizens, Kostof says, protect and guard these sources of income through special urban codes. They establish distinct boundaries that constitute "some physical circumscription, whether material or symbolic, to separate those who belong in the urban order from those who don't." People are required to activate, enforce, and maintain the credibility of these codes, resulting in specialization and differentiation of roles. The city thus fills with well-differentiated urban actors, becoming a place "where people are priests, or craftsmen, or soldiers—and where wealth is not equally divided." This inequity creates professional specialization and social-class hierarchies. Cities come to house diverse populations and to possess an unstable interior dynamic.

The city also acts as an attractor to inhabitants of a larger region, offering specialized goods and services not readily available elsewhere. Great imperial capitals in the European heartland, European colonial cities in inhospitable outlands, or postmodern installations like Eurolille have all functioned as focal points for the material and cultural flows of their regions and have connected with global systems of transportation and communication. Beyond the surrounding areas or "basins" of attraction in which their influence is strongest, cities' areas of extended influence may overlap with those of other cities. Kostof argues that cities originally came in clusters, "urban systems" in which each city related to every other, and adds that both an agricultural hinterland and a great state (represented by a resident monarch) supported every great preindustrial city. He writes:

Diagram of shrinking Europe: impact of high-speed rail. (Eurostar, 2004)

> There were only a handful of genuine metropolises in antiquity, among them imperial Rome in the 2nd century AD and Chang'an in the 8th. In the Middle Ages this prodigious size is matched by Constantinople, Cordoba, and Palermo, the last two of which may have been in the 500,000 range in the 13th–14th centuries. Baghdad may have had as many as 1,000,000 inhabitants before it was destroyed by the Mongols in 1258. Again we have Chinese parallels for such phenomenal concentrations—Nanjing in the 15th century, and, in the late imperial era, Beijing, Suzhou, and Canton. Beijing remained the world's largest city until 1800, with a population of 2,000,000–3,000,000, when it was overtaken by London. Its close rivals in the 17th century were Istanbul, Agra, and Delhi.[10]

In contrast, most towns in classical antiquity were relatively small: a population of 2,000 or less was, Kostof says, "not uncommon" and one of 10,000 would have been "noteworthy." Among 3,000 towns of the Holy Roman Empire, only about 10 or 15 (Cologne and Lübeck among them) had over 10,000 inhabitants.

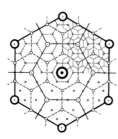

*Walter Christaller:
Dutch cities node
and network
diagram, 1930s*

*Enclave and
armature,
Amsterdam, 1603*

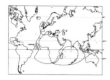

*Dutch East India
Company (VOC):
global trade
network, 1700s*

Kostof thus sees the city as an attractor with specialized functions and diverse populations that is set within a larger urban network. In this view, the city never exists in isolation but is linked to other cities and to its hinterland by powerful trade relationships and draws energy from them. It redistributes this energy inequitably within its boundaries, where its inhabitants and institutions process flows of energy, material goods, information, and ideas. The city acts as an attractor or magnet in a larger field, a node within a network; its internal order and structure depend on flows from outside. This concept inspired Walter Christaller in the 1930s to model the small, evenly spaced cities of the Netherlands (with their local hierarchies) as a single system, the Dutch "ring city."

Kostof also categorizes cities using a typology that highlights the dominant actor or activity in a city or a city's geographic or topographic situation. His city types include the *riverine settlement* (river town), *natural harbor* (port town), *defensive site* (castle town), *linear ridge* (ridge town), *hilltop town* (hill town), and *sloping terrain* (terraced towns). There can also be valley towns and water towns,[11] while the industrial world has produced its own crop of town types: mining towns, mill towns, factory towns, railway towns, specialized manufacturing towns like the "auto city" (Detroit), and spa towns or vacation towns in exotic or exciting settings (like Blackpool or Las Vegas). Yet cities are not static, Kostof insists: they are "organisms" that grow in particular patterns in response to specific conditions, and which change over time. Separate towns, for instance, can merge into one, a process Kostof calls *synoecism*, following Aristotle's coinage. His favorite example of such growth is the three hilltop towns that grew into Siena, nucleating around the piazza in front of the new city hall.

As described by the dictionary, the hierarchy of urban influence extends downward through metropolis, city, town, village, and hamlet, each embedded in a larger system. Smaller towns are conventionally described as being "in the orbit" of nearby, larger cities, while villages and hamlets identify themselves by their proximity to the largest neighboring town. Kostof cites Fernand Braudel's argument that "a town only exists as a town in relation to a form of life lower than its own . . . It has to dominate an empire, however tiny, to exist."[12] This analogy suggests a colonial relationship of domination and attraction, reflecting the hierarchical structure of the European urban tradition. This tradition constantly bends the flows of the urban system toward a place of central order and control, perhaps a national capital or metropolis.

One result of this constant pressure and compression is the formation of a series of interrelated urban institutions that structure the internal processes, networks, and flows of the city: government councils, trade councils, labor unions, libraries and universities, water supply systems, sewage disposal systems, and so on. These institutions manage the city, keeping records that are essential to the monitoring and maintenance of the system. "It is through writing," Kostof says, "that [merchants] will tally their goods, put down the laws that will govern the community, and establish title to property—which is extremely important,

because in the final analysis a city rests on the construct of ownership."[13] Records, laws, and ownership are intimately linked to the needs of the institutions and individuals that own the land and organize the various flows of the city.

To own land in the city—an inherently limited resource—is one way to control and profit from the city's processes and flows. In the European tradition, the great landowners of the city, together with the collective interests of small landowners, have powerfully influenced the city's form. This is why the legal codes governing and recording landownership are one of the earliest and most constant of written urban memory-structures. Urban actors create physical institutions (monuments, libraries, archives, and the like) that are charged with the maintenance of memories and codes of activity essential to the identity, organization, and stability of a given urban setting. These memorials and storage areas are meant to stand outside of the flow of everyday life and time. They reflect and invert normal and everyday flows, and their fixed visual order is important to a community's sense of place and continuity. They are meant to be static, resistant to progress, a "negative utopia," in Manfredo Tafuri's phrase (*Architecture and Utopia*, 1976). Following Tafuri, Kostof stresses the role of the monument and memorial, which entails "a set of public buildings which give the city scale, and the citizenry landmarks of a common identity."[14] These symbolic signature-markers give the city an atemporal aspect, a "diachronic" dimension that stands outside of time. Serlio's Noble scene, with its visual references to ancient Rome and its memorials, reflects this diachronic dimension.

The streets, squares, and monuments of the central city are the places where—at least in the traditional European view, and despite their partial exclusion of many groups (e.g., women, slaves, foreigners)—history is made. This has prompted twentieth-century totalitarian regimes in Germany, Italy, Russia, and elsewhere to co-opt these traditional city spaces in their attempts to

Left *Medieval memory-system; nested enclaves—a city of rooms*
Right *Armature approach as steps in a hierarchy leading to the center*

rewrite history. Commercial forces in the later part of the twentieth century made similar (though less obvious) attempts. The intermittent democratic re-liberation of public urban spaces demonstrates their ongoing symbolic value to the citizenry, especially in an age of "placeless" global media. These urban spaces still symbolize the city's promise of freedom from oppression. The reopening of the Brandenburg Gate in Berlin or the democratic occupation of Wenceslas Square in Prague during the "velvet revolution," both in 1989, carried this celebratory message all over the world via satellite television.

From the dictionary, Serlio's images, and Kostof's list of specialized urban resources we can conclude that a "city," at least in the European setting, is a complex, compressed, organizational structure that relates to a large local hinterland and a network of long-distance trading systems. It has traditionally been organized around the visual order of streets and squares that constitute the symbolic, public realm of the city. In the sixteenth century, Serlio represented the visual order of the city's public spaces as perspectival constructs, each with its own system of internal organization and activity. In this European tradition, highly specific social organizations and institutions accommodate the nobles, merchants, and peasants. In the Piazza San Marco in Venice, for instance, there was in Serlio's day a kiosk at the base of the campanile with a seating area reserved for aristocrats, where they could be seated to watch the passing crowds and be seen, in turn, in all their own splendor. Such institutions are semipermanent; they require land and employ particular physical structures under particular social codes.

We can also conclude that the city is "compressed" or "pressurized" in the sense that it draws people and activities from the surrounding countryside and squeezes them into a relatively small space. The result is a highly stratified society—functionally differentiated, politically divided, dynamic, always slightly off-balance—whose energy and diversity emerge from the mixing and intermingling of its diverse life-worlds. The pressure inherent in such a setting creates forces and fractures or organizational patterns that channel various flows, both material and intangible, through the city. What is more, under similar contextual conditions these patterns tend to recur, though never in quite the same way.

1.2 CITY MODELS AND CITY THEORIES

Theory is not written for entertainment, yet when it is a successful and succinct explanation of the inner workings of a formerly confusing phenomenon, it is by its nature absorbing to read—difficult, perhaps, but unforgettable once grasped. Think only of Darwin's central ideas, or the fundamental laws of mechanics. That urban theory is so boring is more than discouraging. It must be a sign of deeper difficulties.
—Kevin Lynch, *A Theory of Good City Form*[15]

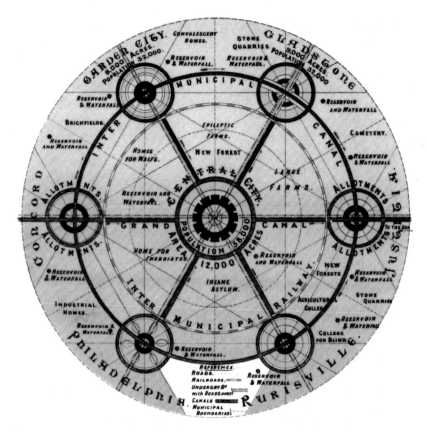

In considering what makes a city, we have been building a mental model of the urban network: a complex structure with compressed nodes of activity and areas of widespread sprawl that vary from low-rise development to the agricultural settlements which support city life. Kevin Lynch, one of the most influential theorists of urban form of the late twentieth century, saw urban models as an expression of *city theory*, an expansion of the concept of *urban design*. Traditional urban design busies itself with making small fragments of the city work, creating the settings for specific actors, whereas city theory is "normative"—that is, it explicitly addresses the question of what a city, including its relationships to the larger urban network, *should* be. Lynch elaborates this view most thoroughly in his last book published in his lifetime, *A Theory of Good City Form* (1981). Here he describes three traditional "normative theories" of the city, that is, three "coherent set[s] of ideas about proper city form and its reasons": the city as sacred ceremonial center, the city as a machine for living, and the city as an organism.[16] One or another of these theories, Lynch argues, has been held by the dominant or "leading" urban actor (i.e., individual, group, or institution holding preeminent power in the city) in most cities at most times.[17]

Ebenezer Howard: "A Group of Slumless, Smokeless Cities," Tomorrow: A Peaceful Path to Real Reform (Plate 7), 1898

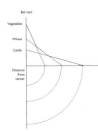

Paul Krugman: diagram of Von Thünen's Central Place Theory of 1826, The Self-Organizing Economy *1996*

In creating his city theories and city models Lynch was involved in the "systems revolution" that, according to British town planner Peter Hall (*Cities of Tomorrow: An Intellectual History of Urban Planning and Design in the Twentieth Century*, 1988), took place in city planning in the 1970s. In place of producing finished plans frozen in time, planners suddenly began analyzing shifting situations in complex, self-organizing systems, with no final, perfect, finished state in sight. For Hall, predecessors of this revolution range from the physical "survey" planning methods of Adshead and Abercrombie at Liverpool University in the 1910s to later German location theory (e.g., Christaller's and Lösch's network theories, described in more detail below). Hall stressed the importance for the German theorists of testing their theories against reality using scientific methods, techniques that were adopted by American economists like Walter Isard (*Location and Space-Economy*, 1956), creating what Hall calls an "instant revolution." He quotes Michael Batty on the result: "[T]he discipline of physical planning changed more in the 10 years from 1960 to 1970 than in the previous 100 years, possibly 1000."[18] Cities and regions were now viewed, in Batty's words, as "complex systems," with their spatial distribution of material elements (buildings, pipelines, power lines, roads, etc.) as only "one physical subset" among "many other classes of systems" that might be relevant to the actor-designer. In the systems approach to design, as described by Francis Ferguson in *Architecture, Cities, and the Systems Approach* (1975), the actor-designer was seen as being actively and continually engaged in monitoring these systems.[19]

The systems approach borrowed ideas from the new science of cybernetics (inaugurated in the 1950s by Norbert Wiener), among other sources. Feedback in urban systems was used to generate computer models; these models were used to simulate such interactive systems as traffic flows, employment patterns, and land-use patterns starting in Detroit in the mid 1950s (with disastrous results) and later in Batty's work for British new-town planning in the Midlands in the 1960s and 1970s. Batty, with Paul Longley, went on to write one of the first books outlining the urban impact of self-organizing patterns, *Fractal Cities* (1994).

Lynch drew on earlier city models from well-known works in city planning and economic geography in constructing his three "normative" models, cataloguing them in a lengthy appendix to *A Theory of Good City Form*.[20] Regarding the City of Faith, for instance, Lynch refers to Von Thünen's Central Place theory of 1826, which represents city growth as a relatively stable, concentric series of rings expanding around a single, central marketplace in a flat, agricultural plain.[21] This self-organizing network possessed a single center or attractor, forming around it a hierarchical system of agglomeration. It broke down when tiny differences in land rent, land use, and transport costs allowed subcenters to develop, first within the city fabric as specialized areas and later on the edges of the city.

In discussing his City as a Machine model, Lynch cites Walter Christaller

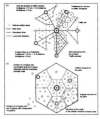

Walter Christaller: diagram of Central Place theory and attractors in network, 1930s

(1933) and August Lösch (1940) for mapping the breakdown of the Central Place system into a symmetrical hierarchy of hexagonal subzones.[22] This results from the introduction of a system of industrial production that can move to different sites in the transportation network. In *The Self-Organizing Economy* (1996), Paul Krugman describes how the introduction of such a system in the Industrial Revolution disturbed the existing agricultural equilibrium and so encouraged the generation of new urban forms, a process he called "urban morphogenesis" (from the Greek *morphos*, shape or pattern, and *genesis*, origin). Krugman notes that in 1952, Alan Turing, the British computer pioneer and Second World War cryptologist, provided a mathematical model for the emergence of two specialized satellite centers on opposite sides of the old center. These twin centers would dominate the "racetrack" ring of development around the edge of the city.[23] They grow because they are the most unstable subcenters, drawing energy from their more stable surroundings. In London in the eighteenth and nineteenth centuries, for instance, a center developed on either side of the traditional city center comprising the City of London and its Roman walls. The West End became a center of wealth and conspicuous consumption, while the East End became a center of poverty and industrial production.

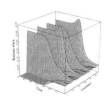

Paul Krugman: diagram of Alan Turing's 1952 "RaceTrack" model of peripheral development, The Self-Organizing Economy, *1996*

In discussing the Organic City, Lynch refers to ideas developed by Walter Isard in *Location and Space-Economy* (1956) and Jay Forrester in *Urban Dynamics* (1969), who hypothesized that siting decisions for industrial facilities and other urban elements are made by actors working in multicentered networks.[24] As distances increase and the system develops multiple, unstable points of equilibrium, communication networks become important. Subcenters grow and combine into a complex, self-organizing system. Such multicentered city systems have had a long tradition in city planning theory. Ebenezer Howard, for instance, proposed in *Garden Cities of Tomorrow* (1902) to build a ring system of 12 new towns around London beyond a green belt, intending that this network would replace the old, central city.[25]

In *The Self-Organizing Economy*, Paul Krugman adapted Turing's computations to model 12-centered and 16-centered systems of cities evolving over time. For Krugman, the basic principle of self-organizing networks was that order emerges from chaos through the activities of actors following their own private interests (much as in Adam Smith's "invisible hand" theory). Using Turing's formulas to describe the frequency and intensity of the growth of new cities in the ring, Krugman found that subcenters observed Zipf's power law for the size and hierarchical ranking of cities in a network (also referred to by Lynch).[26] Zipf's law predicts a constant, proportional, hierarchy of city sizes based on statistics of area and population; in Krugman's model, as cities ascended the multicentered network hierarchy they doubled in size and population and became less numerous. This followed from the inherent limits of the organizational capacity of urban actors. Further, Krugman found that this pattern of self-organization held true for United States census data over more

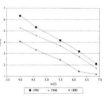

Krugman: diagram of Zipf's power law, Self-Organizing Economy. *There is a constant ratio between city size, distribution and population in the USA*

than a century of industrialization. The largest US city, usually New York, was always about twice the size of the second city, usually Chicago, which was in turn twice the size of the third city, Los Angeles, and so on. Krugman wrote that the accuracy of Zipf's law in predicting the relationship between size, scale, and frequency of large cities was "astonishing."[27]

Lynch not only drew on the conventional, scientific, rational approach of urban economists, geographers, and city planners concerned with self-organization in constructing his conceptual city models, but also sought to allow for the less quantifiable influence of the collective unconscious. Feedback from large numbers of less-powerful urban actors, Lynch maintained, allowed new patterns to emerge through a process of trial-and-error learning. Feedback empowered the end user, the *local* actor-designer. Informational systems allowing feedback flattened the hierarchy of command and control that had developed in highly centralized, modern industrial systems such as Fordism, with its single, mass-produced, standardized product.

Based on a similar trust in feedback and the collapse of Modernist hierarchies, Peter Hall, Cedric Price, Reyner Banham, and Peter Barker argued against the possibility of successful master plans for vast, modern city-regions in their article "Non-Plan: An Experiment in Freedom" (1969).[28] Hall and his collaborators were optimistic about the flexibility and adaptability of local control in global systems. Price attempted to incorporate rapid feedback into his own designs, such as *Fun Palace* for the run-down East End of London (1962–67). The Fun Palace proposal envisioned a three-dimensional matrix of services in which capsules and building elements could be shifted at will by mobile, overhead cranes attached to the building's frame. Price's *Potteries Thinkbelt* project (1966) proposed a mobile university of especially equipped rail carriages (mobile enclaves) for an abandoned industrial area, using a rich rail infrastructure (a redundant system of flows) to re-educate unemployed workers.[29]

Price assumed that the actor-designers in his buildings could read feedback patterns in the city and change their built environment accordingly. They could monitor global and local systems, watching the shifting flows, energies, time frames, and miscellaneous preferences of a changing society. The British group Archigram, whose work was later cited by Lynch as exemplary of the City as a Machine mentality, pushed this flexible, systemic feedback logic even further, visualizing mobile cities (e.g., Ron Herron's *Walking City*, 1964.) Archigram's mechanical fantasies supposed a surface skin of fast-changing individual housing capsules that would be moved, in the case of Archigram member Peter Cook's *Plug-In City* (1964), by permanently installed cranes. Cook imagined his Plug-In City as providing new forms of public space within an infrastructure of gigantic frames termed "urban forums," interior or exterior places of spectacle and consumption filled with media screens. Here, too, feedback and monitoring would enable the system to respond to changes in demand. Cook's *Instant City* project (1968) took this idea even further, envisioning the temporary creation of media-saturated public spaces in the landscape, foreshadowing the American pop festival at Woodstock, New York (1969).[30]

Lynch, in the spirit of Italo Calvino—whose fictional *Invisible Cities* (1972) he praised in *A Theory of Good City Form* for its description of a series of fantastic cities, each housing a "society that exaggerates the essence of some human question"[31]—believed that each city *model* corresponds roughly to a specific city *theory*. Values, in other words, shape cities. And because values can only be understood imaginatively and sympathetically, Lynch stressed the role of imagination in the understanding of cities. This makes his city theory one of the few recent attempts to construct a pluralist city in our imagination, emphasizing the possibilities of multiple interpretations.[32]

Lynch defined *model* in accord with the word's traditional usage as an adjective meaning "worthy of emulation," explicitly distinguishing his normative usage from that current in scientific and academic circles. In academia, Lynch said, *model* usually means,

> an abstract theory of how something functions, in which the elements of a system, and the relations between those elements, are clearly specified, preferably in a quantitative mode. . . . For our purpose, a model is a picture of how the environment *ought* to be made, a description of a form or a process which is a prototype to follow. Our subject is environmental form rather than the planning process, but models for form must take the creation and management process into account.[33]

Lynch was clear that actors use models to create order among the chaos of the city. "Creating order," Lynch says, "is the essence of cognitive development." Urban actors seek "a simple and patent first order structure which allows a more extensive ordering as it is more fully experienced, and which encourages the construction of new meanings, through which the inhabitant makes the world his own."[34] He constantly stressed the importance of urban actors' values in the creation of order in cities, and how differences between urban actors could create compartmentalization and specializations.[35] He also "unmasked" his own values, concluding that "that settlement is good which enhances the continuity of a culture and the survival of its people, increases a sense of connection in time and space, and permits or spurs individual growth: development, within continuity, via openness and connection."[36]

Models, he wrote, are in fact a practical necessity. "Models of some kind *must* be used: one cannot manage complex, real problems, under the pressure of time, without employing prototypes already in the head."[37] He described how the "process of design always uses models, although a basic model may be obscured by a surface innovation, or an alien model may be converted to some surprising new purpose."[38] Models range from "detailed prototypes followed habitually, almost unconsciously—such as sidewalks at the street edge—to major patterns put forward for consciously developed reasons—such as the idea of the satellite town."[39] For Lynch, "The most useful model is one in which the dependence on the situation in which it is to be applied is carefully stated, and in which the expected performance of the model is also specified. Then the model is open to test and improvement."[40]

Lynch thought that in *A Pattern Language: Towns, Buildings, Construction* (1977), Christopher Alexander and his colleagues had outlined a testable, empirical system for the production of models, a methodological system of morphogenesis.[41] Alexander sought to reduce the activity in the city to a mass of small, universal algorithms or simple formulas connected in precise networks of relationships. He created a long list of such components, all very pleasant and small scale, ranging from the bay window to the threshold to the local street with gardens. These elements can be combined according to various rules and codes to create specific local environments. The city as a whole is constructed by local networks of citizens cooperating in a semiautonomous system of interactive relationships. Asymmetrical neighborhood units are oriented toward the center of the conglomeration, where a linear pedestrian spine serves as a commercial and cultural armature that is surrounded by low-rise, high-density housing and entered by car from the periphery. The breakthrough made by Alexander and his colleagues was to create simple, small-scale feedback loops, algorithms or formulas that allowed for feedback at a small scale within a system. The result was that small-scale end users or consumers could customize products, in this case housing and civic forms, and ultimately alter large-scale outcomes by their cumulative, local activities. N. J. Habraken provided an elegant restatement of this thesis in his book *The Structure of the Ordinary: Form and Control in the Built Environment* (1998).[42]

Christopher Alexander: tree diagram of top-down hierarchy, 1964

Alexander's "patterns" were local *algorithms*, that is, formulas operating on local decisions but cumulatively creating larger, unintended structures. These larger structures—e.g., segregation, specialized enclaves, agglomerations, urban sprawl—emerge from the behavior of multiple actors, each of whom is located in a cell and relates to their neighbors according to set codes. (Juval Portugali, in *Self-Organization and the City*, 2000, later investigated the complexity of the often unintended larger patterns that can emerge from local actors' desires.[43]) Alexander called these local, bottom-up, open networks of decision-making "semilattices" and argued (in "A City Is Not a Tree," 1964) against closed, top-down, hierarchical systems of decision-making, exemplified for him by Howard's hierarchical *Garden Cities of Tomorrow* ideal. Patterns generated from open semilattice networks challenge designers accustomed to making top-down decisions for others.

Lynch viewed *A Pattern Language* as "a most important book" and thought that Alexander's proposed patterns "are full of much good sense, especially for our own culture and situation."[44] Although he rejected Alexander's claim to have found "timeless," "natural" patterns based on the community's life-cycle, his own concept of the Organic or Ecological City was deeply influenced by these bottom-up concepts. In describing his own ideal society or "place utopia" in the last chapter of *A Theory of Good City Form*, he constructs a "muddled landscape" model based on people caring intensely about their own place of habitation in the landscape. Land is managed by not-for-profit trusts and through "place educated" people reshaping their city from the bottom up.[45]

Nor is Alexander's influence limited to Lynch. David Smith, a student of Lynch's from MIT, pioneered participatory planning in America, setting national standards for community review boards in the RUDAT (Rural/Urban Design Assistance Board) process endorsed by the AIA after the 1967–69 riots in American cities. David Gosling, a fellow student of Lynch's from 1957 to 1959, describes David Lewis' career trajectory in *The Evolution of American Urban Design* (2003), highlighting the way in which Lewis's concern for the community (*The Pedestrian in the City*, 1965) led to his pioneering work in community participation in the 1970s and 1980s. (Lewis settled into a New Urbanist mold in the 1990s, having *The Urban Design Handbook: Techniques and Working Methods* [2003] written for his office practice, Urban Design Associates.[46]) Will Wright, creator of the bestselling computer game *Sim City: The City Simulator* (1989), in which players create their city from the ground up, lot by lot and cell by cell, acknowledged his debt to Alexander's concepts of pattern emergence, pattern language, self-organization, and urban actors' pattern-recognition skills.[47]

Alexander: semilattice, open-city diagram, 1964

For Lynch the central problem or paradox of urban modeling is that although *individual* actors seek freedom in the city, urban patterns emerge as a by-product of *group* behavior. Lynch develops his own language of city patterns in a short appendix to *A Theory of Good City Form*, then offers a long "Catalog of Models of Settlement Form."[48] His pattern analysis shares many features with the work of Arthur Gallion, Dean of the School of Architecture at the University of Southern California (1945–63), who identified three competing patterns of urban form in his *Urban Patterns* (1950).[49] Lynch and Gallion were both influenced by Lewis Mumford's description of linear technocratic structure in *The Culture of Cities* (1938). For Gallion, a Modernist, form followed function, so each urban pattern was directly linked to one of three competing technological systems. The first form/function pair was the traditional, craft-based European city; the second, the industrial city of the nineteenth century; and the third, the modern industrial city, especially in its American city-region format.

Lynch recasts Gallion's formulation and argues for his own pattern system, which makes a fundamental distinction between movement and stasis. "Settlement form," Lynch wrote, "[is] the spatial arrangement of persons doing things, the resulting spatial flow of persons, goods, and information, and the physical features which modify space in some way significant to those actions, including enclosures, surfaces, channels, ambiences, and objects."[50] Lynch had been long preoccupied by the difference between movement and stasis. In an early article entitled "A Theory of Urban Form" (written in 1958 with his mentor

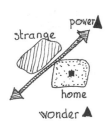

Kevin Lynch: stasis and flow diagram, A Theory of Good City Form, *1981*

at MIT, Lloyd Rodwin), Lynch proposed a language of urban forms based on the activities of urban actors, either those locally active in a place or enclave (creating a matrix of "adapted spaces") or those in transit, who need pathways or armatures (creating "flow facilities").[51] Lynch referred to René Thom's theories of the balance between flow and stasis in the generation of spatial patterns in fluids. Basing his ideas on Thom, he developed a theory of morphogenesis (the emergence of form and order) from flows in "A Theory of Urban Form" and later in his account of "functional theory."[52]

From the basic distinction between flow and stasis, Lynch unfolds a systematic examination of settlement patterns in terms of (a) flows of energy, information, and people and (b) localized "place settings" that consume energy and produce useful products.[53] He then explores the psychological geography of such a system, asserting that each citizen constructs a mental city-map consisting of a system of fragments, each with its own characteristics, building types, and even microclimate. This mental map, Lynch contends, contains nodes as attractors that draw citizens to various points depending on their preferences. He speaks of urban "grain" to describe the mix of uses in each area of the city and describes the city as a series of "patchworks" of various intensities of mixture, held together by focal patterns and networks of transportation.[54] He accents his vision of the basic elements of this city theory with hand-drawn diagrams of the various networks of flow and stasis that create channels of movement and enclosures for place-based activities of actors ("armatures" and "enclaves," respectively, in my terminology).

Lynch creates his own favorite "imaginary model" from this matrix of elements.[55] In this "alternating net" model, he reintroduces the concept of time geography, pioneered by Torsten Hägerstrand of the Swedish Lund School of urban geographers in the 1950s (from whom he also borrowed the concept of "attractor basins" focused on "milieux" or nodes within networks, concepts which will be discussed in the next chapter).[56] The "patchworks" in Lynch's alternating-net model have a time component, working either at a "slow" or a "fast" pace, served by support networks that are also "slow" or "fast." Lynch proposes a democratically governed city that is controlled from the bottom up by citizens who can elect to live in "fast" or "slow" worlds and to move between them. The network is a loosely defined grid, with "fast" or "slow" channels of movement alternating in a tartan pattern. Fast-paced enclaves would assemble along the fast-movement system, while slower, more rural or bucolic elements would assemble along a parallel but rambling set of paths surrounded by woods and fields. Occasionally the system would change and a new fast channel would cut through the slow, low-density environment, but at the same time other fast channels would be abandoned to sink slowly back into a slow mode. Thus, he concludes, "the settlement maintains a permanent reserve of circulation space and may gradually accumulate a 'layering' of notable structures saved from successive epochs."[57]

Lynch based his 1981 concepts of city theory and city models on his earlier research in Boston, described in *The Image of the City* (1960). There he describes how he interviewed citizens on neighborhood streets in an attempt to discern their shared cognitive map of the city. He asked children and adults to draw maps of the city, then compared these to the physical city, looking for telltale distortions and repetitive patterns. Through this process of interviewing and map-collecting he reconstructed the "image of the city" that was shared by those who used it, graphically including neighborhoods, barriers, links, centers, and edges in a coherent perceptual and cognitive system. On this basis he identified the basic elements of the pedestrian city as the *path*, *edge*, *node*, and *marker* (which together define the *neighborhood cell* or *district*). He worked in the old pedestrian core of downtown Boston, and this period of research followed a deeply influential stay in the hill towns of Italy and a visit to Rome that he recorded in his *Travel Journals* (1952–53).[58] Lynch found that inhabitants of Boston's historic core could read their own part of the city with clarity and precision, while areas produced during the Industrial Revolution and automobile age lacked this readability. He went on to investigate other cities in the United States using his mapping system, with similar results. He consistently found that the physical scale of industry and the automobile was inimical to the old residential and pedestrian order.[59]

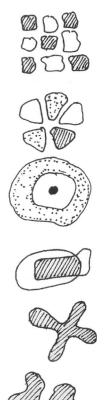

Lynch was mapping a disappearing city. His research coincided with the construction of Boston's central arterial highway, which was slicing through the center of the old city to make an approach to a new Charles River crossing. Begun in the 1950s, this six-lane elevated highway stood in stark contrast to the 30-foot-wide historic streets of north Boston, with their intimate neighborhood scale dating from the 1600s. A photograph of the new highway and north Boston in *Site Planning* (1962) exactly illustrates this contrast; the caption dramatically points out how the new roadway "slashes through the old city fabric" and a small diagram in the margin drives home this point.[60] Lynch was very conscious of the different urban codes governing the two sides of this stark urban contrast. Here the City of Faith (broadly defined) confronted the City as a Machine, the latter now dominated by the automobile. *A Theory of Good City Form* encapsulates this contrast in two graphics which face each other across the open book. On the left are photographs of an "accidental visual sequence" along a narrow street of Cordoba that "draws one forward as it twists and opens out." On the right is Lynch's diagram depicting a "sketch for an imaginary highway progression" not unlike that encountered while driving a central artery out into the western Boston suburbs, with marker buildings, rivers, bridges, and changing views all annotated.[61]

Kevin Lynch: patchworks diagrams

Two different philosophies—two different urban theories or urban models, one "fast" and the other "slow"—had met with devastating effect in downtown Boston. Lynch recorded this contrast just when the suburbanization of American cities was first impacting traditional downtowns. In reaction, he proposed the

Lynch: alternating net diagram, A Theory of Good City Form, *1981*

*Central Boston
urban design,
1945–2005*

a) *J R Meyer, Kevin
Lynch and Donald
Appleyard: study
for Boston City
Hall Plaza, 1959*
b) *Raised central
artery (1956) in
historic North End,
2001*
c) *I M Pei: aerial
view of Boston City
Hall Master Plan
1961–68*
*d) Gerhart Kallman
Noel McKinnell and
Paul Knowles: city
hall, 1962–68*
e) *Benjamin
Thompson and
Associates: Faneuil
Hall Market Place,
1971–76*
f) *Faneuil Hall
Market Place
armature, 2005*
g, h) *Demolition of
the central artery—
the "Big Dig," 2004*

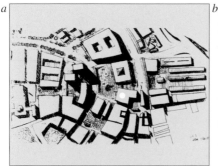

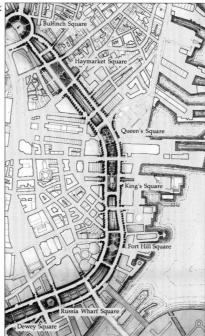

Bulfinch Square

Haymarket Square

Queen's Square

King's Square

Fort Hill Square

Russia Wharf Square

Dewey Square

Central Boston urban design, 1945–2005

i) *North End with central artery removed, 2005*
j) *Lawrence Chan, Alex Krieger and Associates with Hargreaves Associates: Boston City Hall Plaza renovation plan, 2003*
k) *Chan, Krieger and Associates: master plan for central artery corridor, 2003*
l) *Chan, Krieger and Associates: detail of central artery corridor, waterfront area, 2003*

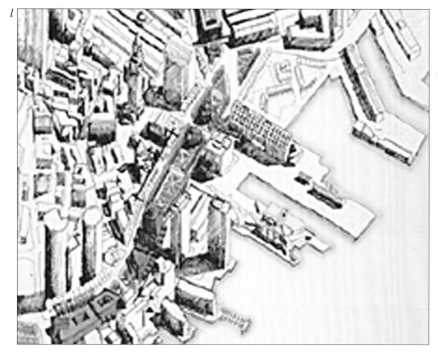

idea of small-scale conservation in his research for the Boston Redevelopment Authority (led by Ed Logue in 1961), which was beginning to reconstruct the central city. Lynch pointed to J. R. Meyer's 1959 plan to conserve Quincy Market and connect to the site of the new town hall.[62] In *The Evolution of American Urban Design* (2003), David Gosling reproduces a plan, developed in 1959 by Lynch, Meyer, and Donald Appleyard, to connect under the new highway to a series of new developments along the waterfront and piers.[63]

These ideas influenced the redevelopment authority's work, beginning with the new low-rise design for the city hall plaza district (with only two towers) as laid out by I. M. Pei's 1961 master plan and continuing with the competition for the low-rise city hall won by Gerhart Kallman, Noel McKinnell, and Paul Knowles in 1962. The completion of the city hall in 1968 was followed by the redevelopment in 1971–76 of Quincy Market as Faneuil Hall Market Place, a successful downtown mall (the first "festival market place") developed by the James Rouse Company and designed by Benjamin Thompson.[64] It took another 30 years for the failure of the central artery to be recognized. Its burial in the "Big Dig" of the early 2000s, with an urban design plan prepared by Alex Krieger and Lawrence Chan, is the largest, most complex, and most expensive Federal public works project ever undertaken.

Having recognized the confrontation of "fast" and "slow" city models in central Boston in 1960, Lynch bemoaned the paucity of alternatives in *A Theory of Good City Form*. "A well-developed stock of models which integrated process and form would be of immense value to [city design]. These models and theoretical constructs must be sufficiently independent and simple, however, to allow for that continuous recasting of aims, analyses, and possibilities that is inherent in the conduct of city design."[65] In order to partly remedy this lack, Lynch offered a long list of "models of settlement form" in Appendix D of *A Theory of Good City Form*.[66] I have reproduced his summary of this list on page 41 to

Left *Kevin Lynch: "The visual form of Boston ..."diagram with key,* The Image of the City, *1960*
Right *Lynch and Donald Appleyard: diagram of journey to the suburbs,* The View From the Road, *1964*

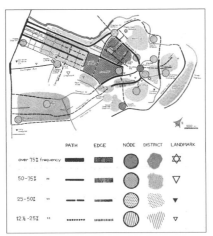

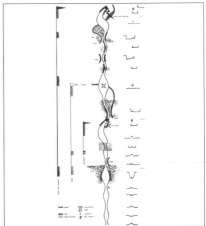

illustrate the range of combinations that he was able to create from his basic model of stasis versus flow (enclave versus armature). The first two sets of models, "General patterns" and "Central place patterns," concern the general organizational relationships between armatures (flow) and enclaves (stasis). Lynch identified such growth patterns as central-place agglomerations, star shapes, nested hierarchies, and large-scale patterns of centers. The next set of models, "Textures," concerns enclaves, particular patches, mixed- or single-use fragments, and housing typologies that form the fabric of the city. The last three sets of models—"Circulation," "Open space patterns," and "Temporal organization"—concern armatures, linear flow patterns (including information systems), corridors of "open space" in ecological systems, and sequencing issues such as the rate of change and timing of renewal.[67]

Lynch thought that actors use urban models to combine elements of stasis and flow to make urban patterns that work for their purposes at particular times, and that these patterns could in turn be recombined over time to form a large variety of urban models. Further, he associated particular actors with specific city theories and models. He wrote, "value-coherent normative theories will tend to favor certain models over others, or (mistakenly, as I have tried to explain) to propose one set of models as the universal solution. Thus the 'city-is-a-machine' view will be attracted to clear, repetitive patterns, made up of rather uniform, replaceable, separate parts: regular grids, isolated buildings, and the like."[68] Lynch's models thus did not pretend to be neutral or scientific; they were "imaginary," imbued with actors' values and normative preferences, their notions of how things *should* be.

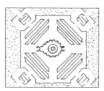

We will now examine Lynch's three normative city models, the City of Faith, the City as a Machine, and the City as an Organism (or the Ecological City). Their power, in Lynch's words, is that they are based on "great normative metaphors . . . [that] combine motive, form, and a view of the nature of human settlements in one connected statement."[69]

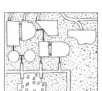

1.3 THREE NORMATIVE MODELS AND THEORIES

In devising his three normative urban models, Lynch considered how dominant urban actors would structure and organize the relationships of the city if they had absolute power and acted logically. The models are thus deliberate simplifications. The first two, for example—the City of Faith and the City as a Machine—each assume top-down control by entrenched elites. In the City of Faith, feudal warlords and priests favor stasis, place-making, and a land-based agrarian economy; in the City as a Machine, corporate executives and capitalists prefer systems of flow and exchange, of consumption and production, embedded in a space-based, capital-intensive, industrial economy. In the third model, the Ecological City, Lynch imagined a more complex structure in which an *elected* elite responds to feedback from the city's inhabitants.

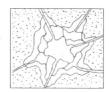

Spiro Kostof: three city models, The City Shaped, *1991*

1.3.1 The Theoretical Context

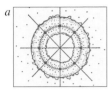

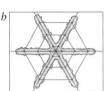

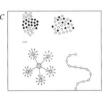

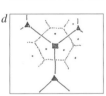

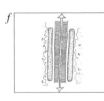

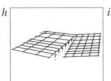

During the 1960s and 1970s, many other theorists posited triple models of urban operation, each to characterize a successive epoch of civilization. These other tripartite schemata form the background to the patterns of Lynch's city models and may be best described in terms of three major revisions of Modernism and contemporary functionalism.

The first revisionist approach examines the different forms of knowledge available to urban actors in different versions of the network city, drawing on the phenomenological analyses of architect-critics like Christian Norberg-Schultz (*Existence, Space, and Architecture*, 1971). This analysis seeks to uncover prescientific logics in order to discern patterns of relationships better suited to humanity than those imposed by modern science.

The second revisionist approach surveys the "supplementary" systems of signs and mechanisms necessary to control, coordinate, and communicate in a network city. Françoise Choay, in her article "Urbanism and Semiology" (1969), gives a complex reading of how the different signs, systems, and languages available to actor-designers over time provide the basis for this account, which distinguishes between premodern, modern, and contemporary systems of networked urban communication.[70]

The third revisionist approach analyzes the effects of the acceleration of communication systems in network cities. It bases itself on concepts such as the necessity of a social "milieu" for face-to-face meetings, as described by Manuel Castells in *The Informational City* (1989). This revised systems approach stresses the role of communications and local pattern-recognition in the making of global city-network patterns and distinguishes between cities in agricultural systems, industrial systems, and informational networks.

Lynch implied that the three basic forms "that a city should take"[71] that he described in *A Theory of Good City Form* and other writings—the City of Faith, the City as a Machine, and the City as an Organism (or the Ecological City)—tend to succeed each other through historical time and, furthermore, that each theory tends to shape the city in its own image, giving rise to a city type or "urban model" corresponding to itself. Each urban *model* mirrors a dominant urban actor's city *theory*. This is the result of the dominant urban actors' power (direct or catalytic) to pattern the city's activities in accord with their normative theories. These urban patterns, in turn, give rise to a view of the city that is shared by a majority of the city's inhabitants, so model shapes

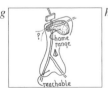

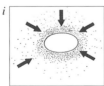

Table 1. Lynch's Summary of Models of Settlement Form

1. General Patterns	2. Central Place Patterns	3. Textures
A. The star or asterisk	A. Patterns of centers	A. Cells
B. Satellite cities	B. Specialized and all-purpose centers	B. Sprawl and compaction
C. The linear city	C. Linear centers	C. Segregation and mix
D. The rectangular-grid city	D. Neighborhood centers	D. Perceived spatial textures
E. Other grid forms	E. The shopping center	E. Housing types
F. The baroque axial network	F. Mobile centers	1. High slabs
G. The lacework		2. Towers in the green
H. The "inward city"		3. Dense walkups
I. The nested city		4. Ground-access walkups
J. Current imaginings		5. Courtyard houses
		6. Attached houses
		7. Freestanding houses
		F. Housing innovations
		G. Systems and self-help
4. Circulation	5. Open Space Patterns	6. Temporal Organization
A. Modal choice	A. Distribution of open space	A. Management of growth rate
B. Circulation patterns	B. Map shapes	B. Strategies of development and renewal
C. Modal separations	C. Open space classes	C. Permanence
D. Managing travel distance	1. Regional parks	D. The timing of use
E. Channel prototypes	2. Urban parks	
	3. Squares or plazas	
	4. Linear parks	
	5. Playgrounds and playfields	
	6. Wastelands and adventure playgrounds	

Kevin Lynch: city diagrams, A Theory of Good City Form, *1981*

a) *Ring or central-place model after Von Thünen*
b) *Star or radial-finger model*
c) *City grain diagrams, linear and satellite city models*
d) *Net city model, after Christaller*
e) *Node, interchange diagram*
f) *Linear city diagram after N A Miliutin and A Sprague,* Sotsgorod: the Problem of Building Socialist Cities, *1974*
g) *Home and range diagram*
h) *Grid and interstices diagram*
i) *City node, attractor diagram*
j) *The "inward city", (medieval/Islamic)*
k) *Patchwork city diagram*
l) *Cellular city diagram*
m) *Lacework city diagram*

Lynch: city diagrams, City Sense and City Design, 1990,
n) *Polycentric net City diagram*
o) *Galaxy city model*

l  *m* 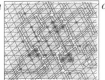 *n* 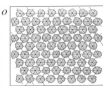 *o*

theory even as theory shapes model in a feedback loop.

For Lynch, all three city models are built from basic functional elements assembled in relationships that are determined by the city theory of the dominant urban actors. In the City of Faith or "Cosmic City" (as it was later termed by Spiro Kostof in *The City Shaped*, 1991), the shaman or priest rules, magic dominates the world-view, and magical proprieties determine the relationships of the urban elements. In the City as a Machine, managers and engineers sharing a scientific world view dominate and utilitarian concerns are determining. Citizen-planners govern the Ecological City and affirm an organic, ecological world view that sees values beyond mechanistic utilitarianism. In each model, as I will now examine in more detail, the philosophy of the dominant urban actor—priest, utilitarian, or eco-citizen—shapes the disposition of elements in the urban constellation.

1.3.2 The City of Faith

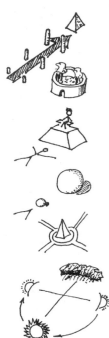

Kevin Lynch: City of Faith—common concepts of form, A Theory of Good City Form

A set of "magical" rules governs the relationships between urban elements in the City of Faith, which, Lynch writes, is based on "a magical model of the universe and the gods."[72] Priests promulgate prohibitions and rituals that can be endlessly elaborated. Codes about hygiene, food, clothing, time, prayer, and everyday events and habits set up clearly prescribed ritual relationships between heaven and hell, earth and sky, that unfold in the daily life of the city. Sacred warriors enforce the rules within the sacred precincts. These rules may strike some moderns as arbitrary superstitions, but for many people, over many centuries, they have provided security and reassurance in a shifting and uncontrollable world.

The design of the City of Faith typically obeys a cosmological geometry, being oriented to sacred axes in the heavens and on the earth. Through geomancy or divination, the priests establish magical "enclosures" (i.e., temples and sacred sites) on propitious sites.[73] These enclosures or enclaves are arranged about a single, central reference point, a place of calm, stasis, and order amid the chaos of the world. They are often guarded by gatekeepers and surrounded by sacred perimeter walls. Through a surfeit of order, organization, and controlled information that is deployed along axial symmetries of approach to the sacred, the warrior-priest seeks to exclude the uncertainties and irrational flows associated with the anger of the gods or with demonic forces. As Lynch's illustrations demonstrate, the priests (who are also warriors and rulers, or are at least closely associated with those groups) tend to express their power in the social hierarchy by elevating themselves on central ziggurats.[74] From these enclaves they distribute intelligence and information from the top down, much as in Noam Chomsky's "totalitarian propaganda model." (Chomsky and Edward Herman distinguish this premodern, hierarchical style of media control from modern "democratic" methods of decentralized, oligarchic, self-censoring media control: *Manufacturing Consent*, 1988).[75]

Cities of Faith such as ancient Beijing tend, as a result, to be cellular structures organized around approaches to dominant sacred enclosures. They stand out from the countryside as centers of hierarchy comprised of nested enclaves: the temple stands within the sacred precinct, the sacred precinct stands within the sacred district, and the sacred district stands within the walls of the sacred city. Clarity and hierarchy are built into the city plan. Axial armatures and symmetrical compositions connect the enclaves that symbolize the power and control of the dominant actor, the ruler-priest. Lynch shows that similarly magical and hierarchical power relationships between armatures and enclaves can be found in imperial Rome and ancient Aztec temple-city complexes.

The landscape outside the city also participates in the "magical" system. Meanings are hidden in hills, rocks, caves, and streams, and these are made evident by divination. What I term "stretched armatures"—axes of movement and organization that extend far from their nodes of origin, even beyond the city itself—act as symbolic intermediaries, extending paths of sacred meaning and pilgrimage across the landscape in a network linking various "attractors" (sacred sites). In the City of Faith, enclaves anchor cosmic stasis while armatures channel sacred flows.

Lynch applied his City of Faith model primarily to holy capitals such as Kyoto, Madurai, and Rome, but I will use the City of Faith as a catchall category for the premodern city. This allows me to include under this head many important cities founded in the preindustrial era that were organized not only or primarily around their magical or sacred aspects but were important mercantile or industrial production centers as well. Medieval Florence or Bruges, for instance, functioned as manufacturing centers, weaving silk or wool for export, while also building large cathedrals as signs of devotion and wealth. American cities like colonial Boston were founded on a mixture of Puritan piety and ferocious trade, and set enclaves of religious calm amid their bustling economic activity.

Lynch: City as a Machine diagram, Good City Form, 1981

1.3.3 The City as a Machine

Lynch's second urban model, the City as a Machine, also features enclaves and a connecting system of stretched armatures or communication corridors. Flow (armatures) and stasis (enclaves) are separated, as in the City of Faith. In the City as a Machine, however, flow is particularly important, as it physically connects pieces of the city that have been segregated and separated by industrialization. In Lynch's schematic diagram of the City as a Machine, lines and arrows (both dashed and solid) signifying flows connect small cellular structures to form a grid of separate but interlinked cells or enclaves.[76] Individual cells can be removed and replaced without affecting the operation of the overall system, and new cells can always be added, making the system potentially unbounded. A key refinement to the City as a Machine model that will be discussed extensively in

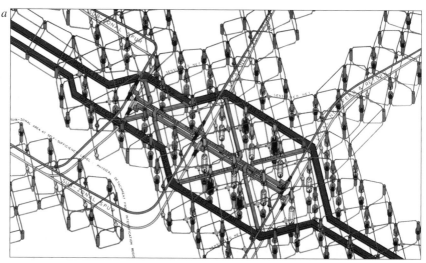

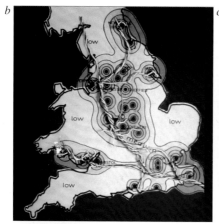

EACH WALKING UNIT HOUSES NOT ONLY A KEY
ELEMENT OF THE CAPITAL, BUT ALSO A LARGE
POPULATION OF WORLD TRAVELLER-WORKERS.

A WALKING CITY

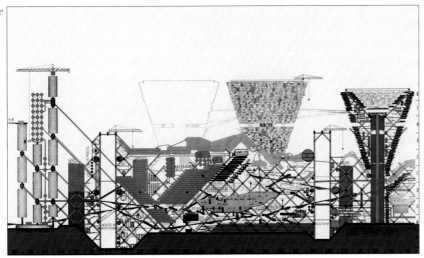

e

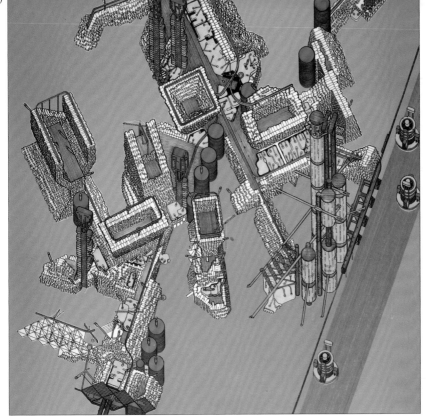

f

City as a Machine: Archigram, 1960s

a) *Dennis Crompton:* Computer City, *1964 (© Archigram Archives)*
b) *Dennis Crompton:* UK Network, *1964 (© Archigram Archives)*
c) *David Green:* Living Pod, *1966 (© Archigram Archives)*
d) *Ron Herron:* Walking City, *1964 (© R Herron Archive)*
e) *Peter Cook: Plug-in City, section, 1964 (© Archigram Archives)*
f) *Peter Cook: Plug-in City, axonometric, 1964 (© Archigram Archives)*

Chapter 3 of this book is expressed by the fact that most of the cells in Lynch's diagram are uncolored, signifying normative spaces of various kinds, while a few are shaded, signifying *heterotopic* cells, that is, those containing unwanted, excluded, or non-normative functions.

The theory underlying the City as a Machine assumes that a city is a system of mechanical parts that interact in a network and are not bound to any particular place. To illustrate the stretched-armature, linear form of the City as a Machine, Lynch cites the linear city proposed by Ivan Leonidov for Magnitogorsk, USSR, in 1930, and shows a typical (idealized) node of such a city as sketched by Antonio Sant'Elia in 1914—"a futurist fantasy of towers and dramatic transportation."[77] He also mentions the British group Archigram and its vision of a mechanical city "in which the whole environment is mobile or demountable," a reference that calls to mind Ron Herron's aforementioned Walking City (1964). In this extraordinary image, a machine city comprising four enormous, interconnected pods on stilts (homes for various United Nations agencies) promenades in the East River with the skyscrapers of New York in the background.[78]

Walking City is apropos because Lynch constructs a dynamic model of the City as a Machine in his diagrams, text, and citations. The City as a Machine can grow, and it can do so in generally predictable directions and in large, mechanical increments. Lynch compares its parts to the cogs and gears in a machine, all of which make physical contact and are harnessed to a program of linear production, consumption, and growth. He shows, furthermore, that what I have called "stretched" armatures form a network among the cells of the city. These armatures need not all involve material transport; the dashed lines connecting some cells of Lynch's diagram of the City as a Machine might be read as high-speed communication lines carrying the city's mediascape, accelerating response-time between cells. It is also notable that landscape and topography do not appear in Lynch's diagram of the City as a Machine; the white of the surrounding page acts as a featureless, desert-like space. The City as a Machine is essentially placeless. It might as well be, and often has been, imagined as floating in outer space.

Lynch was critical of the simple rules of combination, repetition, and connection implicit in the City as a Machine. These were the essence of the Modernist city of C. E. Jeanneret (Le Corbusier), CIAM (the Congrès Internationaux d'Architecture Moderne), and the 1933 Athens Charter, all influential on American postwar city-planning practices. The Athens Charter specified that functional uses should be segregated for maximum efficiency, specifying a simple, mechanical urban taxonomy of four functions and three densities. These Modernists wanted to reform the bipolar schema of the industrial city of the nineteenth century, with its segregation of consumption and production, rich and poor, culture and nature. They proposed that the twin poles of the industrial city—the enclaves of production and of consumption,

CIAM grid, 1933

connected by systems of communication and transportation—be split up and reclassified into four new categories set in a green landscape.

In this codification, each cell or platform belongs exclusively to one of four functional categories: (1) residential, (2) work (industrial or office facilities), (3) leisure (sports, entertainment, or shopping), and (4) transportation and communications. (There was to be a fifth, miscellaneous or nonconforming category of heterotopic elements, e.g., old, mixed-use areas.) Each cell can be high-, low-, or medium-density, depending on its position in the city (center, edge, or in between). Corridors of transportation and communication connect all cells.[79] Similarly, Le Corbusier, in his plan for Chandigarh (1951), proposed categorizing movement flows into seven types, expanding the American highway engineers' systemic hierarchy of feeders, arteries, and highways. Lynch incorporated these Modernist taxonomies of flow and function in his City as a Machine model.

Sim City 1
packaging, 1989

The Athens Charter's City as a Machine includes not only four functions and three densities, but also a rule of "pavilionization" (dictating that every function must be housed in a separate building or "pavilion," as in the Beaux Arts system). This rule sets the stage for the proliferation of specialized, standardized building typologies within cells, and forms the background for a further rule of systemic growth by cellular incrementation. Anyone who has played the computer game *Sim City* (1989) will recognize this model. *Sim City* allows the player to construct a virtual city consisting of monofunctional cells (housing, offices, factories, commercial centers, parks, etc.) that can be connected by transportation systems across a universal grid stretched over the landscape (plain, island, mountain, etc.). The original game had a single feedback loop from the press to the mayor, who occupied a crucial, central control point in the city system. (A "feedback loop" is an information-transmitting link that enables a system or structure to correct itself so that it maintains a constant state or remains oriented toward a constant goal; a ship's rudder and helmsman constitute a classic mechanical feedback loop.) Its built-in feedback marks *Sim City* as an advanced version of the City as a Machine model, construing the city as a self-organizing system that produces order out of chaos, driven from the bottom up by actors' micromotives. *Sim City* also, in good City as a Machine style, presumed the existence of an economic engine that would act as a pump for never-ending growth.[80]

Fritjof Capra: The Web of Life, *1996, feedback diagram*

In his book *Ladders* (1996), Albert Pope provides a brilliant description of the real-life impact of *Sim City*-style growth as played out in the American grid structure (first established as a national policy by Thomas Jefferson). Pope documents the "collapse" and "implosion" of the universal coordinates of the Jeffersonian grid that was caused in the twentieth century by the arrival of the highways, with their few exits at long intervals. These exits created an access hierarchy within the grid and set in motion a rearticulation of the city space. Using contemporary Houston as an exemplary case, Pope describes this

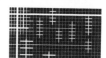

Albert Pope: grid versus ladders diagrams, Ladders, *1966*

implosion into the controlled, cellular structures (enclaves) that he terms "ladders." Places were no longer theoretically equal, as they would be in an open, universal, Cartesian grid; there was a new "logic of Centralized Polynuclear Expansion" that produced "spirals of exclusion."[81]

Pope drew diagrams of these new "ladder" enclave structures with their single, controlled entrances, echoing Hilbesheimer's analysis of suburban growth in the 1950s.[82] Ladders represent a new, hybrid form combining the place-centering capacity of the traditional urban enclave with the linear-sequencing ability of the industrial armature, often in a three-dimensional spatial matrix. Ladder enclaves can be organized both horizontally and vertically, as for instance in multilevel malls and atria—the specialized, repetitive typologies of the City as a Machine of the late twentieth century.

The City as a Machine model possesses clarity of organization and precision of taxonomy. This clarity and precision is descended from Ildefons Cerdá's *The Five Bases of the General Theory of Urbanization* (1867), which was in turn based on the methodology of Darwin's *The Origin of Species* (1859) (discussed further in the next chapter). Indeed, it might be argued that this "mechanical" model is also evolutionary and biological insofar as each specialized cell type—residential, industrial, or other—can be endlessly improved in terms of efficiency, that is, evolve. Despite this pseudo-alive quality, there is, as Lynch remarks, nothing "magical" about the City as a Machine. All aspects of the city are "cool," mathematical, systemically predictable; it is composed of clearly defined parts—enclaves, armatures, and heterotopic elements—which can be sized according to the flows and capacities required.[83] The city theory underlying the City as a Machine involves a simple, mechanistic calculus: four functions, three densities, a rule of noncombination that separates everything, and the repetition of specialized, standardized building typologies in special zoning enclaves. These simple rules, endlessly reapplied, extend the city across the landscape in a boundless grid of mechanical efficiency.

Or inefficiency. One of Lynch's criticisms of the City as a Machine is that its commitment to always constructing anew is wasteful. It has, he says, no way to adapt old cells to new uses, and thus inevitably abandons the old downtown for new business centers or for peripheral growth. This pattern of growth means that the City as a Machine is doomed to sprawl ever outwards, leaving behind it the devastation and abandonment that are only too familiar in American cities (e.g., the abandoned core and inner-city margins of Detroit, as documented by photographer Camilo Vergara in *American Ruins*, 1999).[84]

Still, the City as a Machine model obviously has great power. This can be seen in a brief examination of the projects portfolio of a successful "New Urbanist" design firm such as that of Andres Duany and Elizabeth Plater-Zyberk. The size of their projects quickly grew from 80 acres at Seaside, Florida, in 1982 to 9,400 acres in Avalon Park, Florida, in 1989 as a result of their skill in designing and marketing small neighborhoods organized around scenographic armatures. These skills were much appreciated by giant, landowning sponsors on the periphery of megalopolitan conurbations. While these designs were an improvement on previous suburban models, at the level of city theory they do not fundamentally alter the growth system of the City as a Machine.[85]

Camilo Vergara: American Ruins, 1999
a) *Downtown Detroit*
b) *Empty people-mover Detroit*

1.3.4 The Ecological City

Lynch's third urban model, the Ecological City, was also constructed from enclaves and armatures. He based it on the logic of his teacher Frank Lloyd Wright, who had sought an organic relationship between the elements of his Broadacre City (1935), turning each home into a miniature farmstead. (Lynch, with other apprentices, helped build the Broadacre City model at Taliesin West, Wright's home, headquarters, office, and school in the desert on the edge of Phoenix, Arizona in the late 1930s.) In the Broadacre City model the landscape and larger ecological systems play an important role in merging the city into the countryside. *This* kind of sprawl, Lynch believed, is not necessarily bad. Indeed, Lynch wrote positively in his article "City and Regional Planning" (1973) of "looking forward to the urban countryside" that combines the openness of the country landscape with the sophistications of city life. In this, he echoed Ebenezer Howard's town-and-country "twin magnets" diagram in *Garden Cities of Tomorrow* (1902).[86]

In the Ecological City, urban actors struggle to maintain a delicate, "organic" balance; the city is almost literally an organism. Lynch stresses the self-organizing dynamism of all organisms and thus of the Ecological City and reminds his readers that "it is a homeostatic dynamism: internal adjustments tend to return the organism to some balanced state whenever it has been disturbed by an outside force. So it is self-regulating. It is also self-organizing. It repairs itself, produces new individuals, and goes through a cycle of birth, growth, maturity, and death."[87]

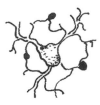

Kevin Lynch: Ecological City diagram, A Theory of Good City Form, *1981*

Lynch describes the tenets of this relatively recent city theory. "The first tenet," he states, "is that each community should be a separate social and spatial unit, as autonomous as possible." Within itself, furthermore,

Ryonji temple, Kyoto Japan, 1499

the healthy community is a heterogeneous one. There is a mix of diverse people and places, and that mix has some optimum proportions, a "balance." The parts are in constant interchange with each other, participating mutually in the total function of the community. But these parts, being different, have different roles to play. They are not equal or repetitive, but are diverse, and support each other in their diversity. . . . [T]he healthy community is stable by virtue of maintaining its dynamic, homeostatic balance. . . . [T]he optimum state is the stage of ecological climax, with a maximum diversity of elements, an efficient use of energy passing through the system, and a continual recycling of material. Settlements become ill when the balance breaks down, when the optimum mix degenerates, . . . recycling fails, parts dedifferentiate, or self-repair ceases.[88]

Lynch thus stresses that "balance" in the Ecological City pertains not only to the ecology of the individual cell or enclave, but to the ecology of the system as a whole.

The city theory underlying the Ecological City is concerned with an overall dynamic, with heuristic learning, with a sense of balance that includes social justice. Lynch often referred to an "ecology of learning" as the basis of his vision of the organic city.[89] The elements of this city are thus more complex and hybrid than those of the City as a Machine. In the Ecological City, boundaries are not always clear and hybridity is the norm, making heterotopic conditions more common. In describing this complex situation, Lynch says: "Melting transitions are a very common feature, and ambiguities are important, for reasons of choice, flexibility, or the evocation of complex meanings."[90]

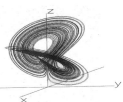

James Gleick: Punctuated equilibrium diagram, Chaos: The Making of a New Science, 1988

"Organic"—a key concept in the Ecological City model—denotes, for Lynch, a set of elements from Darwin's evolutionary model updated for the age of cybernetics and heuristic feedback loops. The iterated behavioral patterns of urban actors can, on this view, slowly change toward new "attractors" (a primarily cybernetic, not biological, metaphor), shifting the balance of the urban model either gradually or in unpredictable leaps as urban actors encounter the limits of their ecological setting. Economists like Paul Krugman have called this picture of sudden shifts the "punctuated equilibrium model,"[91] explicitly referring to an important revision to gradualistic Darwinism first introduced by biologists Stephen Jay Gould and Niles Eldredge in 1972. Urbanists recognize these jumps as incremental growth-spurts with periods of steady-state maintenance in between. Lynch thus sees the Ecological City as a cybernetic or pseudobiological system that includes a network of information flows and feedbacks to designers. He describes the Ecological City as "self-organizing" and makes reference to biological and cybernetic concepts of the 1970s.

Lynch's melding of cybernetics and biology was in harmony with certain intellectual fashions of the 1960s that were out of favor by the 1980s but which returned in the 1990s in the writings of authors like Fritjof Capra. Capra, though not a student of urban form, sheds additional light on these questions in *The Web of Life* (1996). Capra pictures *any* self-organizing system as an ecology, that is, a system capable of maintaining a dynamic balance, learning from past mistakes, and repairing itself. Lynch ascribes all these properties to the Ecological City. Capra contrasts dynamic, self-organizing systems with the previously dominant world-view, which was based on Newtonian science and its clockwork concept of mechanism—the world-view that shaped the City as a Machine. Capra and Lynch both argue that this world-view is changing. Capra quotes Thomas Kuhn's description of a scientific "paradigm" as "a constellation of achievements—concepts, values, techniques, etc.—shared by a scientific community and used by that community to define and legitimate problems and solutions," and proposes that a major, discontinuous, revolutionary break in world-view has occurred in the last century, creating what Kuhn termed a "paradigm shift" (albeit one occurring at different rates in different disciplines).[92]

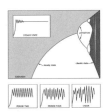

Gleick: Complexity theory diagram, Chaos

This shift, Capra believes, is from the old Newtonian world-view toward an ecological, systems-conscious one. He notes that the word *ecology* derives from the Greek *oikos*, meaning "a household," traditionally a female domain. The dictionary defines a *system* as a whole compounded of parts;[93] Capra states (attributing the observation to Heinz Von Foerster) that the word is derived from the Greek *synhistanai*, meaning "to place together." He writes that to

Frank Lloyd Wright: Broadacre City model, 1935

A G Tansley: ecosystem diagram, 1930s

Richard Gregory: Gestalt theory diagram, Eye and Brain: The Psychology of Seeing, *1966*

"understand things systematically literally means to put them into a context, to establish the nature of their relationships." Biologists, he says, pioneered this relational network approach to self-regulation early in the twentieth century, emphasizing "the view of living organisms as integrated wholes." In the 1930s, for example, the British plant ecologist A. G. Tansley defined an *ecosystem* as a self-organizing system of relationships, a "community of organisms and their physical environment interacting as an ecological unit."[94] Capra believes that scientists have removed man from the center of their ecological picture, creating a nonanthropocentric, posthumanist "deep ecology" and engendering a widespread change in values. It is, of course, not necessary to believe in a "Gaia" system or in the more mystical forms of global intelligence, à la Teilhard de Chardin, to see the advantages of this ecological systems approach.

As mentioned above, the organic tradition was shared by Lynch's teacher Frank Lloyd Wright. Capra extends Wright's analysis by emphasizing that this tradition has stressed relationships and flows over rigid parts linked by simple chains of cause and effect (the Newtonian view), an emphasis paralleled in the field of quantum physics. In both fields, workers found that the older scientific assumption of fundamentally discrete entities acting deterministically upon each other was inadequate: objects' boundaries could no longer be conceived of as perfectly clear. Quantum mechanics made it clear that at the subatomic level objects dissolve into wave-like patterns that represent not simply the probability of discrete objects being present or not, but the probabilities of interconnections or relationships in a network of interaction or "observation." As physicist Werner Heisenberg wrote, "The world thus appears as a complicated tissue of events, in which connections of different kinds alternate or overlap or combine and thereby determine the texture of the whole."[95] For Capra, the shift to the ecological model resembles the shift to quantum mechanics in that it involves a move away from the analysis of parts (science in the Cartesian, Newtonian mode) to the study of the sense or "texture" of the whole. All knowledge thus becomes approximate knowledge, dependent on the means of observation employed and on a sense of the whole.

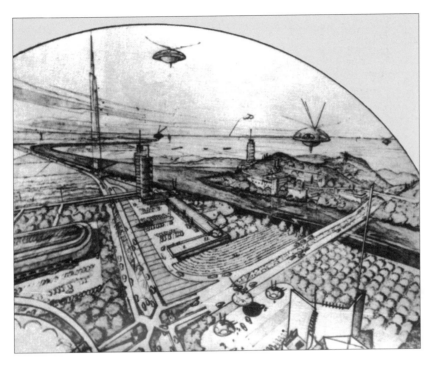

Frank Lloyd Wright: Aerial view of Broadacre City, 1935

This "sense of the whole" is fundamental to pattern recognition in the Ecological City. As a concept it derives from Gestalt psychology and its holistic analysis of perception and pattern-making activities in the human brain. Capra emphasizes that the German *Gestalt* means organic, *living* form, as distinct from *inanimate* form (denoted in German by *Form*). Gestalt psychologists, he writes, saw that "[l]iving organisms . . . perceive things not in terms of isolated elements, but as integrated perceptual wholes—meaningful organized wholes, which exhibit qualities that are absent in their parts."[96] Capra argues that the human brain is itself an enormously complex self-organizing system and that it is attracted by self-organizing patterns wherever it may find them: in relationships, in fluid dynamics, or frozen as geological records in rocks; in evolving hierarchies in social organizations; or in works of art. In Gestalt theory, the individual parts making up these patterns gain their value from their participation in the pattern of the whole Gestalt. The brain not only seeks these patterns in the world, but projects them as hypotheses *about* the world which may or may not be confirmed by experience. Pattern-making, pattern recognition, pattern-testing and self-organization are therefore fundamental to the Ecological City. Capra proposes to redefine the new ecological paradigm in terms of "a constellation of concepts, values, perceptions, and practices shared by a community, which forms the basis of a particular vision of reality that is the basis of the way the community organizes itself."[97]

Since urban actors are constantly scanning their environment for patterns, they are likely to detect a changing situation. After a while they project or recognize a pattern in the event, communicate with others about it, and test their perceptions through interventions designed to evoke particular feedbacks. Capra makes this appear a simple operation of pattern recognition and projection, but in *The Projective Cast: Architecture and Its Three Geometries* (1995), Robin Evans reveals the complexity of this task, which involves the use of multiple projection systems by different actors in the construction process as well as multiple symbolic means of representation that range from spoken commands, legal documents, and conceptual analyses to drawings and photography. Evans distinguished between three different projective systems, each with its own geometry, that may be mixed and matched by actors as needed in the process of perceptual construction. He provides an elegant diagram of this complex situation at the end of his book that has much relevance to Capra's projective hypotheses.[98]

Capra sees patterns in self-organizing systems as a special kind of "dissipative structure" sought by urban actors. A dissipative structure appears in a particular location in a network or larger system of forces as a response to specific pressures, then disappears when no longer required: for example, the vortex that forms as a bathtub drains. Such structures exist in a state far from equilibrium; that is, they depend on imported energy for their dynamic stability. They must expend (dissipate) energy in a process of exchange with the larger scheme of systemic flows in their environment. A similar structure or pattern of relationships will recur whenever the same set of flows occurs in the network; however, despite similarities recognizable by our pattern-making abilities, each dissipative structure is unique in detail (for example, no two bathtub vortices are identical, though all are recognizable as members of the same class of events.) Every self-organizing, dissipative flow system is different and takes on unique attributes as determined by the local network. Finally, if adjacent flows or pressures increase or decrease, the dissipative structure can disappear or dissolve.

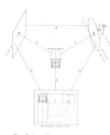

Robin Evans: architectural design diagram, The Projective Cast, 1995

Lynch, toward the end of his life, saw cities in terms of flows and waste products—that is, as systems with enough complexity, scope, and surplus energy to serve as hosts for dissipative structures, urban vortices. In his last book, published posthumously (*Wasting Away*, 1990), he looked unflinchingly at the question of waste and pollution in the emerging, global, consumer society.[99]

Capra's interpretation of ecological systems points toward the tendency of structures in the Ecological City to shift and change: urban pattern and structure are part of a process, part of larger network of visible and invisible flows of information and energy. Capra, like Lynch, emphasizes that in the ecological paradigm, feedback loops are crucial to the process of pattern recognition and to the formation of structures. Self-regulating structures depend on actors' feedback and process to maintain their form, striking a sensitive, dynamic balance far from equilibrium, a balance under constant pressure and stress, a assesses the drawbacks and uses of stereotypes and the problem of limited objectives, motives, and community input. He stresses the need for multiple actors, multiple and complex goals, and "fluidity" or flexibility with respect to time and form—the avoidance of a single, final image or "picture."[110] He recommends a dynamic, shifting balance between enclaves, areas of stasis, and channels of transportation and concludes with a critical review of the rather conventional 1960 master plan for Philadelphia, which was prepared under the leadership of Ed Bacon, a pioneer of urban design.

In his second broadside, "City Design and City Appearance" (1968), which is also included in the Banerjee and Southworth anthology, Lynch defines the role of *urban* design as the limited field of "project design" and sketches a far wider design agenda for *city* design. Project design is performed for a specific client in the service of a concrete program and is targeted within a specific enclave. It has a set time frame and assumes total control over some urban form (e.g., a new town). City design, in contrast, crosses disciplinary boundaries and includes architectural design, object design (i.e., design of a single article, such as a chair or bridge), system design, and environmental (ecological) design issues. For Lynch, system design is the design of "a functionally connected set of objects, which may extend over large areas but do not make a complete environment" (e.g., a highway or lighting system).

In this article, Lynch for the first time defines city design in an expanded, interdisciplinary field as the "general spatial arrangement of activities and objects over an extended area." City design, he wrote, deals with,

> the spatial and temporal pattern of human activity and its physical setting, and considers both its economic-social and psychological effects (of which latter the sensuous aspect is one part). The concepts and techniques for manipulating this complex pattern are as yet half-formed. The ambiguity of our graphic notation system, and its lack of inclusiveness, is one symptom of this inadequacy. The goals for which this pattern is manipulated are not clearly stated, and their relation to pattern is imperfectly known. Our vocabulary of city form is impoverished; the need for innovative ideas is correspondingly strong. Yet it is clear that city form is a critical aspect of the human environment, and design we must.[111]

This extensive field of endeavor set Lynch's approach at odds with the increasingly specialized field of urban design that was developing on the east coast of the United States in response to rapid suburban growth and urban sprawl (detailed further in the next chapter). Dean José Luis Sert , Le Corbusier's student and author of *Can Our Cities Survive?* (1942),[112] convened the first annual Harvard Urban Design Conference in 1956. He established the urban-design program that year, and continued a series of conferences through the 1960s. By 1973, the American Institute of Architects recognized urban design as a special subdivision of architectural practice.[113]

For Lynch, urban design was at its best in the regional malls, the new subcenters of the expanding urban network of the new regional city. This belief reflected the origins of contemporary urban design, but was hardly likely to endear Lynch to its leading practitioners, like I. M. Pei. (Pei progressed from designing the open-air armature of the Green Acre Shopping Mall in Long Island in the late 1950s to designing the Boston Government Center master plan in 1961.) Lynch admired malls because they created efficient new nodes at strategic intervals in the new urban networks, even while objecting to them at a particular, local, tactical level in terms of their closed-design approach. He would have confined contemporary urban design to such large-scale, local centers, and wrote as follows in the 1974 *Encyclopaedia Britannica*:

Reyner Banham: diagram of mountain and coastal ecologies, Los Angeles: The Architecture of the Four Ecologies, *1971*

> Some of the most sophisticated work in urban design has occurred in commercial centers. This is hardly surprising, considering the large investments in those centers, the effective control of form that is possible, and the importance of attractive form for increasing profits. . . . The regional shopping center is now a successful and much-imitated model, more closely based on behavioral knowledge than any other type of environmental design. Now rather artificial, specialized, and physically isolated, they could nonetheless be integrated with other functions to become true social centers.[114]

American shopping malls were, in fact, gaining increasing recognition at that time as urban centers; Reyner Banham, for example, wrote of malls as devices that created new suburban subcenters to counter the outward expansion of the network city in *Los Angeles: The Architecture of the Four Ecologies* (1971). Banham dedicated a chapter to the "Art of the Enclave," praised theme parks such as Disneyland, and highlighted the work of pioneering shopping-mall designers based in Los Angeles, such as Welton Beckett and Victor Gruen. (This work is also discussed further in the next chapter.)

Urban design, in its initial, postwar, suburban formulation, inherited a Modernist and functionalist base. Its narrative was fundamentally mechanical, in the Newtonian tradition, but was applied to urban fragments instead of whole cities. Lynch was broadly critical of contemporary urban design because of the scale of the large incremental additions it assumed. This top-down approach, Lynch argued, would lead to major mistakes. Perhaps he had in mind the fate of the $6 million Framingham Shoppers World Regional Mall in the Boston suburbs, which in the early 1950s closed after six weeks of operation due to major faults in its design, bankrupting its sponsors. Lynch described this approach as "the risky business of big pieces" because such new incremental additions might or might not work. The "failures of urban design are many," Lynch wrote, while successes are rare (citing Vallingby, a new-town center in

Shoppers World, Framingham, MA, 1950s (photograph courtesy of Richard Longstreth)

Sweden, also much admired by mall designers like Gruen, as one such success). "Distinguished historical, unplanned areas," he adds, "are much easier to find" than examples of successful urban design.[115]

Large incremental additions to American cities were in vogue when Lynch wrote his encyclopedia article. Banham describes many of these giant projects, but not the community opposition to them, in his *Megastructure: Urban Futures of the Recent Past* (1976). In New York, for instance, Paul Rudolph's design for a colossal megastructure covering the Lower Manhattan Expressway (1970) would have obliterated the historic SoHo district. Along with the Moses Westway project (first outlined in 1971), it would have transformed Lower Manhattan into a vast highway interchange. Community opposition halted this project. In this same period the Port Authority of New York and New Jersey overcame the opposition of the proprietors of the Cortlandt Street ("Radio Row") electronics stores, the Washington Street fruit and vegetable market, and local real estate industry leaders to build the twin towers of the World Trade Center (dedicated 1973).[116] Nor was the United States alone in its preoccupation with megastructures. The Greater London Council proposed the demolition of the Covent Garden market area, though it was successfully opposed by the Covent Garden Association Community Group in the late 1960s and early 1970s (as described by Brian Anson in *I'll Fight You For It!: Behind the Scenes in Covent Garden*, 1981). Community groups were less successful in trying to halt the demolition of Les Halles market in central Paris.[117] Banham also discusses a variant of the megastructure, the horizontal "megaform" (which includes landscape elements), instancing Arthur Erickson's design for the Vancouver Civic Center Project (1973).[118]

Vallingby new-town center, Sweden, 1949

Lynch was clear that Modernist city-planners and architects had become more and more out of touch with the way urban actors were operating on the ground. He saw the protest movements as positive and useful feedback from urban actors closely affected by planned changes. He saw a place for historic preservation. But also, unlike many urban designers (such as Modernist José Luis Sert, Dean of the Graduate School of Design at Harvard), Lynch was not opposed to suburban growth and, in his view, not all sprawl was bad. His personal theory of an "alternating net" model envisaged dense, "fast" growth literally interwoven with rural, low-density, "slow" growth in a tartan-like pattern. Like his contemporary Ian McHarg, author of *Design with Nature* (1969), he outlined areas of permitted growth and would have reserved vast areas for agriculture. While urban designers concentrated on megastructures, Lynch took a panoptic view of ecosystems and landscapes. His drawings for "A Temporary Paradise? The San Diego Region" (1974), for instance, made in association with Appleyard, were sketched as if seen from a height of 30,000 feet to give a regional, landscape view.[119]

Covent Garden protest, 1970 (photograph Peter Bairstow)

Toward the end of his career, in "City Design: What It Is and How It Might Be Taught" (1980), Lynch disclosed that he chose the term *city design* "in some desperation." He added that this term is "the best I can think of just now [because] the field has been an ambiguous one, seeming to lie between city planning and architecture or landscape architecture."[120] He also describes this emerging discipline as an interdisciplinary field that crosses established boundaries and includes a disparate set of activities. "City design," he continues,

> is no longer confined to the public regulation of private actions, or to the design of public works, or to map-like arrangements of legally defined uses—although all these continue to be important. It expands to include such topics as programming for an activity and character, creating prototypes for the environment as they will be used, making "framework" plans, engaging in environmental education or participatory design, thinking about the management of places, using incentives, and building the institutions of ownership and control.[121]

City design, in this view, forms a "framework" for participatory design from the bottom up, linking itself to institutions that manage, service, and control places of public activity, creating prototypes for the housing fabric and transportation systems, and generating new, adaptive programs in the city.

Kevin Lynch and Sasaki, Dawson and Demay Associates: landscape survey of Martha's Vineyard, MA, 1973

Lynch continues this argument in "The Immature Arts of City Design" (1984, the year of his death), the fourth and last of his articles in *City Sense and City Design*. He attacks three "accepted models" of top-down city design. The first is large-scale urban design, which targets specific "parts of the city with aesthetic intent," creating an incremental "collage city" or "city of big parts" (a reference to urban design as put forward in Colin Rowe and Fred Koetter's *Collage City*, 1978, discussed in the next chapter). The second is conservation of "parts" of the city that already work well (a reference to the historic preservation movement that grew worldwide in the 1970s, also discussed further in the next chapter). The third is the largely invisible "preparatory planning process" undertaken by planners.

Lynch goes on to suggest six "neglected techniques" which could contribute to city design. The first three are concerned with armatures of movement and actors' conceptual "images" or mental maps of cities. The first is "structure design," which operates on the perceptual and conceptual models of citizens, that is, on their mental maps of the relationships between armatures and enclaves. Structure design culminates in "image design." The second is "framework design," that is, design of large-scale infrastructures (e.g., networks of parks) that are closely associated with the paths or armatures navigated by citizens and that also help form the citizen's "image" and "structure." The third neglected technique is "sequence design," which concentrates on spatial armatures and their narratives, that is, on serial sequences of images seen by pedestrians or drivers on their paths, making up the experience of a "journey" (and that also help form "structure" and "image").

The second triad of neglected techniques emphasizes not movement but its complement, stasis. Number four is the art of enclave or "place making," which seeks to create a sense of belonging, including participation in "home design." The fifth technique is "routine design" or "system design," which is based on Lynch's concept of industrial design as the profession that designs the anonymous objects that inhabit public space and provide infrastructural services. Lynch mentions the rationalized "street furniture" of Georges Haussmann's mid-nineteenth-century boulevards as a preeminent example of a flexible, place-making, top-down "systems design." Sixth and last, there is "prototype design." Lynch mentions Christopher Alexander's *A Pattern Language: Towns, Buildings, Construction* (1977) as exemplifying this approach, in which community input and participation motivates enclave design and housing prototypes for adaptive reuse by citizen builders from the bottom up.

Making better use of these six techniques would open city designers more to change and a pluralism, which Lynch sees as the essential "art" at the base of a participatory aesthetic in urban design. He writes that city designers should be "comfortable with continuous change, partial control, pluralism, and participation; these are creative arts eliciting an aesthetic response."[122] In his own practice, Lynch tried to base city design on partial control, participation, narrative structures, paths, and image construction as made available to all sectors of society, even those who were not well funded, well organized, or articulate.

Lynch worked at both the global, strategic scale of the city-region and the scale of local, tactical intervention. His goal was to create narratives that supported urban image-spaces in which actor-designers could participate in the creation of urban space. He made many plans for Boston neighborhoods, including the first plans for the Government Center in central Boston (which replaced Scollay Square, beside Quincy Market and Waterfront, c. 1962). He also advised suburban communities on the location of highway projects and commercial subcenters based on studies of visual form (e.g., the Brookline Study of 1964–65) and planned the renovation of the poorest and largest public housing project in New England, Columbia Point (designed by Carr/Lynch Associates), where he worked with an eight-person committee of residents as clients.[123] With Donald Appleyard, he was involved in plans for the entire San Diego region, which included the border with Mexico (1974). And he played an important role in envisioning an attractive, linear, lake-park corridor in the center of Phoenix, Arizona (Rio Salada Development, 1985).

Kevin Lynch and Donald Appleyard: Rio Salada plan, Phoenix, AZ, 1985

1.4.3 City Design Since Lynch

City design is the art of creating possibilities for the use, management, and form of settlements or their significant parts. It manipulates patterns in time and space and has as its justification the everyday human experience of those patterns . . . [City design] thinks in terms of process, prototype, guidance, incentive, and control and is able to conceive broad, fluid sequences along with concrete, homely details. It is a scarcely

developed art—a new kind of design and new view of its subject matter.
—Kevin Lynch, *A Theory of Good City Form* [124]

Since Lynch's death in 1984, the practice of city design has continued but has divided into two scales of operation to deal with the emerging fragmentation of the city across vast regional landscapes. The tradition of large-scale city design has continued as a remedial practice in the work of Peter Calthorpe, who recently produced two 100-mile-long metropolitan corridor plans, one for the Portland-Willamette Valley and the other extending north and south from Salt Lake City, between the mountains and the desert. These are given in his book *The Regional City* (2001), written with William Fulton,[125] which includes a chapter on "designing the region" based on global plans to shift cities from "edge cities" to "regional cities." The "building blocks" of the regional city are *centers*, *districts*, *preserves*, and *corridors*. Each building block works as an autonomous system or layer in the city composition.

Calthorpe's "regional city" thus includes a layer of linear, regional features such as parklands and continuous ecological corridors that operate at the scale of mountains and rivers, much as Lynch imagined for the Ecological City. A separate layer contains highways and transportation corridors that also work at the megascale along alternating linear corridors, not unlike Lynch's "alternating net" model. Within these two frameworks Calthorpe and Fulton place a texture of residential enclaves, with New Urbanist district plans termed "neighborhoods." This enclave concept is based on Calthorpe's early work with Doug Kelbaugh, the *Pedestrian Pocket* (1989). These "pockets" are small-scale, local, prototype enclaves for clustered, pedestrian-friendly new towns centered about a "central park" and linked by light rail and highway to their "mother" metropolis; they are thus enclaves designed from the top down by architects, unlike Lynch's prototypes.

Lynch's large-scale Ecological City design strategy drew heavily on the work of landscape architects and regional planners such as Frederick Law Olmsted, Howard Odum, Benton MacKaye, and Lawrence Halprin.[126] Lynch himself made an early contribution to this field with his popular textbook *Site Planning* (first published in 1962 and revised many times in association with Gary Hack). Simon Swaffield's reader *Theory in Landscape Architecture* (2002) contains two selections from *Site Planning*, "The Art of Site Planning" and "Site Design" (both from the last, 1984 revision with Hack). Lynch's large-scale city design work included studies of landscape types, often as seen from the road or the air, as in his Martha's Vineyard research for the Vineyard Open Land Foundation with Sasaki, Dawson, and Demay Associates (1973.)[127] In that project, Lynch helped formulate development guidelines based on landscape type, treating the landscape as a patchwork of local ecosystems connected by various flows. Monica Turner, Robert Gardner, and Robert O'Neil developed a very similar technique at a more sophisticated level (without reference to Lynch) in *Landscape Ecology in Theory and Practice: Pattern and Process* (2001).[128]

techniques or "scenarios" that simulated numerically the results of various design decisions and applications of specific codes. City-modeling took on a new life in this highly computerized, digital environment, and was extended to imaginary city images. The Dutch architectural group MVRDV, for example, projected various futures in their *Costa Iberica* study of tourist areas on the coast of Spain, including a fantastic image of a hyperdense tourist city by the sea.[139]

1.4.5 A Place Utopia

Lynch did not seek to make diagnostic or prognostic use of his three normative models, despite his early interest in such applications (e.g., *The Image of the City*, 1960). However, in Chapter 17 of *A Theory of Good City Form*, "A Place Utopia," he does describe a utopia (literally, a "no-place") that is a complex urban system combining elements of all three of his urban models. These elements exist in parallel, with institutional methods for conflict resolution and built-in provision for expected change. He writes of the "recycling of settlements" and says that in this utopia—unlike most—"change is expected." There are strategies for decline as well as growth; Lynch posits "rituals" for closing an old place and opening a new one. He also imagines the devolution of New York into a cluster of communities devoted to fishing, special recreation, and the mining of the neighboring museum of skyscrapers for stone and raw materials, all functioning as a tourist attraction inside a vast regional landscape inhabited in a low-density sprawl. Land management and "place creation" are much-appreciated arts in Lynch's place utopia.[140]

Kevin Lynch: alternating-networks diagram, A Theory of Good City Form, *1981*

It also includes important elements that are absent from his declarations on city design. Lynch, for instance, imagines that most people will live most of their life in one place and in one group, and travel intermittently: "Mobility is tempered by ties of place."[141] But some people will move to seek a better environment, opportunities for work, and so forth. He envisions such movements as part of a worldwide system for maximizing the use of the world's resources, and as involving negotiations between interregional authorities. Some groups are constantly mobile, their home being on the road or aboard ships or planes, servicing the larger ecology of migrations.[142]

One of the most striking elements of Lynch's place utopia is that there are special enclaves dedicated to "environmental" experiment and change (places of the sort I term *heterotopias* and examine in detail in Chapter 4). He writes:

> Environmental change has also been formalized in experimental centers. Volunteers give a trial run to some hypothesis about a modification of place and society—a new type of group family in a specially designed structure, for example . . . The volunteers monitor their own experiment and may abandon or modify it. Should it prove workable, the experiment becomes a demonstration. Others repeat the experience for themselves—

for pleasure, for confirmation, or to help them choose a way of life.[143]

It is not hard here to see Lynch incorporating contemporary social experiments, such as hippy communes like Ant Farm's Drop City (1963–69) or alternative communities like Christiana in Copenhagen (which is discussed extensively in Chapter 4).

Through the lens of Lynch's place utopia one can see city design as a management system for a complex system of urban patches and patterns that are linked together by channels of communication and transport. Some enclaves or patches are remnants of previous normative city models. Others are places of change and experiment. Cells are constantly emerging and dying as the needs of the citizens evolve; old cells are being reinhabited and adapted to new uses as new cells are being created elsewhere.

Normative city *theory* is the working system of shared belief that ties all these patches and channels (armatures and enclaves) together and that manages change from within. City *design* is the management system that monitors and constantly rebalances the overall system in the landscape and ecology of regional and global networks. The latter is concerned with affairs at all scales, from the global perspective—the view from 30,000 feet or even from orbit—down to the most place-specific details. The connecting catalyst between all scales is the involved and sensitive urban actor, whose personal choices—which are based on the city theory he or she holds—create larger patterns in the system, generally in conformity with "power laws" such as Zipf's (seen to govern the distribution of American city sizes over the last 100 years).

Lynch's problem was that most designers did not share his panoptic vision of city models, city growth, and city transformation. As we saw with current practitioners of city design, it is rare to combine the ability to see large-scale patterns, often associated with top-down design, with focus on small-scale detail, incorporating feedback from the bottom up. Lynch's reliance on Christopher Alexander's "pattern language" to describe the emergence of city form from below severely limited his appeal to design professionals, who foresaw their own redundancy in the strategy of "partial control." Furthermore, designers in advanced industrial societies tend to specialize to one end of the design spectrum or the other and rarely master both. An easier compromise was the strategy of urban design, which posited a middle ground between the two extremes as a separate world unto itself.

1.4.6 A Glance Ahead

In the remainder of this book I will investigate three recurrent urban structures or organizational patterns: the *armature*, the *enclave*, and the *heterotopia*, all of which we have encountered under different names in Lynch's city models. For the moment, the *armature* may be envisioned as the traditional European street. It is a linear organizational pattern or sequencing device, perspectival in structure. The *enclave* may be exemplified by the traditional public square. It is a centering device, a static enclosure with a single center and, often, a single function. The *heterotopia* is a special form of enclave that contains exceptions to the dominant urban system. It is hybrid, with multiple subcenters and subcompartments, and is differentiated from its surroundings; examples include a monumental church, hospital, or any public institution standing out from the surrounding urban fabric. Heterotopias often handle flows and manage change for the larger-scale urban networks in which they are embedded.

Heterotopias are real places, but many include a utopian component, an element of displaced dream or illusion. Michel Foucault stressed that although Utopia is a dream of a *good* place, the word itself means *no* place.[144] Utopia is thus unreal, imaginary. It is a dream . . . yet this dream, or a fragment or ghost of it, is embedded in the real space of the heterotopia. This ambiguous and contradictory construction frees heterotopias, in part, from their particular locations and connects them with a larger system of values, beliefs, and hopes that is centered elsewhere.

This chapter has been centered on the work of Kevin Lynch. Lynch pugnaciously attacked the urban designers who were his contemporaries, but did not live to articulate his own theories in all their complexity. In the next chapter I will take up the task of unfolding and extending Lynch's insights by first going deeper into urban design, the "middle ground" that provoked Lynch's ire and set him against his contemporaries, thus limiting his influence and ensuring his rapid disappearance (with exceptions as noted above) from design theory and practice in the 1980s and 1990s.

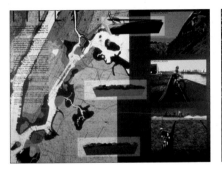
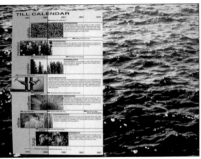

Landscape Urbanism

Victoria Marshall and Steven Tipv: Van Alen Institute East River Competition, New York; Competition winner 1998 (http://www.vanalen. org/competitions/east _river/first.htm)

Ecological City

a) *Kevin Lynch and Donald Appleyard; San Diego plan, 1974*
b)*Metro and Peter Calthorpe Associates: Portland Metro Area plan, 1996–2005*
c) *Michael Sorkin Studio: Brooklyn waterfront plan, 1993–94*
d) *Bolles+Wilson Architects: Eurolandschaft sketches, ca. 1994*
e) *Field Operations: Freshkills Park, Staten Island, New York, layered design analysis, 2003 (http://www. fieldoperations.net/ projects.htm)*

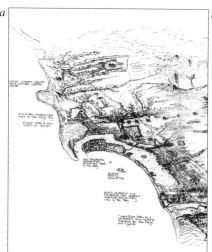

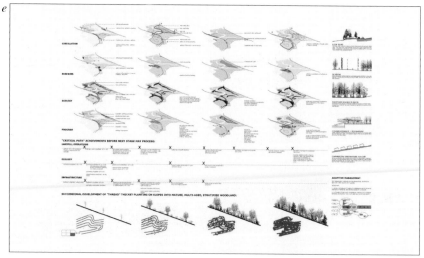

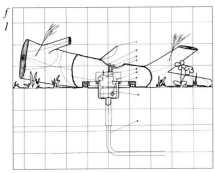

f
1

f
2

Ecological City

f 1) *David Green:* Rock Plug, *1969*
f 2) *Green:* The Bottery, *1970*
g 1) *Dennis Crompton:* Computer City, *1964*
g 2, 3) *Mike Webb:* Suitaloon, *1967*
g 4) *MVRDV: Dutch Pavilion, Hanover Fair, 2000*
h) *ISoCaRP Conference: three city models, 2001*
i 1, 2) *Paola Viganò et alia: Lecce City Territory, dispersal and concentration scenarios, 2001*

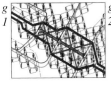

g
1

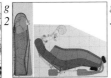

g
2

g
3

g
4

h

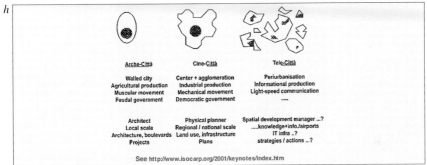

See http://www.isocarp.org/2001/keynotes/index.htm

i
1

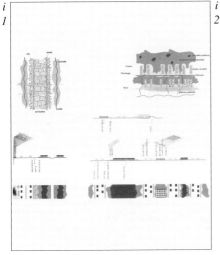

i
2

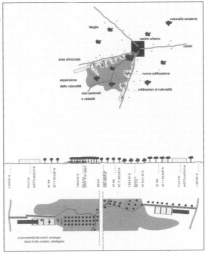

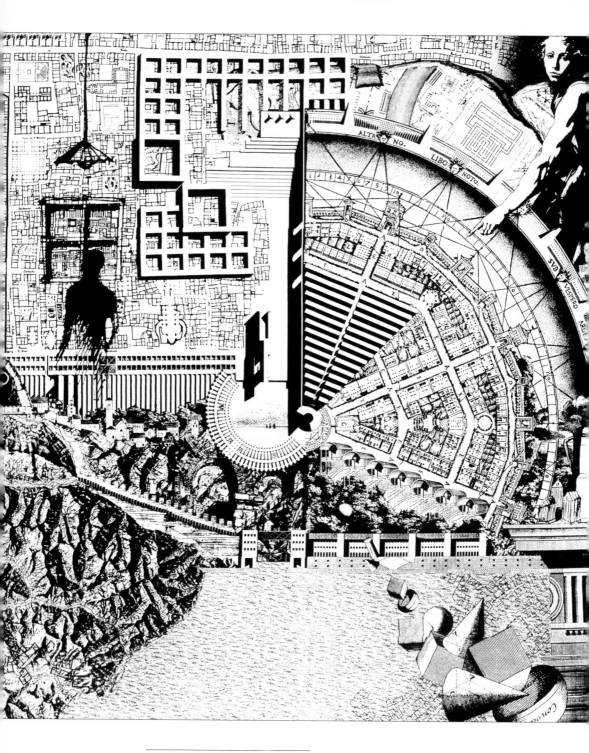

Chapter 2

What Is Urban Design?

2.1 WHAT IS URBANISM?

> When several villages are united in a single complex community, large enough to be nearly or quite self-sufficient, the *polis* comes into existence.
> —Aristotle

Thanks to Serlio, Kostof, Lynch, and the dictionary, as reviewed in Chapter 1, the traditional European definition of *city* is relatively clear. It should therefore be equally straightforward to define the term *urban*. According to the Oxford English Dictionary, *urban* means "of, living or situated in, a city or town," while according to Webster's it means "relating to, characteristic of, or constituting a city." Webster's also states that *urbanism* is "the characteristic way of life of city dwellers," that is, of their life-world, and that to *urbanize* is "to cause to take on urban characteristics . . . to impart an urban way of life" to a place or space.

Our concern is with the characteristic way of life—the life-world—of city dwellers, an urban pattern of activity that repeats over time but, like a fractal, is never exactly the same twice (see discussion of Capra in Chapter 1). As we saw in the previous Chapter, the "city" has comprised a wide range of urban conditions over time. In his three normative models, Lynch indicates the range of these conditions, including the compact enclaves of the City of Faith morphology (based on agricultural support systems) and the stretched armatures and dense nodes of the City as a Machine (with its star-shaped morphology based on modern transportation and communications and with its split between production and consumption). Recently, the more evenly distributed network morphology of the Ecological City (a.k.a. the City as an Organism) has arisen, with its various hybrid nodes of various vintages and sizes, reconditioned by informational systems and constant feedback from a vast constellation of cellular enclaves scattered across the globe. These three urban patterns are roughly equivalent to the Archi Città, Cine Città, and Tele Città morphologies.

The first part of this chapter will examine how the collective urban actors corresponding to these morphologies define their models of urbanism in terms of their own life-worlds and activities, their control of public space, their need for privacy. The second part will look briefly at how these voices define design, that is, the methods by which their model of the city shall be realized. The third part will study a crucial shift in the approach to design that occurred after the collapse of Modernism. This shift was the emergence of the practice of urban design in New York in the 1960s as a background to the writing of *Collage City* (1978) by Koetter and Rowe. This seminal book, which has been criticized for

Aldo Rossi: Analogical City, *1976*

creating the "Museum City," presented an urban-design approach very different from that proposed by Lynch in *A Theory of Good City Form* (1981).

The last part of the chapter will explore the variety of design approaches available to designers at the turn of the twentieth century, a collection of recombinant techniques I call the seven "-ages" of the contemporary, postmodern city (decoupage, collage, bricolage, photomontage, montage, assemblage, and rhizomic assemblage). The thesis of this chapter is that both Lynch and the Koetter–Rowe team, in attempting to juggle and balance the recombinations of the fragmenting city in different but related ways, staked out a fourth position beyond the discourse surrounding the usual three normative models.

In the first chapter we saw a diagram from Robin Evans's *The Projective Cast: Architecture and Its Three Geometries* (1995), based on Buckminster Fuller's favored tetrahedron structure, that shows the relationships between the multiple actors who build buildings and the difficulties of their communications. It is useful to keep this diagram in mind as we move between actors' viewpoints and their techniques for realizing the city. Evans's diagram is relevant to our study of the city because it portrays three actors—the client, the builder, and the architect—and the relationships that link them, *plus* a fourth position from which all the systems in the built object can be seen. We can use this diagram to map the relationships of Lynch's three city models and their actors, then position ourselves with Lynch at a fourth point overlooking the system.

2.1.1 Constructing the Urban Life-World

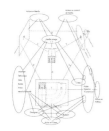

Reflexive architectural design, based on a diagram in Robin Evans The Projective Cast, *1995*

In this section we examine the three competing voices that inhabit Lynch's three cities: three classes of urban actor that determine three distinct urbanisms, each with corresponding urban patterns and life-worlds suited to its creators' needs and technological capacities. We will first hear the dominant actors of the Archi Città arguing for the importance of top-down management, a clear geometric order based on divine inspiration, and the importance of a single, central place from which all others can be seen and commanded. We will then listen to a dialectic debate in the Cine Città between two opposed parties, one representing the old way of the closed city and the other representing the new, expanding city. In this context, all actors are expected to make a choice for the old center or the new edge-city. Finally, we will hear a polyphonic chorus discussing the possibilities of a city where the old city center is just one of many centers making up the Tele Città.

Christian Norberg-Schulz, in his *Existence, Space, and Architecture* (1971), defines the phenomenological concept of an urban actor's "life-world." Each life-world exists within a perspectival construction or framework, and each life-world's perspective has its central vanishing point, mirroring the position of the observer or actor. Norberg-Schulz argues that every individual's life-world is different, arising as it does from the interaction of personal knowledge, communal knowledge, and scientific knowledge. Each of these three knowledge types is "true" within its own framework, but can be falsified or contradicted by the others. Further, each knowledge type implies a corresponding life-world; for example,s the life-world of a scientist or engineer in the laboratory is different from that of a merchant in the marketplace or a homemaker at home. Yet difference does not imply disconnection or irrelevance. Each of these three systems—laboratory, market, and home—is present in the other two: the scientist is affected by market forces, the homemaker by engineering developments, and so on. Thus, for Norberg-Schulz every individual's life-world represents a different balance and interaction between three elements or knowledges that are interlinked by feedback loops. Like Serlio's tripartite schema, this model of the urban dweller's life-world describes a field of *dynamic* discourse and interaction.[1]

"Personal" knowledge comprises notions of the world based on purely individual experience modified by discussions with family and friends and by rather fuzzy (usually) background notions of modern science. A person who rarely leaves their home and has relationships only with friends and family moves largely in this private or personal sphere. Early American sociologists of the Chicago School imagined that many people inhabit such a small-scale social world, a "neighborhood unit" or local universe that they rarely leave. Such a person's "spatial schema" or path through the city would be formed in terms of this private world or enclave.

The urban life-world of "communal" knowledge is based on unwritten law, shared discussions, and interactions among community members guided by implicit rules of thumb. Actors in the sphere of the communal-knowledge life-world put personal and scientific knowledge in the background. Norberg-Schulz emphasizes that much practical knowledge resides in the community, where skills are developed by individuals and passed down from generation to generation by word of mouth, with relatively little being written down. The individual might build a personal knowledge base along particular lines of interest, but this knowledge only comes to fruition when shared with the group. Communal knowledge tends to survive as folk culture, outside the realm of modern science.

Vernacular urban cultures are rich in communal knowledge. Here local customs and practices are memorized within a group as the unwritten codes and rules handed down from father to son or mother to daughter within a trade or tribe. Local builders, for instance, may lay out courtyard houses and vary their section by rule of thumb to catch the prevailing wind, with large eaves on porches and overhanging roofs for shade. Public space, in the city of communal knowledge, is deeply wedded to community activity; it is also a contested space where authority figures need constantly to assert themselves. The advent of the radio, television, air conditioning, and globalization have tended to stress or dissolve the local, urban, communal knowledge of the small-scale village or

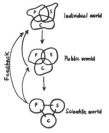

Christian Norberg-Schulz: Three worlds of knowledge, Existence, Space, and Architecture, *1971*

town that is (or was) close to the earth but conscious of the sky.[2]

The older vernacular urban world-view also included small elements of scientific thought; these would eventually develop into a full-fledged scientific world-view. For later nineteenth-century commentators such as Idelfons Cerdá (discussed further below), this meant that the work of Italian Renaissance architects and urban designers like Donato Bramante or Michelangelo could be seen as precursors of a more rational and scientific approach. (In the next chapter, these precedents are discussed in terms of combinations and recombinations of urban elements.)

According to Norberg-Schulz, the scientific life-world contains personal and communal components but discounts them as subjective material, incapable of verification. This is in accord with the views of phenomenologists such as Henri Bergson and Edmund Husserl, who argued in the late nineteenth and early twentieth centuries that in the modern world all knowledge is atomized and partitioned, categorized and segregated, rendering the relationships *between* things invisible. Each piece is perfect in itself, best represented as an atom or sphere that forms links to other such atoms and spheres in a carefully segregated network. The phenomenologists criticized the empirical tests of the "scientific method." These tests, they argued, could only prove what scientists initially hypothesized in their research parameters. Such knowledge was carefully constructed and self-referential, and had no wider relevance.[3]

Ildefons Cerdá: Barcelona extension, plan, 1859

Thus the scientific logic of modern city-planning and architecture seeks clearly defined and segregated monofunctional zones in the city, to be connected by clear lines of transportation and communication infrastructure. Lynch's City as a Machine is constructed in this fashion. Today's city-regions are the product of such thinking, which allows city planners and architects to distribute urban functions scientifically or rationally (it is hoped) across a large regional landscape. Yet scientists inevitably distort or elide personal and communal knowledge or logic in their atomistic schemes, which cannot take into account the fuzzy and nonlinear (but not necessarily invalid) logic of nonscientific thinking. Public space disappears into the channels of communication and transportation, leaving an empty shell where community participation once was—the Modernist's empty plaza or parking lot sprawling at the feet of great towers. In place of *community* spaces there emerge privately owned "public" spaces, recentering the city on multiple subcenters whose constellations form privately controlled edge-cities.

"Scientific" knowledge, as defined by Norberg-Schulz, contains the world of industrial production and consumption. In this world, knowledge is organized on Cartesian, mechanical principles. This system construes the world in terms of linear chains of action and reaction and amplifies oppositions between binary pairs (yes–no, off–on, up–down, in–out, figure–ground, etc.). These binaries limit and repress personal and communal knowledge-systems in the pursuit of an "objective" world-view because their communication requires the simplification or reduction of complex messages and of ambiguity. In addition, the mechanization of vision (the development of photography and the cinema) extended this scientific field so that the city itself was seen in a new way—through the lenses of machines. A simplified image of the city, captured on film and edited in a montage, moves through the flickering gate of the projector. The machine gate places frames between light and darkness at a set rate to create a moving picture whose precise character depends on lenses, film stock, processing, and lighting. This image of the city on film, of the Cine Città, is a technicized fragment, an edited version of the full city seen from certain preferred, mechanically accelerated viewpoints and paths. The dream or vision of the dense, megalithic modern city thus became a part of mass culture in the 1920s via movies like Fritz Lang's *Metropolis* (1927), even while its dispersal was accelerating under the impact of the automobile.

2.1.2 The Emergence of "Scientific" Urbanism: Cerdá and More

Françoise Choay notes in *The Rule and the Model* (1997) that Ildefons Cerdá coined the terms *urbanism* and *urbanization* in his *Theory of Urbanization* (1867).[4] For Cerdá, "urbanism" was the science of human settlements at various scales and times, including countryside networks. Choay argues that Cerdá was the first to outline a self-conscious, autonomous, modern, scientific theory of the city, albeit in a highly personal and bombastic style. Cerdá's new science of urbanism would study the relationship of stasis and movement in the city, both ancient and modern. In his view, the new technologies of steam, telegraph, and electricity were creating a new civilization, entailing an enormous jump in scale and speed for the nineteenth-century European city.

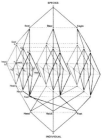

Claude Levi-Strauss: diagram of he totemic operator

Choay suggests (to reduce her complex argument to its essentials) that Cerdá articulated the goals of the emerging modern design profession by merging the combinatory, bottom-up matrix of Leon Battista Alberti (1404–72) with the frozen, top-down, Utopian ideal of Thomas More (1478–1535) and then subjecting the result to Darwinian testing in the field. Though both Alberti and More presented an image of a dense city with public spaces that still belonged to their local communities, the former envisaged a matrix built from the decisions of local builders following a set of combinatorial rules and the latter presented the image of an ideal, dense city frozen in perfection for all time.

Choay associates the combinatorial discourse of the dense city with the publication of Alberti's *On the Art of Building in Ten Books* (1450), which followed his treatise on perspective (*De Pictura*, 1435). *On the Art of Building in Ten Books* emphasizes a flexible, combinatorial logic, implying that the city itself, like a big building, could be made from the proper combination of elements within the closed visual mechanism of the perspectival domain. In effect, Alberti took the informal combinatorial matrix of the vernacular medieval city and subjected it to precise rules within a three-dimensional spatial

*Streets in
perspective*

a 1, 2) *Michelozzo
Michelozzi:
Dubrovnik
(Ragusa) extension,
main street and
plan, 1470s*
b) *Sebastian Serlio:
Comic Scene, 1540*
c) *Leon Battista
Alberti: personal
medal with flying-
eye emblem,
ca.1470*
d) *Balbassare
Peruzzi: theatrical
perspective (©
1990, Photo
SCALA, Florence)*

*a
1*

b

*a
2*

c

d

coordinate system based on the discovery of perspective. He claimed these rules were descended from the Romans, in particular, from Vitruvius, who in the first century BC described how to lay out cities and buildings.

Alberti set up recognizable, formal patterns as locally stable algorithms or recurrent structures that would temper and channel the chaos and flows of the city. These patterns resided inside a perspectival matrix that helped the designer organize parts and elements into symbolic wholes. His logic was ultimately linguistic (descending from Latin grammar and syntax, which operated according to a simple set of rules for combinations and exceptions), but his formulas also had mechanical aspects, setting fixed, invariable relationships and ratios. Alberti's Palazzo Rucellai in Florence (begun 1453), for instance, established the new norm for a cubic patrician palace, with its etched classical facade and elaborate surfaces of rusticated stone.[5] His system of combining fixed, invariable elements with structures and relationships that could change to accommodate new situations established a new professional language. This dual system was both top down (mandated by fixed, hierarchical, organizational structures) and bottom up (employing combinatorial elements that could accommodate innovation).

Thomas More: Utopia, *1516*

Alberti's system was thus a transitional structure, both ancient (hierarchical, with a single center) and modern (open and combinatorial) in character. The public space of the city was controlled by the new science of perspective, and each building had a place in the visual hierarchy of the city corresponding to the social station of its owner. Alberti's ideas on public space influenced following generations of Renaissance designers, who could align these two aspects (ancient and modern) through a mathematical and proportional matrix that included ideal typologies based on Platonic solids (cube, sphere, cone, etc.). Choay compared this Renaissance double structure, part machine and part combinatorial matrix, to structuralist theories created by twentieth-century anthropologists and linguists like Levi-Strauss or Noam Chomsky, with their dual "deep" and "surface" structures and hidden central reference point.[6]

Thomas More's *Utopia* (1516) presented a very different image of the city's life-world. He stressed the formal and spatial dimension of urban organization as an expression of social rules and, ultimately, of ethical behavior. Public space was, in this vision, sacred space, an idea descended from classical ideals about the Greek agora and Roman forum. Although these spaces had historically often been irregular, forming gradually and in response to circumstances, topography, and the desires of spirits and deities (as divined by priests and seers), More's city was, like Alberti's, strictly rational. His discourse was, however, more critical of the status quo than Alberti's, and he imagined a radically alternative social arrangement.

Utopia, as Choay notes, initiated a discourse on the ideal social organization of the city. More wanted to freeze social relationships in a formal and spatial pattern fixed for all time. Utopus, his fictional founder of the state of Utopia (literally "no place"), decreed that its capital city Amaurotum should be hyper-orderly and symmetrical in all directions. The largest temple or meeting place dominated the center of the main square; smaller temples occupied a smaller square in each quarter of the city. Two of these subsidiary temple squares had markets. Townhouses were grouped around community leaders' houses on the streets leading to the temples. All the houses of Utopia were standard, namely, three-story townhouses with roof gardens. Large glass windows in each house faced communal back-gardens. Gardening was the chief leisure activity of the inhabitants, who were never to number over 6,000. The idea of a fixed population became a recurrent theme of utopian thought, resurfacing in the late twentieth century in the American New Urbanist movement's definition of an ideal neighborhood unit.[7]

More's static Utopia was an implicit critique of contemporary London, a dynamic, disorderly civil society expanding in an age of global exploration and Atlantic trade. Utopia mirrored London's position on a small island off a large continent, with an abundant agricultural hinterland of farms (communal, in Utopia) and a network of smaller towns. Utopia's orderly townhouses contrasted with the messy, irregular, still-medieval fabric of London. More also sought to correct many of London's social flaws. In Utopia there would be no religious intolerance, no licentiousness, no drinking to excess, and no sexual promiscuity; women would be equal to men, being allowed to own property and to be priests. (However, Utopians would still have slaves working in their hospitals, communal farms, and jails outside the walls.)[8]

Mies van der Rohe: German Pavilion, Barcelona, 1929, (reconstruction; photograph 2003)

Little could change in the design of Utopia; later generations could only refine and fulfill the design laid out by Utopus. When the design was fulfilled, a new colony on the same model would have to be started elsewhere. Choay speculates that this extreme spatial rigidity and attachment to a fixed image of the city was the product of More's insecurity, his fear of the changing world around him. She cites More's anxiety at the discovery of the American continent, the founding of new colonies, the expansion of trade on a global scale, and religious wars in Europe.[9]

More's goal was to optimize urban social processes through design for social justice, religious freedom, social harmony, and gender equality, thus providing a more regulated and moral urban life. To achieve these goals, More imagined the city as a totality, a theocracy, a self-balancing system. Anticipating behavioral psychologists of the twentieth century, he thought that spatial arrangements shaped the social behavior of urban actors; physical closure and structuring of the urban life-world was therefore important. In particular, Utopia would encourage better social behavior through a rationalized system of religious visual surveillance. "The Elders" were the dominant actors; each Elder watched all the life on his street through the glass backs of the houses.[10] This fishbowl existence reinforced good behavior. The patriarchs would further reinforce their control of the social hierarchy via their sermons in the prayer halls. Perspectival vision and visual inspection, which had previously helped display the power of the Prince in Renaissance theater (as in Serlio's Noble scene), here became an instrument for the maintenance of a puritanical urban virtue.

More, seeking to mandate a perfect network of social and economic relationships within a fixed frame of spatial relationships, thus created an imaginary urban life-world that was transparent to its monitors and frozen for eternity in one ideal form. Although this imaginary, ideal city was admittedly "no place," not real, it was nevertheless intended as a goal for those who sought a better world, and More hoped that his readers would deem the image attractive, the goal worthy. Manfredo Tafuri, in *Architecture and Utopia: Design and Capitalist Development* (1976), observes that such idealized, perfect models, "negative utopias," were indeed eventually integrated into the industrial production process. Tafuri contrasts the fixed, negative utopias of More or of Mies van der Rohe, who in the early twentieth century sought a classical stillness in the midst of change, with capitalist entrepreneurs' restless drive toward perfection—their habit of tossing earlier models on the scrapheap of history—and modern designers' devotion to a shifting, positivist utopia.[11]

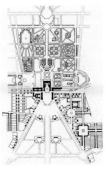

Plan of Versailles: France, 1687

Michel Foucault argues that perspective and visual inspection played a particularly important role in this new, impersonal, utopian, scientific, spatial approach to public space, an approach that reflects and services the power relationships in our polarized society. Following Herbert Marcuse, Foucault emphasizes the "one dimensional" quality of the new, scientific man. He observes that the new, scientific apparatus in architectural and urban practice is designed to establish simple, disciplined, everyday patterns of behavior in carefully designed spatial and typological arrangements. This entails a transparent life-world based on a bipolar system of observer and observed, subject and object, establishing a fundamental split in society (and strongly recalling More's project). The state system enforces the code of modernity through visual inspections and secret surveillance. Foucault cites the design of Jeremy Bentham's Panopticon prison as symbolic of the power of public space and vision to shape activities in the utopian program of the eighteenth-century Enlightenment. This prison, a specialized heterotopic device designed by Bentham to reform its inmates, constituted a miniature model of the modern life-world. Everything was classified and in order, demonstrating the principles of a new life-world based on segregation, separation, inspection, transparency, and distance communication.[12]

Foucault's critique of the public space of the modern life-world continues the long Neoplatonic tradition in France of questioning the predominance of vision. Visual surveillance and the pursuit of "good" public behavior is as pervasive in the Panopticon as in More's Utopia. The "eye of power," the hidden jailer of the Panopticon, sat in a central, dark tower like a hidden god, replacing the Sun King at Versailles. This "eye" lay at the center of a three-dimensional spatial matrix forming the basis for the new building typology. It was integral to the system:

unseen, yet able to see into all the well-lit cells on the prison's periphery. Bentham took pains to isolate all prisoners and to provide the jailer with the means to discipline and punish misbehavior. His was a Newtonian universe of action and reaction, cause and effect, crime and punishment, a closed, mechanical mechanism designed to maintain a social equilibrium. This mechanism's express aim was to make prisoners internalize the hidden jailer so that they would return to society reformed, able to behave according to modern society's norms. The Panopticon's officially engineered power relationship between center and edge, observer and observed, supports Foucault's bipolar analysis of the mechanical relationships implied by modernity.

The urban life-world engineered in Bentham's rationalist, utilitarian approach to design—preoccupied with top-down control, segregation of functions, classification of fixed typologies, concentration of power, and an overarching visual and social order—was mirrored in the nineteenth century in a series of utopian designs for new industrial communities isolated from existing cities. These projects were conceived as critiques of the pollution, squalor, and disease of the nineteenth-century industrial city. Here public space took on the utopian values of freedom and control prescribed by More. This rationalist, utopian, socialist critical tradition of public urban space, further exemplified by Charles Fourier in France and Robert Owen in Britain, continued in the Beaux Arts school system at the end of the century in projects like Tony Garnier's *Cité Industrielle* (1901–17). Modernists inherited this concept of a reformed public space, descended from dense urban cores, as they projected new cities with wide open spaces (e.g., Le Corbusier's *Contemporary City for Three Million Inhabitants*, 1922).[13]

Choay argues that Cerdá provided the rational basis for the new scientific urbanism and life-world in his treatise on urbanization as a modernization process. Cerdá uses Darwin's theory of evolution to combine More's fixed Utopian typology of urban public space with Alberti's rules of combinatorial generation. In *The Origin of Species* (1859), Darwin argued that the evolution of natural "design" is an autonomous process that can be observed and understood step by step. Darwinian natural selection is an unguided process that matches form to function through testing against local ecology. Darwin described this

near a city"; thus, even at this early date the term *urban sprawl* is specifically linked to an urban life-world consisting of housing and shopping centers of a sort made possible only by the automobile. It denotes the extension of a new organizational and distribution pattern in a continuous belt of new growth that extends beyond old city-core and industrial grid expansions, beyond the reach of Cerdá's streetcar and railway "commuter belts." Indeed, "urban sprawl" implies a new form of "conurbation" (i.e., "an aggregation or continuous network of urban communities"—Webster).

In its definition of urban sprawl Webster was referencing the massive wave of American suburban development that occurred after 1945, when 40 million citizens moved to the suburbs in just 15 years. By 1961 Jean Gottmann could describe the northeast-coast corridor of the United States from Boston to Washington as a "megalopolis" containing 38 million inhabitants. Most lived in low-density suburbs, a "nebulous structure" merging with the landscape.[20] The rise of the Anglo-American suburban megalopolis prompted not only the concept of "urban sprawl" but the question "What is 'urban'?" The new conurbations contained multiple centers of different formats; Howard's ring-radial model was no longer adequate. Should there be, or could there be, a new urban science to account for the new situation?

Jean Gottmann: regional water-supply map, Megalopolis, *1961*

Some theorists took up the task of creating one—or at least refurbishing the old urban science. In Chapter 1, we saw that Lynch cited Walter Isard (1956) and Jay Forrester (1969) in describing the emergence of a new network theory of multiple centers in the 1960s. As early as 1965 the British geographer R. E. Pahl, in *Urbs in Rure: The Metropolitan Fringe in Hertfordshire*, questioned the usefulness of traditional central-place theory in explaining the new situation. Pahl considered that the growing specialization of uses, proliferation of private development, and segregation of classes on London's "metropolitan fringe" in Hertfordshire, beyond London's Green Belt, constituted a new pattern of urban organization.[21] Twenty years later, in *Bourgeois Utopias*, Fishman described a new urban life-world in which all the functions of conventional cities were now available within a 20-minute highway ride of the suburban home, making the public spaces of the traditional central core unnecessary for the fulfillment of most of daily life's requirements. These new technoburbs or "burbs" (Fishman's term) are subcomponents of megacities that rival their central city in size, if not in terms of world-class cultural facilities. Yet each family in the technoburb would require one or more cars to participate, as its low density could not support public transportation.[22]

The full implications of the scale-jump to a multicentered, regional-city system only emerged some 20 years after Gottmann's seminal study *Megalopolis* (1961). Architects and city planners were struggling to get a clear picture of the new, nebulous conurbations, developing terms and techniques to measure its patterns and flows. Not until the end of the twentieth century had a broad consensus formed as to the nature of this new urban matrix: the "ruralized urbanization" of a vast, peripheral territory (apparently fulfilling Cerdá's prophecy of a century earlier). Below, I outline the emergence of consensus on the "post-urban" dissolution of the American city into the landscape, a product of special and privileged conditions in the United States. I include this survey as an example of the intense professional search that has been conducted for the rules of the new life-world in the new, dispersed, network city in the last 10 years.

In *Edge City: Life on the New Frontier* (1991), Joel Garreau brings into focus the vision of a megacity network dispersed into the peripheral landscape. He demonstrates that there is a marketing and scientific rationale behind the sprawling suburbs and emphasizes the speculative real-estate logic of land development as a driving force in the creation of the new "edge cities." He gives this new, dispersed city not only a popular name but a precise statistical and marketing definition: it occurs along the highway corridors around large American metropolitan areas, with growth nodes at highway intersections. According to Garreau, each "edge city" has on the order of 5,000,000 square feet of office space, a mall of at least 600,000 square feet (with several large department stores), and more jobs than bedrooms. It acts as an attractor, is perceived as one by residents, and, lastly, is "nothing like a 'city' thirty years ago."[23]

The hybrid architecture of the new city is also described by Stephen Kieran and James Timberlake in their article "Paradise Regained" (1991), which restructures the Robert Venturi, Denise Scott Brown, and Steven Izenour team's earlier arguments in *Learning from Las Vegas* (1972) about speed and the dispersal of the city to fit the edge-city's hybrid buildings and "perimeter centers."[24] The result is the creation of new, extended megacity regions that network with each other to form a global economic system, with many local, national, and transnational repercussions. Deyan Sudjic's *The 100 Mile City* (1992) describes the new set of urban morphologies: airports and container ports, business centers, cultural centers, office centers, and commercial campuses dispersed across the regional landscape. "The traditional city," he writes, "has finally shaken off its nineteenth-century self." In *The Global City* (1991), Saskia Sassen describes the economics of the new megacity regions, with their contradictory aggregations of wealth and poverty. Sassen is careful to detail the strategic role of the persistent central area and its specializations as well as those of the periphery, and to highlight the role of immigrant labor and the service sector.[25]

Stephen Kieran and James Timberlake: "Paradise Regained," 1991

The dissolution of the "urban" into the landscape has prompted many theorists, despite the larger process of global urbanization discussed further below, to speak not only of a "landscape urbanism" but of a "post-urban" situation. Yet Corboz points to the huge gap between the European and American urban experiences. The typical European city has not seen the degree of sprawl or diffusion experienced by the American city (especially as exemplified by Los Angeles). Yet, he adds, Europeans will find no reason to feel superior if they look at what is happening to their own new towns or suburbs, where racism, poverty, and crime are just as rampant among and against new immigrant populations as in some American cities.[26] Taking another approach to the question of what the city has become, or where it has gone to, Celeste Olalquiaga gives an intimate sense of what it is like to inhabit American and Japanese city spaces saturated by communications media, spaces in which the body becomes dematerialized and conceptually dissolved in the media (*Megalopolis: Contemporary Cultural Sensibilities*, 1992).[27]

In his essay "Post-Urbanism" (1992), Antony Vidler associates the "urban" (as opposed to the "post-urban") with the traditional European city, and especially with the monuments and urban "rooms" that are cut into its texture to form, in the phrase coined by Francis Yates in *The Art of Memory* (1966), a "mnemonic structure."[28] Yates describes how the "classical system of memory" consisted, metaphorically, of a series of rooms or chambers. Each had its niches and architectural elements such as balconies and corresponded to a branch of knowledge that, upon entry, unfolded around its central axis to reveal its main supporting texts in niches along the walls and subsidiary texts marked by plaques. Scholars would memorize texts and then assign them to their appropriate memory slots, niches, or plaques in the conceptual memory system, which could be shared with others trained in the same method. Yates shows from contemporary descriptions and drawings how Shakespeare's Globe Theatre could be interpreted as a "memory theater," giving another conceptual dimension to Shakespeare's words "All the world's a stage and all the men and women merely players" (*As You Like It*). Vidler points out that the city itself can be seen as such a hierarchical mnemonic structure or memory system, organized to provide a sense of orientation and comfort for its inhabitants.

Frances Yates: Robert Fludd's memory theater, The Art of Memory, *1966*

But not all the memories encoded in the city are comforting. Jean-Paul Sartre, Vidler notes, wrote that he was disturbed in the city by a sense that somebody was missing, an awareness of the exclusions needed to make the bourgeois city comfortable for the middle class. For Sartre, the modern city was haunted by these exclusions. Vidler argues that the disappearance of the (old-style) city, while a cause for concern, also creates an opportunity to include those formerly excluded and thus to lay the ghost. Echoing this sentiment in *SMLXL* (1995), Rem Koolhaas has also welcomed the "death of the city"—though with characteristic irony—seeing in it a chance for a new urbanism.[29]

The disappearance of the traditional city is also described in *X-Urbanism: Architecture and the American City* (1999), by Mario Gandelsonas. He charts the transformation of the modern, American, monofunctional, residential, postwar suburb into a new form of multifunctional "suburban city." This transformation spells the doom of the traditional urban form. What forms is an "X-urban" city—an "out-of-the-city city"—not only along the car-based periphery but also at the old city-core. This core "becomes one more semiautonomous urban 'village'" in the metropolitan constellation of X-urban centers; that is, the core of the American city disappears as an exclusively business-and-industrial district and reappears as a mixed residential, shopping, and entertainment area (still including some business), all uses also found on the periphery.[30]

In 2000, several more commentaries on the sprawling diffusion of the "urban" in America appeared. One such was *After the City* by Lars Lerup, which explores urban sprawl in terms of points of stimulation or attractors and large service areas without distinguishing features. Lerup accurately maps the multicentered system of attractors in privately owned spaces ("stims") against the background of miles and miles of housing estates ("drek") that are customized for every level of income, set in the landscape, and cloaked by a threadbare suburban canopy of trees.[31]

A science of multiple urban subcenters emerged within this new world after a long and painful process of trial and error, supporting new urban life-worlds based on the automobile. In postwar America, this system of multiple subcenters has been based on the mall. Malls initially serviced their local suburbs, then grew to be regional attractors rivaling traditional downtown shopping districts. The architects of the American mall system from the mid 1940s to the 1960s created a network of scattered urban subcenters that was a triumph of the modern science of mass-market real-estate advertising. Starting in the 1960s, developers sought to apply this highly successful, mall-centered real-estate methodology to many other fragments of the postmodern city, as in the redevelopment of Quincy Market by the Boston Redevelopment Authority (examined in the previous chapter). Market research discerned pools of potential buyers; manufacturers and marketers lined up to supply and stimulate the markets. Large institutional builders such as the Levitt Brothers on the east coast applied a similar marketing logic to the provision of standardized middle-class housing in large enclaves on the suburban "frontier." For a time, the Federal government used tax breaks and direct subsidies to encourage big corporations, including mall developers like the Rouse Corporation, to develop and market large residential projects similar to European new towns. Few such projects were as well located, well designed and successful in the long run as Reston, Virginia, designed for New York developer Robert Simon Jr., by Conklin, Whittlesey, and Rossant (1961).

Conklin, Whittlesey and Rossant: new-town center, Reston, VA, 1961

In *The Image of the City* (1961), Lynch looked at the importance of flow and stasis in cities. His view was predicated on identifying pedestrian and automobile networks as separate systems. On the pedestrian network, actors move through or between enclaves along "paths" or armatures and use conceptual "markers" (spires, towers, visually prominent urban features) that enable them to orient themselves and to construct conceptual maps or "images" of the city. Mall developers, Lynch recognized, had learned to manipulate the form this pedestrian narrative practice had taken in the age of the suburb and the cruising automobile, exploiting the "image of the city" utilized by actors navigating the automobile network. Malls and new subcenters became the new "markers" in the landscape of the sprawling city; marketing specialists developed highly efficient computerized models for predicting the "paths" taken by citizens both within the multicentered regional highway system (as drivers) and within the mall itself (as pedestrians).

This system arose because with or without a conscious theory, developers and architects had to create new suburban structures to accommodate the flows and institutions of the new suburban life-world. They were charged with making small enclaves of order within the apparent chaos of the larger, sprawling metropolis. All the settings of the traditional city—administrative, market, banking, military, religious, and leisure centers—had to be reformatted as enclaves within the new network of extended armatures.[32]

Lynch recognized that American mall designers such as Victor Gruen and Welton Beckett pioneered this recentering on (or decentering to) the suburban fringe in the 1950s. This emphasis on commercial real-estate development and its calculations as the basis for urban design need come as no surprise. We have already seen that for Lynch the best place to study urban design was the American mall, where the relationship between commercial node and suburban network is defined by deliberate quantitative calculations. And crucial to the success of these calculations was the science of marketing as employed by the real-estate development industry, the new "behavioral knowledge" (discussed by Lynch in his 1974 *Britannica* article).

In the *The Heart of Our Cities* (1964), Victor Gruen described how early marketing research determined that to be viable, a regional shopping center needed to be within a 20–30 minute drive of about half a million people. Such a center requires 40 acres or more of parking space hugging the perimeter of the building at grade level, as people are unwilling to walk more than 100 feet (or climb) to an entry from their car. Once inside the mall armature, they need to encounter a diversion, such as a fountain or a carousel, food court or waterfall, every 600 feet along the linear armature of the mall. Such diversions prevent the consumer from becoming bored by the shopping experience, which keeps them shopping longer. This was crucial because, as researchers showed, after about 20 minutes in a store or center otherwise rational shoppers tend to begin making "impulse buys." Formerly directed shoppers suddenly start making irrational decisions prompted by a euphoric sense of displacement, fatigue, and the drive to release pent-up frustrations, displaying what is known in marketing jargon as the "Gruen effect" or "Gruen transfer."[33]

Victor Gruen and Associates: interior atrium, Rochester Plaza, Rochester, NY, 1956–61

This marketing terminology reflects the fact that Gruen developed a variety of methods for prolonging a visitor's stay in the mall; these ranged from garden squares to covered multistory atria with such tourist attractions as "town clocks." Gruen also solved the problem of access to the second floor by developing split-level parking lots. An active second floor helps finance the enclosure of the mall and its heating and air-conditioning. Lynch, in 1970, hoped with Gruen that such shopping centers—completely interior, self-contained visual environments—could become the "new Main Street" of suburban communities, lessening their monocultural isolation and autodependence. (Both architects failed to anticipate the mass marketing in the 1980s and 1990s of a factory-made, global monoculture—exemplified by Gap, Starbucks, Tower Records, Barnes & Noble, and the like, which can be found in every mall.)

Mall developers tailored the scale and programming of their new subcenters to the traffic flows generated by the regional population. They tuned their attractors exteriorly to the automobile, then themed their interior, pedestrian environments to enhance their scenographic quality with "fairy tale" narratives (as described by Barry Maitland in *Shopping Mall: Planning and Design*, 1986). The extra attractive power of such narratives became necessary with the proliferation of competing subcenters. Krugman's multicentered computer simulations (mentioned in Chapter 1) showed that not all subcenters can survive; a few will grow at the expense of their neighbors.

The resultant new urban life-world of the polycentric network city is only too familiar to readers in the industrial world. The network city appears to consist of suburban or other places of residence called "home" by their inhabitants (for an average of seven years, in America), highways, one's vehicle of choice, privately owned public spaces in malls, workplaces in various pavilions, and recreational theme parks or national parks. When the network citizen is out and about, fast-food chains provide food. The old city-core is merely one entertainment option and must compete with new leisure centers, including multiplex cinemas at the mall and home entertainment systems. In accord with Lynch's City as a Machine model, this city is made up of a network of discrete elements (homes, estates, malls, office parks, industrial parks, leisure centers, national food chains, national parks, etc.) that are scattered over the landscape, optimally located to maximize traffic count.

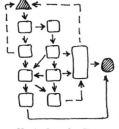

Kevin Lynch: City as a Machine diagram, A Theory of Good City Form, *1981*

2.1.4 The Postmodern Life-World and the Emergence of the Global Network City

The United States's position as a global superpower has enabled this urban diffusion, which is predicated on cheap gas and massive buying power. Few other countries in the twentieth century had such abundant access to the money and oil required to drive automobile-shaped city growth. (The US is not only the world's largest importer and consumer of oil, but its third-largest producer.) The United States's cheap-energy policy, which has shaped its foreign relations with the Middle East, West Africa, Mexico, and Venezuela, has thus directly subsidized the new urban form.

The US census of 2000 revealed the automobile-enabled demographic of the X-urbanism thesis: in 2000 the majority of the American population did not live in regions qualifying as traditional cities, even if those regions were listed not in terms of built-up cores but as more-extended metropolitan statistical areas. "Edge-cities" had grown enormously in the latter half of the twentieth century: 53 suburban cities of 100,000 or more people, all components of larger metropolitan areas based on older centers, had grown by 10% every decade since first being classified as "urban," outpacing their associated central cities. The population of Mesa, a suburb of Phoenix, Arizona, grew from 16,790 in 1950 to 396,375 in 2000, while that of Scottsdale, another Phoenix suburb, went from 10,000 in 1960 to 202,705 in 2000. In the 1990s, Phoenix—if one includes its suburbs—was the fastest-growing US city, a mini Los Angeles in the desert. In *Postmetropolis* (2000), Edward W. Soja identifies seven megacity clusters in the US that together contain the majority of the American population. In the 1990s, the United Nations identified 13 such megacity clusters worldwide.[34]

Lynch's City as a Machine model, adapted to the diffuse network megalopolis comprising multiple enclaves connected by stretched armatures of communication, has therefore become a viable model in many countries, with many local variations. Since Gottmann's 1961 study, other scholars, including Peter Hall, Eichi Isomura, and I. B. F. Kormoss, have applied the megalopolis model to other megacities around the world. These include corridors or megalopoli such as London–Liverpool in Britain, Tokyo–Osaka in Japan, Brussels-Amsterdam and the Ruhr valley in Europe, Los Angeles–San Francisco, Rio de Janeiro–São Paulo, and the greater Hong Kong or Shanghai areas in China. Each of these megacities has its own peculiarities. In Tokyo, for instance, most residential buildings are low rise because of earthquake concerns and land restrictions and not an inch of space is wasted (e.g., garden-city layouts are very rare). The world's largest city, Mexico City, is estimated to have a population of 25 million people, with the majority of the population housed in self-built barrios. Here a postcolonial debate rages over education, poverty, and inadequate infrastructure for public health, sanitation, water supply, electricity, gas, and the like. Almost 140 years ago, Cerdá recognized that the resolution of such issues was central to the creation of a modern city that would be free from the fear of disease.[35]

City Planning Department: Tokyo Second Masterplan, 1968

The networked megacities show local variations of form, often because energy is not as cheap or land as plentiful as in America. In Japan, for instance, urban policies and government supports built into the Tokyo Second Masterplan of 1968 have encouraged the adoption of more-compact urban forms and multiple subcenters. The classical concept of the *polis* still has authority worldwide, and many city-regions seek the illusion of self-sufficiency or near self-sufficiency (always excepting energy imports).[36] As emphasized by Kostof in *The City Shaped* (1991), cities have always depended on their agricultural hinterland for support, manpower, and sustenance. As I have also emphasized, cities are dissipative structures that occur in areas of surplus and redistribute resources within a network of flows (an ecology). Within the postmodern economy, this economic ecology has taken on global dimensions, though everywhere it has a local base of specific actors participating for diverse motives.

The network-city model has dominated European city planning in the twentieth century, relying upon the state as its social and economic sponsor in the "public interest," that is, in the interest of (hopefully) efficient and healthy cities. City planners have sought to implement the network city from Paris to

The net city

a) *Xavier de Geyter:*
different net city
patterns, London
(left column), Dutch
"ring" city (centre
column) and Belgian
conurbation (right
column). 1st row,
built form; 2nd row,
infrastructures; 3rd
row, interstitial left
over space pattern;
4th row, rivers,
topography and
forestation; 5th row,
open spaces, city
and water. After
Sprawl *2002*
b) *Franz Oswald*
and Peter Baccini:
layered analysis of
net city territory,
Netzstadt: Designing
the Urban, *2003*

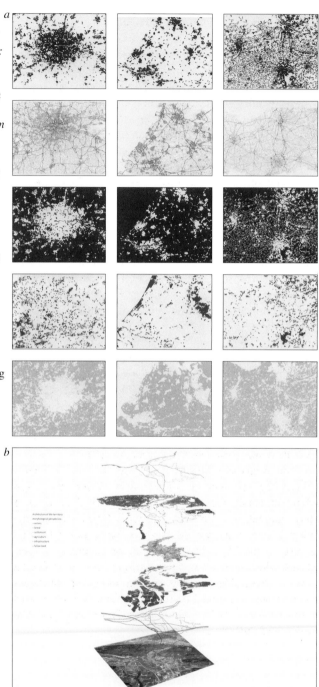

We have seen in Chapter 1 that Serlio created three stage sets to accommodate three different life-worlds for three classes of urban actor in the Italian Renaissance. In Norberg-Schulz's terms, each such actor would have his or her own knowledge base, that is, would operate, in different contexts, according to various schemes of personal, communal, or scientific knowledge. The plan for each of Serlio's spaces reflects its proper occupants, who organize their actions around symbolic props that define their relationships with other actors. These props include the nobles' palaces and monuments of state power, the merchants' port and shop/houses, and the farmers' pub and cottages (which create a hybrid geometry half-dissolved in the agrarian landscape). These settings and props facilitate the activities of Serlio's ideal actors, secure their social and economic status, and give them a distinct sense of place. We might expect such different actors (whether falling into Serlio's categories or into others) to have different concepts of design and different techniques for its practice. Below, I will briefly explore these different design approaches and their implications for the city.

City geomancy and "armchair" of hills, I Ching

2.2.1 Premodern Concepts of Design

Premodern design was concerned with marking out a particular place in what otherwise might appear as a wilderness. Friendly or hostile spirits occupied the landscape, inhabiting special rocks, caves, river bends, river banks, and plains. Design had in part to deal with warding off the evil eye of malevolent spirits, represented by the local climate and its many storms, lightning strikes, typhoons, deep frosts, or floods. Design in this mode was a strategy of defense against supernatural as well as military threats, a marking-off of areas that were protected and safe.

Divination was an essential part of this design system, a practice that still survives in many cultures. In Hong Kong, for instance, the hypermodern Norman Foster design for the Hong Kong and Shanghai Bank had to be vetted by feng shui experts, who advised on the placement of the escalators leading to the banking hall. Distinguished architects in contemporary Japan will tell you that there is no such thing as "urban design" in their country, despite Tokyo's tradition of temple enclaves and the distinct patterns of development around modern railway stations. The important Japanese concept of the space *between* buildings, *ma*, is a semimystical concept not amenable to Rationalistic theories of design.

Actors in the life-world of the Archi Città worked as catalysts to organize a sense of place; they amplified small differences and advantages in the topography, local climate and culture to promote a local sense of identity. Their design process involved much personal experience but was largely shaped by shared, unwritten communal knowledge. Cities were small, local springs and wells could supply water for drinking and sewage removal (if the latter was not to be used as fertilizer). The ancient Chinese and Romans, whose capital cities

Spiro Kostof: City of Faith—bathing in the Ganges, Varanasi, India, 2002

each reached a million people, still operated on the local, village principle, except for the provision of large infrastructures (e.g., the canal system in China or the aqueducts supplying Rome with water). Local codes dominated, codes that were more or less unequal, ranging from the equal subdivision of land in some Greek colonies (grid town) to the unequal linear subdivisions of street-frontage subdivisions along main-street armatures in medieval English towns as documented by M. R. G. Conzens. Chinese towns followed a precise formula, where lot size indicated a family's position on the social hierarchy, leading up to the divinity represented on earth by the emperor.

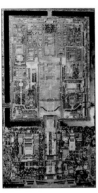

Aerial view of the Forbidden City, Beijing, 2004

Hierarchical organizational schemata abounded in the Archi Città. Nested organizations of enclaves inside other enclaves, as in the Forbidden City in Beijing, were common. Besides horizontal zoning enforced by barrier walls and guards, Cities of Faith also had vertical hierarchies enforced by dominant rulers. Roman temples and public buildings, for example, towered over all private buildings, dominating the skyline as one approached a walled Roman city. Gothic cathedrals in medieval Europe towered similarly over their surroundings. In medieval Islamic cities, the fortress and the minarets of the mosques dominated the skyline. These vertical priorities still remain in place in some cities: in Washington DC new structures are not allowed to obscure the dome of the Capitol building; in Paris, all tall buildings are banned from the center and concentrated in the west at la Defense, the city's mini Manhattan; in London, buildings are kept low around Buckingham Palace, the Greater London Council protects sight lines to St Paul's Cathedral from surrounding hills, and small towers beside the cathedral dome were demolished to clear the view from the north at the request of Prince Charles; in Tokyo, buildings are still kept low around the Imperial Palace at the center of the city; and until recently no building in Philadelphia was taller than the top of William Penn's hat on the statue on City Hall, in accord with an unwritten code observed by local developers.

Further light can be shed on the nature of design in the Archi Città by Françoise Choay's categories of the "diachronic" and the "syntagmatic." Writing in "Urbanism and Semiology" (1969) she terms large-scale organizational structures that last for a long period in a city *diachronic*, that is, standing outside of the immediate time frame. (They are also often heterotopic for this reason.) Normal construction in the city she terms *syntagmatic* if it works on a neighbor-to-neighbor basis as in the self-built vernacular housing of the medieval Islamic or European city. Here design was guided by local codes and customs, local negotiations, and local practices, handed down from generation to generation as local traditional practices and local lore. Local materials and local climatic conditions played a large role in the formulation of these communal practices that were based on the everyday, personal experience of individuals in the city. These rules and their community-based structure represented a bottom-up counterweight to the top-down tradition of the warrior-priests and the edicts by means of which they drew off resources for their monumental constructions.

Looking at the evidence of built cities, there can be no doubt that the builders of diachronic monuments and castles have dominated society for most of history, but the few fragments of old, syntagmatic city fabric that have survived give a sense of the intensity and compression of the medieval Islamic and European rival trading cultures around the Mediterranean, and along the silk route to China and India. These intimate milieux, with their elaborate codes of place-making, speak to us eloquently now even though we inhabit a very different city. We all want to vacation in the Kasbah at Fez, Morocco, visit medieval Spanish towns, or relax in modern hotels close to the core remainders of the Cities of Faith. The concept of a "premodern pattern" of design is nostalgic, the product of a paradigm shift in our urban life-world and urban space that makes the earlier age seem more attractive (neglecting the feudalism, wars, slavery, public torture, arbitrary persecutions, public executions, mass starvation, and plagues of the time). Serlio's image of the Comic scene of the 1540s was already nostalgic, for the chaotic medieval system of syntagmatic city building was becoming rationalized by Alberti's codes and proportional system in new urban extensions such as that at Ferrara in the Renaissance.

Stephano Bianca: Islamic urban elements and assembly Urban Form in the Islamic World, *2000*

Later, Augustus Pugin and John Ruskin, British reformers facing the messy outcome of the first Industrial Revolution in the 1830s and 1840s, would turn back to the image of the medieval city and Gothic church as a symbol of community, communal knowledge, and caring. The same impulse inspired the late-1940s British "townscape" designers, who sought to recreate medieval Italian Gothic hill towns and English villages as a reaction against the sterile, uniform, urban life-world of the British new towns. In *The Death and Life of Great American Cities* (1961), Jane Jacobs appealed to this same village model of self-organization to ensure safety on the New York City streets. In A *Pattern Language* (1977), Christopher Alexander and his associates made a similar appeal to a simpler time when a self-organizing social system governed vernacular, and communal knowledge could resolve complex issues without the intervention of complicated machines or external authorities.[43]

2.2.2 Design in the City as a Machine

Design in the City as a Machine requires simple, clear concepts that neatly articulate each piece of a problem and isolate its properties in atomic or irreducible terms. The goal is to achieve maximum efficiency with minimum investment of energy and resources. New technologies and new materials make this goal at least partly attainable; scientific research has inarguably improved the human lot in some ways, producing a surplus of products that are easily available to many people. According to this line of argument, it is the modern designer's duty to seize on the new opportunities offered by the Industrial Revolution (mechanization of the life-world) to provide happiness to the greatest number, following Bentham's utilitarian tenets (which also inspired his Panopticon).

a, b) *Augustus Pugin: Gothic versus the industrial city, 1836*

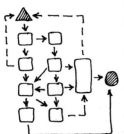

Kevin Lynch: City as a Machine diagram, A Theory of Good City Form, *1981*

We have already reviewed Cerdá's belief in the power of the machine to alter the life-world of the majority of citizens if designers would recognize the logic of the machine age; for Cerdá, this logic lay in the application of a Darwinian process to organization of the city's flows along wide boulevards to facilitate trade and commerce, while providing in each block an island of stasis, half filled with gardens and nature. Cerdá, as I have mentioned, admired the grid as the most rational design basis for the machine city. Lynch accurately represented the topology of this model in his diagram of the city machine as a series of discrete, rectangular cells, all connected by a system of flows in armatures (including the media).

Design in the Cine Città is largely concerned with sequencing and sorting flow, allowing people to find their destinations and to assign goods to their proper enclaves for storage or processing. Cine Città designers hope to construct logically consistent organizations that can process flows and accurately sort and store goods and people for set periods of time, as in the Panopticon (but without its circular plan). The grid plan developed for Chicago in the nineteenth century is often interpreted as exemplary of the machine city. The rapid growth of Chicago (including the invention of the skyscraper as a vertical extension of the grid on a steel skeleton in the 1890s) seemed to prove Cerdá's case, as later designers sought to reform the messy slums and miserable living conditions of the poor using rationalized grid development.

In *Nature's Metropolis: Chicago and the Great West* (1991), William Cronon describes how the city grew from a population of about 25,000 in 1860 to over a million by 1890, despite a devastating fire in the late 1880s that destroyed the downtown area.[44] The city gained 30,000 inhabitants a year for 30 years. This phenomenal growth took place over a marsh; the city was raised 10 feet, building by building, in the 1880s. This engineering feat had the advantage that the drains could now flow into the Chicago River (whose flow had also been reversed so as not to pollute the drinking water taken from Lake Michigan). The meeting of railways from across the Great Plains meant that the city's Board of Trade controlled world grain prices by 1900, while catalogue sales to farmers made the city a giant distribution hub for goods and services.

The railways also brought cattle from as far away as Texas to the slaughterhouses for processing into meat products that were then either distributed in railway freezer cars or canned for distribution to dry-goods stores. With its fast suburban expansion, park system by Olmsted, enormous school system, wealthy suburbs like Oak Park (where Frank Lloyd Wright lived comfortably for a while), Chicago epitomized the modern, American, industrial city. Its grim smokestacks and large slums were counterbalanced by its orderly grid and expectation of upward social mobility from the slums. Chicago's exemplary social and economic ecology was studied by the pioneering urban sociologists Park and Burgess in the 1920s.

Chicago's rapid construction contributed to another aspect of the machine city: the endless repetition of standard building typologies in order to house people quickly and cheaply. Building morphologies varied from detached villas to apartment buildings to repetitious workingmen's houses, advertised in both English and German. Siegfried Giedion, a Modernist historian of the 1930s, described in *Mechanization Takes Command* (1948) how mass production was pioneered in the Chicago stock yards. Animal carcasses were handled in a linear, step-by-step process as they hung from hooks on rails set in the ceiling, being dismantled as they slowly moved along.[45] Henry Ford applied these same principles of sequencing and standardization to the emerging automobile industry in nearby Detroit in the 1910s. This application gave birth to a second wave of modernization in time and motion productivity studies. Ford's product altered the urban life-world by granting actors individual, personal mobility, independent of railway company and streetcar timetables. Le Corbusier was a great admirer of Ford's standardization. In his *Towards a New Architecture* (1927) he opined that modern design was reaching a new peak of standardization and efficiency and compared this new peak to the normative perfection of Greek architecture at the Acropolis in Athens.[46]

Raising Chicago, building by building, 1870s

Norberg-Schulz has described how the scientific life-world is dominated by abstract schema distinct from personal knowledge or communal, vernacular "rules of thumb." Design in the modern world requires professional knowledge learnt from books, not from practice. Modern designers are trained to atomize problems into discrete, isolated elements, parts whose qualities can be classified and known. Each part is a distinct, geometric entity, clearly segregated from its neighbors. Boullée's sublime Cenotaph of Newton (1784) is an early example of this Rationalist approach to design, showing a model of the universe suspended in the center of a sphere that visitors enter from below. The vast scale of this project and its spherical form symbolize the triumph of scientific reason in Newton's discovery of gravity, his uncovering of the rules that governed the design of the universe.

Some designers, therefore, though Cerdá preferred the grid, believed that the basic geometry of nature had been discovered by Newton, whose few simple laws provided a basis for the elaboration of scientific design in place of theological and mystical beliefs. In this view, design should define enclaves with simple geometric forms and link them with a network of straight armatures

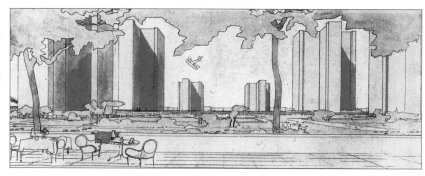

Le Corbusier: view to business center in City for Three Million, 1922 (© FLC / ADAGP, Paris and DACS, London, 2005)

Sant'Elia: sketch of power station, 1914

analogous to lines of gravitational force. The result would be a network with nodes at its junctions, like a diagram of atomic structure. Many designers proposed such pseudo-Newtonian plans for new geometric towns (Claude-Nicolas Ledoux's circular salt works for Chaux with the governor at the center—never built—is one example). Haussmann applied this geometric model to Paris, cutting boulevards through the old city in the 1850s and 1860s.

Such designers employed a "scientific" methodology of analysis, isolating elements as distinct enclaves and connecting them by wide armatures. They rigorously limited the focus and scope of their inquiries in order to obtain clear and precise results. In design terms, this meant that all nonconforming uses and activities were excluded from consideration and placed in special refugia or enclaves (which Foucault identified as heterotopias). Once isolated, exceptions and their attendant uncertainties could be ignored. In New York, for instance, the introduction in 1916 of the first American zoning code distinguished between three types of uses: residential, commercial, manufacturing. The code made a special exception for the vicinity of Wall Street to accommodate skyscrapers, creating the first special district.

This functionalist design approach (derived from algebra, where a function expresses the relationship between known elements or variables) severely limited, in the name of clarity and efficiency, the modern designers' ability to see the existing city. As noted in Chapter 1, the Modernist *Charter of Athens* drawn up by the CIAM (Congrès Internationaux d'Architecture Moderne) in 1933 recognized four categories of use in the city, namely, housing, work, recreation, and transport. Each category implied an associated urban morphology and set of standardized activities housed in a special building typology. A fifth category, *divers* (miscellaneous), held all nonconforming uses such as mixed-use zones or buildings, including the old city. Italian and other delegates at the meeting protested this situation in vain, as they saw most of their historic cities disappearing from consideration.[47]

In *Theory and Design in the First Machine Age* (1960), Reyner Banham highlights the promise of Darwin's organic ideal for Modernist designers, who dreamt of a new freedom, vast open spaces, cheap and flexible construction

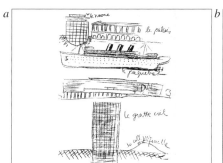
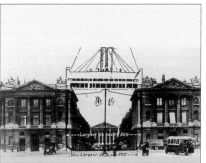

a, b) *Le Corbusier: ship inserted in Rue Royale, Paris. Photomontage, 1921 (© FLC / ADAGP, Paris and DACS, London, 2005)*

systems, and incredibly light structures housing enormous numbers of people in states of luxury previously reserved for princes and the aristocracy. Modernists at CIAM meetings in the 1920s and 1930s wanted to break with the messy, dirty, polluting, nineteenth-century industrial city and its binary opposition between rich and poor, work and leisure, and so on. They decreed a new, universal space with fresh aesthetic norms, stressing the open, "free" ground-plane, the need for pilotis that raise buildings off the ground, flat roofs for roof gardens, strip windows to admit more light, "free" plans, and "free" white facades.

Despite their emphasis on freedom and universality, these Modernists were in fact prescribing from the top down a fixed, utopian vision put together from a kit of combinatorial parts. Banham contrasts the Modernist promise with the grim reality of 1960s design and the fixed, top-down aesthetic canons of the modern masters (e.g., Walter Gropius at the Bauhaus, Harvard, Le Corbusier, Mies van der Rohe). The open promises had become standardized design clichés by the 1960s, manifest in countless utilitarian, inner-city urban-renewal projects and barren luxury slabs and towers in central business districts. For Banham, the fixed canon of formal devices, standardized mass-production methods, and Beaux Arts symmetries of this period all reveal the frozen and fixed nature of the Modernist, utopian design approach. He argues that the Futurists' *Manifesto* of 1911 has more affinity than Modernism with "organic" functionalism that shifts and changes with the environment like a self-organizing system, reflecting the fluid dynamics of the city and its complex section, its noises, smells, and interaction spaces.[48]

Shell spiral on golden section; after D'Arcy Thompson, On Growth and Form, *1917*

The self-regulating balance of form and function in a true ecological system, with its formal elements, typologies, and genealogies, became one of the foundation stones of the modern "organic" approach to design. As we have seen, its transparency was attractive to Frank Lloyd Wright and became enshrined in the work of his student Kevin Lynch as the Ecological City model. The "organic" approach—form follows function with feedback—is also at the core of D'Arcy Thompson's Modernist design classic, *On Growth and Form* (1917). Designers found that the literal transparency between form and function required by the Darwinian philosophy of design was easy to achieve when they sought to maximize the efficiency of the machine based on the mechanics and fixed typologies of the Newtonian universe; but when they tried to incorporate Albert Einstein's Theory of Relativity, as Siegfried Giedion did in *Space, Time, and Architecture* (1941), this match became more difficult. While Einstein was careful to point out that the Newtonian and Cartesian systems worked quite well at earthly speeds and scales, modern designers were fascinated by the special effects he predicted for speeds close to that of light and under other extreme conditions.

Whatever its drawbacks, there can be no doubt about the quick success and power of the Modernist city as a machine-design model. In 100 years it has transformed the fragmented industrial cultures of the world into a global system built on the earlier European mercantile/colonial system. (This transformation has, however, come at a human, psychological and ecological cost that designers are only beginning to recognize.) The City as a Machine design system led to the dispersal of the compact European urban-design tradition and the invention of separate business, production, and leisure centers. The seed of this dispersal was contained in Ebenezer Howard's radial garden city diagram of 1904, which promoted the merging of the city and the country landscape. This was later to become Cedric Price's "fried egg" model, with its fingers of development stretching out from the old core in a star-like pattern. The further expansion of the City as a Machine in the automobile age created a need for new urban subcenters in a polycentric network city. Design came to include vast areas of landscape and "urbanized countryside," as predicted by Cerdá and accounted for by Lynch in his invention of "city design" terminology. Lynch also, as we have already seen, pointed to the new urban subcenters as representing the best of the new science of real-estate-based urban design in network cities.

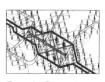

Dennis Crompton:
Computer City, *1964*

The City as a Machine has remained a potent dream for designers despite critics who pointed to its inhumanity and wastefulness, as Lynch does in *A Theory of Good City Form*. Banham and the Archigram group in the 1960s proved correct in predicting the transformation of the archetypal urban machine from the megastructure to a miniaturized device that can be inserted into almost any territory. Mike Webb's *Suitaloon* project (1967), a proposal for a body suit that could inflate to become a house, complete with mechanical services in a backpack, pushed the concept of the urban nomad to a logical and poetic extreme. David Green's *Rock Plug* project (1969) provided a hidden support network for urban nomads, hidden in false rocks and tree stumps. The city is here theoretically and practically dematerialized into the landscape, which in its turn is transformed into a highly complex mass of wired and wireless support machinery. The freedom of the individual becomes absolute and all communal activity contingent on the willingness of individuals to congregate, responding to information in the network to create temporary urban events (like the pop festivals of 1960s) in the middle of the countryside.[49]

Behind this dissolution of the city into the landscape on a global scale lay an electronic-communications revolution that has vastly speeded up information transfer between any two properly connected locations. Archigram anticipated this change in projects like Dennis Crompton's *Computer City* (1964).[50] In the previous chapter, we examined the "systems revolution" in planning that was associated with the city/computer analogy and the early use of computers to analyze traffic networks in the 1970s. Through the 1980s the computerization of architectural design slowly proceeded, accelerating dramatically in the 1990s when personal computers became cheaper and more powerful. This allowed urban conceptual models to be modeled mathematically in a virtual space, a three-dimensional matrix very similar to the perspectival grid constructed by Renaissance architects in the Urbino "perspective laboratory."

In addition, computer-aided design (CAD) programs, once elephantine, became streamlined, allowing the use of multiple layers of information to make composite drawings simultaneously accessible by design teams around the world. Rendering programs made the drawing of perspectives, which had once taken days, possible in minutes. Animation programs allowed designers to walk through virtual models of their buildings. Production programs allowed designers to look at how elements from their project might be manufactured. It seemed that the City as a Machine had found its proper mode of expression in computer modeling, a mode of design widely popularized in the 1990s by the success of video games like *Sim City*.

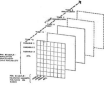

CAD layers for Planners, ca. 1970s

2.2.3 Postmodern Concepts of Design

The controversial advent of Postmodernism does not mean that Modernism has ended as a project. The prefix *post* (Latin for "after") not only does not necessarily imply that Modernism is dead, but can in fact imply the opposite, namely, that Modernism (or Modernisms) continue in other guises. Many authors have pointed to this continuity; Norberg-Schulz's diagram in *Existence, Space, and Architecture*, for instance, folds the scientific life-world of Modernism, along with personal knowledge and communal knowledge, into a kind of trinity of life-worlds that interacted with each other differently in the contemporary experiences of different people. It is possible for a warrior-priest, a person who has never left home, and an engineer-scientist to inhabit the same city and thus for all the three Cittàs to be present in one town built not only over time but simultaneously. As we have seen, Lynch's own *The Image of the City* testified to the abrupt confrontation of two worlds in one city. He also dreamt about peaceful coexistence between "fast" and "slow" corridors of development in his "place utopia" (*A Theory of Good City Form*).

Postmodern design is predicated on the continued existence of the Modernist, Enlightenment project of improving the conditions of the great mass of humanity through design. David Harvey, in *The Condition of Postmodernity* (1989), argues that Modernism did not end or break down but accelerated in the years after the Second World War, taking a new form as an international trend toward globalization of financial markets, manufacturing, informational systems, transport systems, tourism, and more. Accelerated means of transport and communications under the continued Modernist regime shrunk the globe. This acceleration allowed fragmentation, just-in-time delivery systems, flexibility about the means of production, and the systematic marketing of political regimes. The semiologist Umberto Eco, in his book *Travels in Hyperreality* (1986), investigates the world of signs and symbols that resulted from this accelerated Modernism or Hypermodernism, the world of advertising and Pop Art from the 1960s and 1970s also explored by the Archigram group, the Venturi team, and Banham.[51] The modern tradition has also clearly continued in what Jencks calls the "Neo-modern movement," exemplified by the British work of Norman Foster's office, Richard Rogers's office, and the work of Future Systems (i.e., the new Selfridges store in Birmingham, UK, 2003).

Shrinking globe advertisement, 2001

This accelerated modernization process has continued in the 1980s, 1990s, and beyond with the computerization of architectural and urban design and planning using CAD and the geographic information system (GIS) and global positioning system (GPS) software that allows information to be precisely linked to place (as represented by three grid coordinates). The three-dimensional spatial matrix of perspectival construction developed during the Renaissance, along with descriptive geometrical techniques from the nineteenth century, are now coordinated with satellite networks to span the globe. Digital photocollage techniques make it easy to represent both old and new projects, the traditional city or the city of the future.

It might therefore seem foolish to propose the end of Modernism, as did John Thackara in an anthology of distinguished articles entitled *Design After Modernism: Beyond the Object* (1988).[52] Yet the key to this change is in Thackara's subtitle: moving beyond the Modernist *object* to its surrounding and supporting *networks*, as in Christopher Alexander's seminal "A City Is Not a Tree", reprinted in he anthology. This article emphasized set theory and the organizational networks or conceptual models that lay behind various city plans and diagrams. In this context, Kenneth Frampton's earlier article "Place-Form and Cultural Identity" (published in Hal Foster's anthology *The Anti-aesthetic: Essays on Postmodern Culture* in 1983), expanded on his earlier "Critical Regionalism" and heralded the necessity of resistance to globalization and of identifying the power of local, regional cultures as a basis for critical resistance.[53] This shift and this new form of resistance can be associated with the shift from the binary system of the modern city to the polycentric system of the postmodern, Tele Città concept (associated in Chapter 1 with Krugman's multicenter model).

Frampton refers to the German philosopher Jürgen Habermas's article "Modernity—An Incomplete Project," also anthologized by Foster. Habermas, a representative of the Frankfurt School of cultural criticism, argued that the Modernist project was unfinished and should not be abandoned, despite the recent horrors of the Second World War, atom bombs, and concentration camps. The democratic project was still important, as was the question of what constituted the public space of the new network city that was emerging. Frampton recounts that this article was prompted by Paolo Portoghesi's provocative Venice Biennale of Architecture theme and catalogue, *Architecture 1980, The Presence of the Past: The End of Prohibition*.[54]

In the Venice Arsenale, the architects Portoghesi, Aldo Rossi, and John Hedjuk created the *Strada Novissima* (Newest Street) project, consisting of a street armature built by the Cinecittà film studio in Rome. The armature was lined with boutiques designed to show the work of the many postmodern architects who accepted historical references: the Venturi–Scott Brown team, O. M. Ungers, the Krier brothers, Michael Graves, Robert Stern, and many others. Charles Jencks constructed a critics' side-pavilion centering on a tilted big pencil that corrected the street perspective and transformed it into an updated version of one of Serlio's three street scenes (as drawn by Dennis Crompton of Archigram!). The Strada Novissima moved like a carnival or traveling fair to Paris and San Francisco, picking up more pavilions and a terminal square along the way.

Dennis Crompton, Strada Novissima, Venice Biennale 1980

But many (like Thackara) think modern design is a project not so much unfinished as broken. The breakdown of modern design in city planning and architecture has been described by such authors as Charles Jencks, who in his doctoral thesis, published as *Modern Movements in Architecture* (1973), interpreted the Modern movement as a multithreaded network of groups.[55] He continued this theme in his *The Language of Postmodern Architecture* (1977). In *Postmodernism: The New Classicism in Art and Architecture* (1987), he points to 1972 newspaper pictures of the demolition of the Modernist Puitt-Igoe slab blocks as marking the end of Modernism. In *The Condition of Postmodernity* (1990), David Harvey gives an acute and far-ranging Marxian interpretation of the breakdown of Modern planning. Harvey studies the American city of Baltimore, where a festival mall by Rouse, the same developer that renovated Boston's Quincy Market, replaced the industrial port. Harvey provides a wide-ranging cultural commentary that spells out the economic, social, and cultural implications of this paradigm shift.

In *Postmodern Urbanism* (1996), Nan Ellin also describes the collapse of Modern architecture and planning and the appearance of urban-design fragments as a response to the crises of the 1970s and 1980s, which were a period of considerable instability for designers. Ellin writes of a periodic "pendular swing" in the design profession in those years, with many mini oscillations superimposed on the larger swing, which indicated a larger shift in the design paradigm. Not that change was a special feature of those decades; if Jencks's observations are correct, one new actor-designer advocacy group te.g., the Team X Group at Otterloo, Belgium, in 1959, comprising the Smithsons, Louis Kahn, and Aldo van Eyck, or the Archigram group in London in 1963) has emerged every three to four years over the last 50 years. This indicates great creativity in the design profession, with at least 17 distinct actor-designer groups emerging in the postwar years of suburban expansion and globalization. The monumental companion anthologies *Architecture Culture 1943–1968: A Documentary Anthology* (1993, edited by Joan Ockman) and *Architecture Theory Since 1968* (2000, edited by K. Michael Hays) record in detail the process of oscillation, fragmentation, recentering, and breakdown that has gone on within the design, architectural and planning professions.[56]

Most especially, the breakdown of designers' Modern concept of a grid of universal space prompted a crisis in the design profession. Many previously excluded voices were admitted into a polyphonic dialogue, including those of ethnic minorities, feminists, advocates for gay and lesbian rights, and faith-based activists for peace and justice, with racists, nationalists, and totalitarians returning from their disgrace after the Second World War. Design became related to choice, symbolism, differentiation, and specialized actors expressing their needs in a media-rich system of urban communication. The example of the Relativity theory encouraged architects and city planners faced with the enormous variety of actors and special interests in the postmodern city to retreat from universal claims for their designs. The new, polyphonic dialogue was, furthermore, accompanied by an underlying concern for the senses and the body, a concern marked by the reemergence of phenomenology as a philosophy critical of the abstractions of modern science as we saw earlier (e.g., in Christian Norberg-Schulz's *Existence, Space, and Architecture*, 1971). Another example of the widened scope of the postmodern design dialogue, as we have already seen, is the study of the city as a semiological field and system of communication with its own signs, symbols, and rules of combination, as in Choay's "Urbanism and Semiology" (1969).

Design in this postclassical, postmechanical world does not presume the neutrality of the Cartesian coordinates. Velocity and gravity can distort space-time; nor is time itself the same everywhere in the universe. Only the speed of light in vacuum is invariant (i.e., always measured as having the same value, regardless of the observer's situation or state of motion). Furthermore, principles of uncertainty and schemes of probability were introduced into physical relationships by quantum mechanics (at the micro scale) and wave theory (at the macro scale) in the 1920s and 1930s. The flatness and uniformity of the modern, standardized system of typologies thus became stretched and fluidized. Both space and time could be distorted relative to the observer; time could be slowed, accelerated, or even (for some sequences of events) reversed; space could be bent, stretched, and compressed. Local circumstances were crucial. Actors— "observers," in the jargon of the new physics—became critical to the assessment of any particular situation.

Local conditions and observers had been important to Einstein himself, who had pointed out that space was not everywhere the same, not a uniform, neutral medium—one of the fundamental tenets of Newtonian physics. There was no universal or "absolute" space as represented by Cartesian grid coordinates in the rationalist European tradition (though these might be locally and approximately correct under many conditions). Einstein realized that objects would be compressed as they approached light-speed relative to an observer—or, conversely, that the whole universe would be compressed relative to an observer moving near the speed of light; and that both these effects were equally real. Furthermore, single-point perspective was no longer viable under extreme conditions in an Einsteinian universe (and only approximately true even under everyday conditions); at near-light speed, the front and sides of an object, otherwise invisible, could become visible to some observers.

Jane Jacobs's *Death and Life of Great American Cities* (1961) was an early marker of the breakdown of the detached, Modernist, scientific observer and the emergence of the local ecologies or networks as a crucial factor in postmodern design.[57] Jacobs was a highly partisan urban actor-designer, an activist and campaigning journalist for the cause of the old city. Her book opened the door to a positive assessment of the attributes of the city center, with its crowding, mixture of uses, mixture of ethnicities, and complexity, and showcased her bottom-up design approach to public safety based on the "eyes of the street." Jacobs writes:

> Under the seeming disorder of the old city, wherever the old city is working successfully, is a marvelous order for maintaining the safety of the streets and the freedom of the city. It is a complex order. Its essence is intricacy of sidewalk use, bringing with it a constant succession of eyes. This order is all composed of movement and change, and although it is life not art, we may fancifully call it the art form of the city and liken it to the dance—not to a simple-minded precision dance with everyone taking up at the same time, twirling in unison, and bowing off en masse, but to an intricate ballet in which the individual dancers and ensembles all have distinctive parts which miraculously reinforce each other and compose an orderly whole. The ballet of the city sidewalk never repeats itself from place to place, and in any one place is always replete with new improvisations.[58]

Jacobs's vision of the active citizen participant in the street ballet extends to seeing the street life as part of a larger urban system of "organized complexity" that is maintained in a precarious state of dynamic balance by "feedback" and linked to neighborhoods in complex ways. Jacobs argues against the "destruction of diversity" in the city, and participated as a campaigning journalist in battles to preserve Greenwich Village and the SoHo district in New York.

Columbia University planning professor Paul Davidoff, in his article "Advocacy and Pluralism in Planning" (1965), also marked the breakup of the top-down, master-planning tradition of Modernism. Davidoff enshrined Jacobs's

 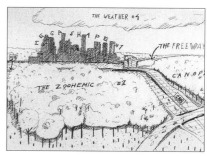

example of an active, participant actor-designer in his theory of advocacy planning, arguing for inclusion of the multiple voices of street people and community groups in the planning process. Advocacy planning can, of course, easily become adversarial planning, since under US law community groups can sue to make sure they are heard. Court cases came to have a great importance in bottom-up advocacy planning and design, as we will see later when examining the emergence of urban design in New York.[59]

Jacobs's influence was not confined to intellectuals like Davidoff. Actively campaigning from her base in Greenwich Village, she had enormous influence in New York. In 1969 the New York City Council voted to reject the City Planning Commission's master plan with its highways and megastructures, largely following Jacobs's arguments for community involvement in decision-making processes. As a campaigning, committed journalist, Jacobs had rigorously attacked Moses's "unwritten" master plans, which evaded public review and had destroyed so many neighborhoods (i.e., the South Bronx, as chronicled by Marshall Berman in *All That Is Solid Melts Into Air*, 1983).[60] There were many active protest groups against such master-planning schemes, for example, multiethnic coalitions like the East Harlem Young Lords movement of the 1960s and the Brooklyn garbage-incinerator protests in the 1970s and 1980s (described by Matthew Gandy in his *Concrete and Clay*, 2003).[61] Bernard Rudofsky's *Streets for People* (1969) shared Davidoff's and Jacobs's enthusiasm for street life and advocated a local, collective building process with a much-reduced role for planners or architects. Such views are also reflected in Lynch's advocacy of "partial control" in *A Theory of Good City Form*.

The emergence of the politics of the local and the personal as a key issue in design is not so surprising, given the enormous increases in computer power recently made available to designers and the "systems revolution" of the 1970s highlighted by Peter Hall. In this milieu, scale became an important issue, as it seemed logical that a designer could move from the details of a design to its global position, looking for recurring patterns, as in fractal theory. It seemed that the secure system of grid coordination that lay beneath every design would ensure that a pattern recognized at one scale would always work at other scales. The computer has tended to undo some of what the Relativity theory did,

restoring absoluteness (the binary 1-0, the Cartesian coordinate system) to centrality, but with a difference, namely, that these things are employed in the service of a flexible overall vision that cannot ever be the same as it was before the theorys. Local conditions and variables take on a tremendous new importance as indicators of larger systems present in a particular milieu. The fractal system recognizes these limits at a local scale, since it must of necessity never be the same twice.

The CAD system of representation has been constantly gaining flexibility since its invention, freeing designers to experiment with customization and more personalized design approaches, including ethnic variations and private narratives. Yet in practice the fractal patterns in large-scale framing devices, like the highway infrastructures of the city and large communal institutions, never easily fit with personal narratives. The local always has to be observed in detail and designs have to be developed from the bottom up as well as from the top down, a feedback process not recognized as legitimate in CAD for many years. But by the end of the twentieth century, designers could frame the choices of various urban actors as "transparencies" or layers, and model their interactions in the city. These complex, interactive models are analogous to the collage techniques developed by Picasso and Braque in the 1910s, but are processed on computers using CAD applications and programs like Adobe Photoshop (an image-manipulating program first released in 1990) and Form Z (a three-dimensional architectural modeling program first released in 1991) to cut up and recombine imagery.

2.2.4 Design in the Three Cities: Summary

In the premodern City of Faith, actors create urban order by mirroring what they presume to be the divine order of the universe. At each city site they make pragmatic and symbolic accommodations to the divine, conforming to formal, self-referential, diachronic geometric systems seen as transcending time and place. In the City as a Machine, actors attempt to create a rational city governed by simple rules, a city whose parts are matched to their functions and where the reliability, efficiency, and standardized mass-production of modern machinery can produce a new spatial environment for the greatest good of the greatest number at the least cost. In the organic or Ecological City, actors seek more individual control over and customization of design, creating a more responsive and flexible design system that incorporates feedback from the bottom up. Design in the City as a Machine is essentially a Modernist project; design in the Organic or Ecological city, a postmodern project. But whether postmodernism constitutes a clean break with a now-defunct Modernist world-view, or joins in dialogue with an "unfinished" Modernist project, is a question on which views differ.

2.3 THE EMERGENCE OF URBAN DESIGN

2.3.1 Collapse of City Planning and Emergence of Special Districts in New York

P Rudolf: Mega-structure plan for the Lower-Manhattan expressway, 1970

In his *Introduction to Urban Design* (1982), Jonathan Barnett, writing as a practicing designer, describes the emergence in New York in the late 1960s of the first professional group to be called "urban designers." He details how Mayor John Lindsay established the Mayor's Task Force on Urban Design in 1966, an advisory group that included Philip Johnson, I. M. Pei (who was working on the Central Boston Urban Design plan), Jacquelin Robertson, and Robert Stern. The task force suggested that Mayor Lindsay establish a new specialized design section within the city planning department to be called the Urban Design Group and to be financed, in part, by the real-estate industry. The group rose to prominence as it became clear that the city council would refuse to pass the city planning department's megastructural master plan of 1968. The planning department faced a crisis of control, as there was no overall coordination legally sanctioned by the council. This situation gave the Urban Design Group an opportunity to substitute locally controlled, small special district plans for specially chosen areas, claiming that such special districts were contained within the 1916 zoning legislation (an unchallenged legal basis for the department's activities). The council's official refusal of the master plan in 1969 prompted the rapid emergence of a new, smaller scale, more flexible discipline that would not rely solely on the universal, rational-scientific context envisioned by Cerdá. *New York Times* correspondent Paul Goldberger called the proposals of this special district system "mini-plans," noting they were tailored to each community.

Jonathan Barnett calmly describes the reinvention of the special district zoning system in New York in his article "Urban Design as Public Policy" (1974), giving scarcely a hint of the momentous shift away from top-down planning the move to urban design involved. The policy of urban design in special districts gave the city council and mayor a way to deal flexibly with the demands of neighborhood pressure groups as well as the new real-estate "science" of the development community and its bankers. The city became a collage of enclaves defined as "Special Use Sections" under the 1916 legislation that had originally designated the Wall Street area as an exception to the general legislation.[62]

between urban actors and a different system of self-organization in the life-world of the city.[80] Each life-world resulted in a different pattern being imprinted in the plan of the city, which could be read in high contrast black-and-white figure-ground drawings, like those employed by Sitte. Using such drawings Sitte demonstrated, for example, that the monuments and small-scale city blocks integrated into the fabric of old Vienna demonstrated the presence of an organic, tight-knit community. For Sitte, the big boulevards and isolated monuments of the Ring Strasse displayed the isolation of modern bourgeois life in the industrial city. In his own designs for "garden cities," Sitte, like Howard, sought to integrate the modern city-region with a small-scale village fabric in a natural setting.[81]

Rowe, as head of the urban design studio at Cornell in the mid and late 1960s, used Gestaltic pattern-reading techniques, following Sitte's example, to identify patterns in city plans. These pattern-reading skills enabled designers to identify the preindustrial fabric, industrial fabric, and modern city fabric, each with its distinct signature and associated imagery. In this system of analysis, repetitive block patterns in an area form "fields" that have boundaries and specific characteristics (and ares similar to Lynch's "districts"). Each "field" has a formal core made up of a monumental building or buildings (e.g., church, courthouse, or post office). The distinguishing characteristic of Contextualist designs was the attempt to link the meaning of this iconic formal core to the surrounding "field." In *Collage City*, Rowe and Koetter illustrate the field as a self-organizing pattern with the barrel-vaulted market roofs of ancient Rome, the equivalent of the covered bazaars in Constantinople or the souks of Islamic society. A "field," if built at one time by a particular set of historical actors, could also be seen as a layer or stratum of the city's history, capturing and symbolizing the aspirations of those actors in a small-scale enclave or "vest-pocket utopia," that is, a miniature utopia that does not seek to encompass the whole city or state in its totalitarian design. Such utopian enclaves record their builders' ideals and aspirations; accumulating through time, they form the text for an incremental reading of the city. London's great estates are "fields" in this sense, as their builders arranged the repetitive units of the townhouses and squares as distinct organizational units on the agricultural fringe of the city.

Having identified fields by their morphological patterns and located their formal, symbolic cores, the Contextualists proceeded to clarify the relationships between these areas by stripping out or opening up the "interstices," the areas *between* fields, often for use as linear parks or routes for highways. In their own designs they retained but modified the large-scale superblock interventions of the Modernism of Le Corbusier's Ville Radieuse (using tall "Redent," slab blocks snaking through the landscape to define large parks and residual street corridors).[82]

The Cornell Contextualists, much like Lynch in *The Image of the City* (1961), had defined "fields" by their "edge" boundaries, by their "node" centers, and by their distinctive "markers" (formal characteristics and key buildings). In *Collage*

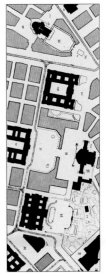

Camillo Sitte: infill project for the Ringstrasse, Vienna, 1889

Cornell University urban-design studio: Buffalo Project, ca. 1978

Colin Rowe:
Comparison between
Palladio and Le
Corbusier Grids
1947

John Hedjuk and
Colin Rowe:
analysis of American
court-house square,
1957

Leon Krier: the
modern versus the
traditional city,
1970s

City, Rowe and Koetter defined the area of each experimental fragment as a "field," each field representing a singular time period and layer in their overall collage. In addition, Rowe, as a student of Rudolf Wittkower (whose *Architectural Principles in the Age of Humanism*, 1949, provided the conceptual framework and methodology of Rowe's early writings, with their emphasis on mathematics, proportion, geometry, and type) saw each field as possessing a symbolic center representative of the primary intellectual pursuit of its founders. Rowe and Koetter saw the city as a system of fragmentary enclaves, small utopias each with its own self-organizing system of order.[83]

This reading of the city's fragments had deep roots in the rationalist and scientific methodology associated with Aldo Rossi's commentaries and the later Rationalists. As we have seen, in Europe a strong reaction against the towers and slabs of Modernism sponsored a return to the old forms of the European city as symbolic intermediaries indicating community and the local culture. While Rossi stressed the "analogical city" of random and surprising juxtapositions inside a ruined order in the 1960s, in the 1970s German Rationalists like Mattias Ungers and the brothers Robert and Leon Krier stressed city design as a modern, rationalist science in the tradition of Cerdá, Stubben, Alphand, and Haussmann. For the European Rationalists, monuments, castles, cathedrals, town halls, markets, factories, and railway stations were distinctive, large-scale, highly differentiated urban elements that gave character to the city—shaped its skyline, and so forth. These buildings acted as symbolic intermediaries between different urban actors and also held the key to the actor-designer's and the city's collective memory, that is, a particular culture's sense of place and history.[84]

Rowe wrote the introduction for the English translation of Robert Krier's *Urban Space* (English version 1979, first published in German as *Stadtraum in Theorie und Praxis* in 1975). Krier provided a systematic model, based on structuralist linguistics, for the manipulation of urban elements as symbolic intermediaries in dialogue between urban actors. Using as a model Levi-Strauss's structuralist network diagram of the "totemic operator" constructing meaning in the network of the Inuit language, he constructed a network diagram of urban terms to describe the city. In this diagram, the primary, Platonic, geometric forms of the triangle, the square, and the circle stand at the top, generating all other forms through a series of transformative operations. City plazas are either open or closed, regular or irregular, overlaid or cut into, dominant or recessed. Building sections are described only in terms of their symbolic surface, the street facade, facing the public street or square. Facades are assembled from overlaying grids, which might contain semantic elements such as a Palladian window or Gothic arch. The language of the city, its image, becomes a three-dimensional construct entirely controlled by the actor-designer as a "totemic operator" manipulating symbolic icons. Krier thought he could account for all possible urban configurations using this system; he joked that a "mad scientist" would one day catalogue all the possible variations

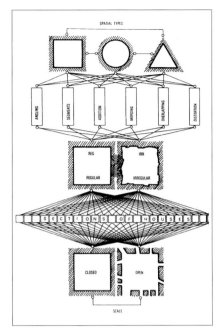

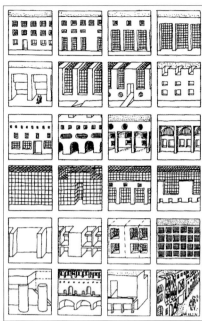

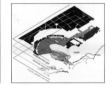

of the system, thus closing its apparently open, combinatorial character.[85]

To Rowe and Koetter, the formal core of each enclave or "field" is a symbolic intermediary by which urban actors communicate with each other. An enclave embodies the ideas of its owners, designers, and (sometimes) inhabitants, and moving through the city means moving between these enclaves. The composite phenomenological experience of this urban promenade, like that of moving through Le Corbusier's *"promenade architecturale,"* is, Rowe and Koetter say, a multifaceted, sequential collage that integrates elements in ambiguous, changing patterns. Like a Picasso portrait, this collage represents a new understanding of form: in particular, a new understanding of urban continuity as a psychic reality and cultural commons that holds together despite all superficial differences.[86]

Rowe and Koetter reject the utopian, total-design aspirations of the early Modernists. Such ideals have, they say, to be limited to vest-pocket utopias; they are not universally applicable. Local variables, individuals, and time flows matter. Space cannot be controlled on a citywide scale, but can and will be distorted and fragmented by local forces, forming highly specific public realms embedded *in* the city. Rowe and Koetter illustrate this collagist design approach with Leo von Klenze's Munich of the 1840s and 1850s. Von Klenze built outside the historic, Gothic, central enclave with its cathedral square; he added a street armature commencing from a new, neoclassical, symbolic gate and terminating near the city center at a copy of the Gothic Loggia dei Lanzi of Florence. Along this street were all the agencies of the modern liberal state: chancellery, foreign

office, university (in an Italianate style), and a Gothic church with a tall steeple. To the north a new sector of the city was laid out on a street grid, which included a new square for a neoclassical, state-owned art museum. The main facade of the royal palace copied Brunelleschi's Pitti Palace. A copy of London's Crystal Palace was built as a palace of industry, and later a new grid of streets and supporting infrastructure was added, crossing the river from the royal palace to a set of hillside gardens. After Munich was bombed in the Second World War it was carefully rebuilt along the same eclectic lines—but with new metro and service systems beneath.

Colin Rowe and Fred Koetter: urban element 1, memorable streets

The city's picturesque variety created the impression of a fragmented, incremental "museum city" symbolic of the passage of time. In the scenographic tradition of Renaissance patronage, a liberal prince here created an encyclopedic, symbolic, cultural landscape collage that encompassed all European history.[87]

At the end of *Collage City*, Rowe and Koetter detail five basic elements of city collage. Each has its own internal organizational logic. The first element is *memorable street*, illustrated by aerial photographs of Fifth Avenue in New York, beside Central Park. This forms a powerful linear organizing element of the sort that I have termed an "armature."

The second element is the *stabilizer*, a self-organizing pattern focused on a single center, creating an enclave. A stabilizer is a structure or figurative pattern, such as the Place des Vosges in Paris, that acts as a self-centering spatial device in a district. An aerial photograph shows the void of the large, royal square, built by royal decree, standing out against the background of the small-scale row houses and small palaces of the surrounding Marais district. The large-scale, geometric gesture of the royal square "stabilizes" (grounds and centers) the smaller-scale operations of local landowners and home-owners in a clearly ordered pattern.[88]

Rowe and Koetter: urban element 2, stabilizer

The third element is the *potentially indeterminable set piece*, any member of that class of similar, small-scale design elements (whether building types, continuous facades, or stylistic details) that, when repeated, produces a highly structured field. Actor-designers recognize these repetitive patterns as areas of visual order and standardization in the city. When it forms around a linear axis, such a pattern yields an armature; to yield an enclave it need not form around a specific center, but it must have boundaries clear enough to define a field.[89]

The fourth element is the *splendid public terrace*: a high place, often an overlook, from which a sense of the city as a whole can be gained. From such a point the actor-designers can see as parts of a larger pattern the fragments with which they are most familiar. This gives a sense of the organization of the whole city, an organization into which the city's various fragmentary parts can be mapped in an exercise of memory. Panoramas and observation decks on hills, towers, or skyscrapers, as well as balloon or helicopter flights, are opportunities to access memory and construct an overview. In a sublime moment of revelation and

Rowe and Koetter: urban element 3, potentially indeterminable set piece reverie, the actor-designer can reintegrate all the fragments of the "collage city."

The fifth element is the *ambiguous or multivalent building*, which can sometimes function as a heterotopia. A building of this type sits at the junction of several urban fields and operates at multiple scales simultaneously; its ambiguity resolves conflict between competing, overlapping fields. As noted by Gestalt psychologists, the same shapes can sometimes be mentally assembled by an observer into two different patterns or wholes (e.g., the famous "two faces vs. one candlestick" figure); this ambiguity is created by the existence of two overlapping or alternative readings, *both* of which are correct. Rowe and Koetter transpose this ambiguity to urban terms as the ability to operate simultaneously at two levels, in the "in-between" space of a network of relationships.[90]

Rowe and Koetter: urban element 4, splendid public terrace

Rowe and Koetter illustrate the heterotopic, ambiguous, or multivalent building with figure-ground drawings of the prince's Residenz Palace in Munich. Here the small scale of the front plaza and courtyard are linked to the old city, with an interior courtyard as an internal organizing device, while another courtyard at the back links to the larger scale of the new von Klenze Frederick Strasse. Yet another large courtyard opens out into the extensive English Garden, with temples and grottos that the prince laid out beside the river. "Ambiguous" buildings, like the overlapping spaces of Cubist collage, are multivalent, operating simultaneously at several scales, layers, and levels. Here the actor-designer can experience the complexity and ambiguous readings inherent in the city plan and fabric as a rich life-world with multiple layers of meaning.[91]

Additional elements discussed by Rowe and Koetter are *nostalgia-producing instruments*—building complexes that displace the observer to another place or time (creating a desire for an unattainable environment, past or future)—and *gardens*, with a distinct emphasis on the Italian formal garden. Their final commentary deals with artists' imaginary combinations of urban elements in paintings and imaginary projects within the context of existing cities, often resulting in a dramatic confrontation. For example, unbuilt Palladian buildings replace the Gothic Rialto bridge and its surroundings in a neoclassical urban scenography in Canaletto's *The Grand Canal, with an Imaginary Rialto Bridge and Other Buildings* (1740s).[92]

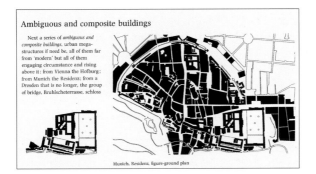

Ambiguous and composite buildings

Next a series of *ambiguous and composite buildings*, urban mega-structures if need be, all of them far from 'modern' but all of them engaging circumstance and rising above it: from Vienna the Hofburg; from Munich the Residenz; from a Dresden that is no longer, the group of bridge, Bruhlscheterrasse, schloss

Munich. Residenz, figure-ground plan

Rowe and Koetter; urban element 5, ambiguous and composite buildings

2.3.3 *Collage City*—Discourse and Application

Collage City initiated a discourse on the logic of relationships between elements and fragments in the postmodern city, even if it did not provide a satisfactory resolution of the question. The strength of *Collage City*'s city concept was that it could accommodate fragments originating in many different systems and organized in many different ways while respecting the internal organization and ecology of each. *Collage City* provided a working method for the handling of a fragmented, multicentered city model through its vision of an incremental growth system comprised of distinctive, competing, self-centered enclaves. Each enclave recorded a separate, incremental layer of city growth. This system of representation could, later, easily be computerized.

The weakness of the *Collage City* approach was that the relationships between enclaves were not examined in detail. The final, overall, autocratic control of the prince in the pluralism of the Munich model did not have much popular appeal in an age of multiple actor-designers (e.g., as advocated by Jane Jacobs) and adversarial battles between public authorities, corporate developers, and community groups. In the *Collage City* vision the promise of a multivocal, dialogic, interactive collage tended to be trumped by the eclectic, symbolic choices of a single, Enlightenment authority. This weakness became obvious in the *Roma Interrotta* (1978) project, organized by Michael Graves and based on Rowe and Koetter's collage theories. A special double issue of *Architectural Design* (1979) replaced the original map panels of Giambattista Nolli's plan of Rome of 1748 with 12 new drawings designed by contemporary postmodern architects. Nolli's plan is well known to urban designers because it showed both public open space and semipublic courtyards and entrances as white spaces against the black of the building mass, emphasizing the continuity of the city. This had been one of the inspirations for the urban design "figure-ground" plan-analysis technique developed by Rowe at Cornell to show urban public space in dense city fabrics. The Gestalt of the whole system, so obvious in the original Nolli map, disappeared in the resultant Roma Interrotta assemblage by individual design stars. Rowe, like Nolli, blacked in the blocks and left the streets white so as to show urban patterns in high contrast. Leading a team of contributors, Rowe fabricated a mostly fictive centuries-spanning history for his sector; other map panels were completed by Rossi, Stirling, both Krier brothers, Paolo Portoghesi, Venturi, Rauch, Graves, Piero Sartogo, Romaldo Giurgola, and Constantino Dardi. No contributor's project related to their neighbor's; each was an isolated display case for its author's talents, separated by a frame from the others.

This chaotic situation exposed the great problem of the *Collage City* approach: how to ensure that the coordination of different actors in the overall composition of the city had a Gestalt, even if a fractured one. Market forces, much like the unintegrated efforts of intellectual designers from around the globe, would obviously create a riot of individual fragments (as in Serlio's

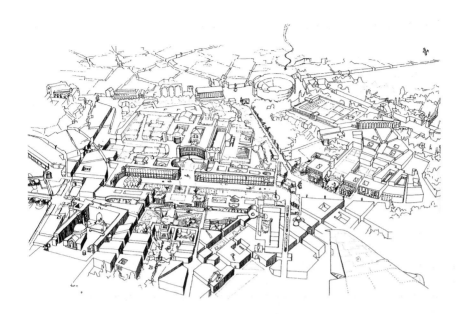

Rowe et alia: Roma Interotta *sector, 1978*

Comic scene). The question was thus how to coordinate the various fragments and allow for individual expression without resorting to the fiction of the "enlightened" prince or princess who would magically bring everything into alignment (as occurred in Koetter and Rowe's favorite case study of Munich, described above).[93]

Collage City did provide a working method for creating successful urban fragments, as Battery Park City demonstrated. I show both the evolution of New York zoning and special districts up to Battery Park City and a series of urban designs from the Cornell School (by associates of Rowe and Koetter) as samples of the *Collage City* approach (pp 124–5). Koetter, in partnership with Susie Kim, worked with Skidmore, Owings, and Merrill on the design guidelines for Canary Wharf in London, the enormous office project in the abandoned London docklands that reoriented the city's direction of growth to the east.[94] In addition, the Koetter and Kim office prepared a series of fragmentary proposals for the incremental redevelopment of other abandoned London docks, anticipating the Thames Gateway proposals of the Greater London Authority. Koetter, previously the Dean of Yale Architecture School, was also in partnership with Michael Dennis, a Cornell professor at the time (later at MIT). Dennis has developed a specialized practice in campus design using *Collage City* principles, as in his Carnegie Mellon campus plan. Further, Steven Peterson and Barbara Littenberg, both graduates of Cornell who worked on *Roma Interotta* with Rowe, won the first urban design competition for Les Halles, Paris, and a high-density project for central Montreal, that were not built. After 9/11/2004 they updated the layered, *Collage City* sectional logic with mixed-use towers (illustrated in the following pages).[95]

Cornell after Collage City

Peterson-Littenberg:
a) *World Trade Centre Innovative Design Competition model, 2002–03*
b) *WTC competition, plan, 2002–03*
c) *Les Halles Competition, axonometric, 1978–79*
Michael Dennis Associates:
d) *Carnegie Mellon University Competition master plan, 1987*
e) *Model*
f) *Aerial view of CMU campus, 2004*
g) *View of new CMU academic quadrangle, 2004*

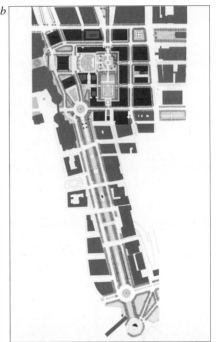

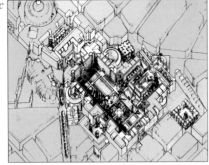

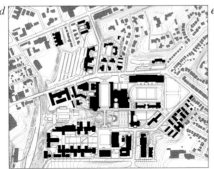

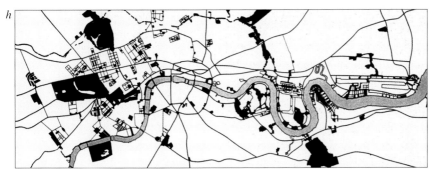

h

Cornell after
Collage City

Koetter and Kim:
h) *Overview of the
West End, the City
and the east London
Docklands, 1997*
*Koetter and Kim:
Canary Wharf,
1988–89*
i) *Waterfront
housing, facade,*
j) *Waterfront
housing,
axonometric*
k) *Urban design
guidelines, 1988–89*

i

j

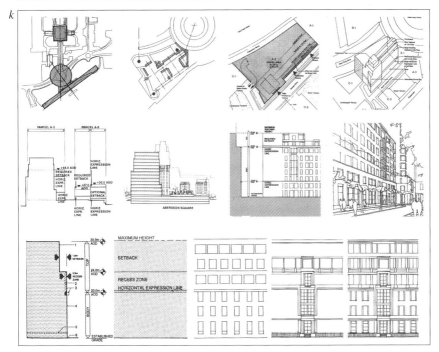

k

Despite its faults, the *Collage City* model of independent fragments became the de facto operating system of the postmodern city. It enabled individual designers to proceed with their fragment with a minimum of coordination with others, closely mirroring the activities of free-market operators in large-scale subdivisions (as in the case of New Urbanism). It became a normative mode of design or planning shared by many different actors with different agendas, a coordinating platform on which many different programs could be assembled. Rowe and Koetter's emphasis on collage allowed for the postmodern pastiche, while their emphasis on the history of fragments opened up the possibility of historical "museum cities" created as marketing simulacra. The example of Munich proved to be a double-edged sword in this respect, with unforeseen results in Prince Charles's support for historical-pastiche designs in Britain or Jerde's mall designs, like *City Walk* (Los Angeles, 1989–93). Later, New Urbanists borrowed its collagist aesthetic and system of fragments, complete with historical references. "Generic city" advocates like Rem Koolhaas rejected its historicism and stressed the utopian, modern, fragmentary aspects of its system, its "vest-pocket utopias," but upsized to the scale of megastructures empowered by the state and by real-estate interests (as at Eurolille).[96]

2.4 THE SEVEN "-AGES" OF POSTMODERN DESIGN

Collage City, published in 1978, marked the shift in design away from Modernism. John Thackara, in *Design After Modernism*, highlights the controversy regarding the "break with Modernism," stressing that the break is in large measure illusory because of the dialogic feedback process that subsists between Modernism and its critics. At the same time, he shows, there *is* a qualitative difference in the response of designers starting in the last quarter of the twentieth century. This was an inevitable consequence of the realization that there was no one actor or designer in charge of everything, with one clock coordinating all events and actions. There are only local actors with global connections, a patchwork of fragments linked to local and global flows. There is no overall logic to this system; this results in surprising, surreal, and dynamic juxtapositions of various patches. Below I examine seven varieties of relationships between actors and patches in a postmodern situation.

2.4.1 Naming the Seven "-ages"

In *Modern Movements in Architecture* (1973), Charles Jencks highlights the numerous and eclectic "-isms" (e.g., Contextualism and Deconstructivism) of the period in which he wrote. Similarly, I would like to highlight the many "-ages" (collage, bricolage, etc.) that have emerged as design approaches in the last third of a century or so.[97] The first was Aldo Rossi's 1976 concept of the "analogical city" as a system of archeological layers and fragments in the city,

Charles Jencks: genealogy diagram, Modern Movements in Architecture, *1973*

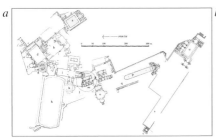

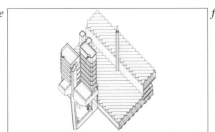

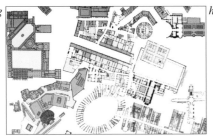

The layered city and the Deconstructive section

a) *Hadrian's Villa, Tivoli, early 2nd century BC*
b) *Hoesli, Rowe, Hedjuk, Slutsky* et alia*: Collage City game, 1956*
c) *Guy Debord:* Naked City *diagram, 1956*
d) *Le Corbusier: view of the Carpenter Center, Harvard, 1963*
e) *Stirling and Gowan: Leicester Engineering Laboratory, UK, 1959–1963*
f) *David Grahame Shane: Covent Garden analysis, London, 1972*
g) *Hans Kollhoff:* Collage City, *1978*
h) *Rowe* et alia*: Roma Interotta, 1978*
i) *MVRDV: Mix City, Costa Iberica, plan, 2003*
j) *MVRDV: Mix City, Costa Iberica, collage, 2003*

which I dub *decoupage*; subsequently there have been *collage* (of the Collage City); *bricolage*, derived from the structuralist writings of the French anthropologist Levi-Strauss; *photomontage* and *montage*, derived from the cinema (1980s); *assemblage*, developed by the protagonists of Generic Urbanism and Deconstructivism (1990s); and, finally, *rhizomic assemblage*, derived from the writing of French philosophers Deleuze and Guattari, which has emerged as a design approach in the network city at the beginning of the twenty-first century.

The Seven "-ages" of Postmodernism

1. Decoupage (Rossi and "analogical city" design)
2. Collage City (plus Contextualism and Rationalism)
3. Bricolage
4. Photomontage
5. Montage
6. Assemblage
7. Rhizomic assemblage

The brief survey of the seven "-ages" below is intended to set up a framework for understanding the return of interest in the traditional design of urban places, an art eclipsed in the triumph of Modernism. This return, despite its protagonists' hopes (as in New Urbanism, for instance), can never be entirely successful because of the continuity of the project of Modernity at a global scale. As the very term *postmodernism* indicates, the base for this return remains Modern. Thus the alluring exterior symbols of a past community (vernacular streets and porches) are often combined with the interior advantages of technocratic, futuristic media rooms with air conditioning and advanced communications (as at Celebration, Florida).

My survey is intended to move fast and is necessarily superficial; it is intended as only a guide for further study. We have looked at Collage City in the previous section and will return to assemblage and rhizomic assemblage in the final chapter. Here I will merely devote some brief paragraphs to each "-age" or design methodology and then return to the problem of feedback and memory between actors and fragments in open systems like those engineered to support the global economy and information systems.

1. *Decoupage: Rossi and "Analogical City" Design*. Strictly speaking, Aldo Rossi's *Analogical City* (1976), is an assemblage, but with a deep sense of memory added that invites use of another category. This memory is not holistic, referring to a hidden Gestalt as in collage, but remains embodied in fragments. Yet this residual presence of memory disqualifies the drawing as an "assemblage" that presumes neutral, ready-made pieces (as in the work of the avant-garde French artist Marcel Duchamp). In order to flesh out my list of

"-ages" I have somewhat arbitrarily called Rossi's drawing a "decoupage," borrowing a film term that (in "classic decoupage") implies that a narrative is being constructed from fragments. In Rossi's case, the narrative is a description of a chaotic state, using "neutral" scientific depictions of the elements of the European city (city plans, sections, facades, and axonometric projections). I might have used the term *"mise en scène,"* employed by Jean-Luc Godard to distinguish his contemporary form of montage using multiple media in the city from the practices of earlier cineastes such as Sergei Eisenstein.[98]

We are not accustomed to hearing the observer-scientist's subjective "voice," nor do we expect from him or her a nonlinear "fairy-tale" narrative structure; yet writing and narrating in an extended, not-entirely-scientific field necessarily involves jumps between "voices" which make no sense by the standards of classical, linear logic. The resulting narrative will seem like a child's fairy story to a committed Modernist, trained in the conventions of "objective" detachment, yet the extended field has a logic of its own, a logic of cinematic assemblage, jump cuts, close-ups, and flashbacks dealing with fundamental psychic realities hidden behind our experience of the postmodern city-region.

Aldo Rossi: Modena Cemetery Competition, sketch, 1971

Postmodern architects and designers have variously narrated this jump-cut logic of the multicentered city. The crucial distinguishing factor of these narratives is their nonlinear quality, whereby the logic of the story is advanced by apparent non sequiturs. Aldo Rossi, an Italian Rationalist architect and painter of the 1960s and 1970s, described this nonlinear method as working by "analogy." An analogy is a "likeness between two things in certain respects; something partially similar."[99] Rossi's *Analogical City* is at first sight a simple collage of built forms erected on the ruins of a centralized, Utopian, Renaissance city-plan. *Analogical City* is a demonstration of the viability of nonfunctional, apparently illogical thinking. The symbolic organization of this city is a centralized utopia, a figure of Renaissance perfection that has, in the drawing, been broken and fractured. Thus, the city's formal center—analogous to that of Bentham's Panopticon or Howard's new-town diagram—no longer holds sway. There is no central jailer, no central observer, no singular narrative, no privileged logic or central intelligence. Foucault's central "eye of power" lies in ruins.

From a Modernist perspective, this "analogical city" is a shocking and aphasic assemblage, yet partial similarity can trigger recognition of shared pattern, even when the two things compared (e.g., the Roman Pantheon and the Panopticon prison) are not identical. This analogical pattern-recognition process implies that the engaged actor-designer can actively construct formal associations and figural correspondences of likeness and resemblance. These associations may appear random to a narrow Rationalism, but manifest an analogical, formal logic of their own. *Analogical City* itself does not observe simple codes of functional segregation, but jumbles up historical and modern examples and typologies, disobeying the modern logic of flows; it combines partially similar elements, stressing their shared urbanity to amplify the complexity of the city, harking back to the crowded, compressed forms of the European street-based city. It keeps the street and surrounds public monuments with built fabric, mixing and matching elements with no apparent (linear) logic.

For Rossi, the seemingly arbitrary logic of analogy best expressed the poetry of the city as an object created by citizens over time. The fabric of the city is a collective effort of individual citizens having its own logic, but the poetry of the city lies in its time-defying monuments. Rossi saw cities as continuously inhabited structures produced by the flow of time and events through a particular place; there is, in fact, no overall (linear) logic controlling the way that fragments and programs come to be deposited in them. Yet the culture of the city stands outside of time as an almost autonomous, analogous by-product of its citizens' lives. Accidents, personalities, cultural traditions, and technical innovations all play their part in the analogical city's poetic narrative.

The design logic of Rossi's "analogical city" is defined by poetic and symbolic relationships between actor-designers in the city, rather than by functional networks. His sense of urban poetry is descended from that of Walter Benjamin in Weimar Germany in the 1920s. Benjamin wrote of the city as one disaster piled upon another, ruin upon ruin, directly opposing the normal bourgeois view of scientific progress. Among these ruins, Benjamin sought out surprising juxtapositions: strange, adaptive reuses of formerly grand structures. He loved, for example (like the Surrealist André Breton), the "subaqueous light" of the decaying, about-to-be-demolished, glass-covered Parisian arcades.[100]

Passage des Panoramas, Paris, 1800–34

Such pieces of abandoned urban equipment serve both Benjamin and Rossi as reminders of the ephemeral nature of fashion in the modern city. Rossi linked his sense of the poetry of past grandeur to an active appreciation of the nobly proportioned and geometric forms that he, like Le Corbusier, considered symbolic of eternal truths. This city of eternal truths could, Rossi thought, best be demonstrated by tombs (following Adolf Loos's aphorism that tombs have the best architecture). Rossi's clearest statement of his urban poetics was, therefore, a miniature city for the dead at the Modena cemetery (1971).[101]

2. *Collage City (plus Contextualism and Rationalism)*. Starting in the late 1950s and early 1960s, collage and bricolage became important techniques for designers handling the complex, fragmented, and ambiguous situation in which they found themselves. Influenced by the Relativity theorys, designers no longer saw themselves as working in a uniform "deep space" of universal perspectival recession. Shallow space, local layering, hybridization of patterns, multidimensional overlaps, and ambiguous transparencies became of more interest (as evidenced by Colin Rowe and Bob Slutsky's two-part article, "Literal and Phenomenal Transparency," commenced in 1955 and published in 1963 and 1971).[102] Rowe and Slutsky explored both the layering of building plans and facades and movement through these layers, creating a *"promenade architecturale"* (an architectural sequence), as in their analysis of the unbuilt Le

Corbusier competition design for the League of Nations (1927) or in their reading of the Villa Stein in Garches, France (1927).

As described earlier in this chapter, Rowe and Koetter's *Collage City* (1978) developed these themes into the operating system of choice for designers working with multiple actors, systems of movement, and a variety of urban fragments. Rowe and Koetter incorporated the earlier work of the American Contextualists (1960s) and European Rationalists (1970s). The distinguishing characteristic of Rowe's work, whether in conjunction with Slutsky or, later, with Koetter, was the role assigned to memory and a residual sense of the whole Gestalt as an active agent in design. Whether in Palladio's villas or Le Corbusier's Villa Stein, memory and geometry, according to Rowe, play a reintegrative feedback role, inserting the fragments into an overall schema or conceptual model (as in Lynch's interpretative reading of interviewees' city models in *The Image of the City*). Like Rossi, Rowe and his partners sought a sense of the continuity of history in the urban experience of dense cities with continuous urban fabrics. Both imply that there is a Gestalt or pattern that is larger than any of its individual parts, a situation that, as Dalibor Vesely wrote in "Architecture and the Ambiguity of the Fragment" (1996),[103] is not only recognized and articulated by poets and painters but unconsciously absorbed by all citizens. In his *Architecture in the Age of Divided Representation: The Question of Creativity in the Shadow of Production* (2004), Vesely expands on the notion that fragments can act as a trigger of a collective memory, arguing that even a fragment of broken whole can be redemptive. [104]

3. Bricolage. As described earlier in this chapter, Rowe and Koetter incorporated Claude Levi-Strauss's concept of bricolage as an example of Gestalt thinking based on pattern-making. In Gestalt thinking, a pattern or whole formed from assembled parts is larger than and different from those parts, addressing a holistic, second-order cognitive layer. This layer remains unconscious in many people who nevertheless get from it much satisfaction. Applications of Gestalt thinking might range from the ad hoc assembly of a garden shed to a self-consciously artistic assembly of discrete objects whose juxtaposition evokes memories of a whole process (like an amateur collage juxtaposing real objects with photographs of a lost home or ship). Levi-Strauss contrasted the holistic thinking of bricolage with the atomized thinking of engineers, who work from part to whole and know the whole precisely in terms of its parts. The French term *bricolage* is sometimes associated with do-it-yourself design, as when a nonprofessional uses a kit of parts to create part of their own environment following their personal rules rather than scientific or communal norms.

Rowe and Slutsky: analysis of Le Corbusier's competition design for the League of Nations (from "Literal and Phenomenal Transparency," 1955)

4. *Photomontage*. Collage and bricolage maintain a sense of a whole that is larger than its parts and that gives one a sense of closure, of mastery. Photography, like painting before it, can be used either to reinforce this sense of

closure and completion or to deliberately disrupt it, as Canaletto did in *The Grand Canal, with an Imaginary Rialto Bridge and Other Buildings*, with its collection of idealized Palladian buildings, or Rossi did in the *Analogical City*. Early in the twentieth century, photographers realized they had an expanded ability to displace well-known images and position them in new, surprising situations. With this process they created a fictive space made of recognizable elements, well-known buildings, and landmarks suddenly piled one upon another, as in Paul Citroen's *Metropolis* photomontage of 1921.

As Dawn Ades outlines in *Photomontage* (1976), the Surrealists seized on photomontage as a way of representing the irrational forces of the darker side of the collective unconscious, which had been exposed by Freud and unleashed by capitalist industrial society.[105] In their hands, photomontage became a powerful tool for triggering repressed emotions and memories. It also became an invaluable technique for modern advertising, and was seen by the leaders of the Bauhaus and Russian Revolution as a key part of industrial marketing. Photomontage techniques remained a staple of advertising campaigns throughout the twentieth century, receiving a new lease of life with the arrival of the Web and of programs like Photoshop, which allow still images from around the globe to be instantly and arbitrarily juxtaposed or recombined with each other in cybernetic hyperspace. An example of the designs made possible by such methods is MVRDV's *Costa Iberica*.[106]

5. *Montage*. Where collage, bricolage, and photomontage largely work with still images, *montage* is a cinematic term referring to the actor or director's ability to construct movement in an imaginary space from footage of real places. That is, short sequences or shots of real places are reassembled or juxtaposed to create a sense of movement in a fictional space, a new, emotional space, a reality that may have lurked, in some sense, behind the original location (or locations) but which is brought to the fore in the cutting room. In a famous montage in Eisenstein's *Battleship Potemkin* (1925), a sequence of shots follows a mother and perambulator down a flight of steps in St. Petersburg, creating a tense, compact space containing people and events that were in physical reality far apart. Eisenstein called the result a "montage of attractions."[107]

I use the word *montage* to refer to the space of experience constructed in systems of movement and the individual's journey along specific narrative paths in the city. Montage in this wider sense can be traced back to the systems of controlled movement engineered for aesthetic purposes in English landscape gardens, as described by Christopher Hussey in *The Picturesque: Studies in a Point of View* (1927) and by John Dixon Hunt in *The Picturesque Garden in Europe* (2002), examined further in the next chapter.[108] Montage survived as a thread inside Modernism in Le Corbusier's concept of the *promenade architecturale* and played an important role in the design process of the British "townscape" group of designers surrounding Gordon Cullen in the 1950s and

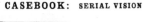

To walk from one end of the plan to another, at a uniform pace, will provide a sequence of revelations which are suggested in the serial drawings opposite, reading from left to right. Each arrow on the plan represents a drawing. The even progress of travel is illuminated by a series of sudden contrasts and so an impact is made on the eye, bringing the plan to life (like nudging a man who is going to sleep in church). My drawings bear no relation to the place itself; I chose it because it seemed an evocative plan. Note that the slightest deviation in alignment and quite small variations in projections or setbacks on plan have a disproportionally powerful effect in the third dimension.

also in the design of Walt Disney's Disneyland, California (1954). In Cullen and Disney's work, the city became the equivalent of the storyboard used by modern film directors (e.g., Eisenstein, Hitchcock) who treated the world as a sequence of preestablished shots that tell a story visually. This highly effective technique, further developed by Cullen, also influenced Lynch's concept of the visual path as a narrative sequence through the city in *The Image of the City* (according to David Gosling in *The Evolution of American Urban Design*, 2003).[109]

Gordon Cullen: townscape storyboard, 1960

As noted by the architect Nigel Coates in his article "Street Signs" (in *Design After Modernism*), the return of narrative space has been one of the characteristics of postmodern design. Coates introduces NATO (Narrative Architects Today), founded in 1983 and devoted to "partial representation" in design. This means the deliberate construction of a filmic architecture with glaring gaps in its construction that reveal the support structures (e.g., Coates permanently retained the scaffolding used for construction of one of his Café

Bongo buildings in Tokyo).[110] This design gesture reveals the quality of the city as stage prop and constructed scenography for the *mis en scène* of city life, a theme Coates further pursued in his *Ecstacity* (2003).

The tradition of narrative and montage also continues in such nomadic artist's projects such as Krzysztof Wodiczko's *Homeless Vehicle Cart* (1988), intended as a rhetorical political intervention raising the issue of homelessness before a mayoral election. Wodiczko developed Mike Webb's *Suitaloon* project for homeless individuals living in the city streets, providing a small mobile shelter in a reconstructed supermarket cart that could plug into the city's infrastructure for essential services (both illustrated in Chapter 1). Such pieces attempt to explode the normal cultural stereotypes and bring design back into the street as a bottom-up process serving those disposed by our society.[111]

6. *Assemblage.* Assemblage differs from collage and bricolage in that this process of design discounts the redemptive quality of the memory and the overall Gestalt valued (even if shattered) by the other two systems of design. Practitioners of assemblage prefer to let each piece or fragment speak for itself in a syntagmatic system based on neighbor-to-neighbor relationships, much like that described by Choay in medieval European and Islamic urban life-worlds. There is no central or overall system of command or feedback, no point from which an overall view can be had that puts everything in perspective. Assemblage design works as an unpredictable, self-organizing system with strictly local rules that can nonetheless produce predictable large-scale patterns, as manifested in Zipf's law or in those patterns of segregation highlighted by Krugman (see Chapter 1).

Venturi, Scott Brown and Izenour: National Football League Hall of Fame, New Brunswick NJ, 1967

In assemblage, ready-made pieces or found objects are picked at random and combined without any overall intent of creating beauty, but rather with an interest in the process and game of combining parts. The hand of the maker is not hidden, but is celebrated in all its messiness (as in Russian Constructivism from the Russian Revolution). The elements combined can be garbage, as in Kurt Schwitter's vast abstract sculptural installation *Merzbau* (1923). Tafuri, writing in *Architecture and Utopia*, saw this project as representing the chaos and pain of the Weimar years in Germany. The work of Duchamp also exemplifies the wit and poetry of assemblage and the use of the ready-made. American Pop artists like Robert Rauschenberg and Andy Warhol followed a similar path, introducing ready-made elements, commercial signs, or hyperreal, mass-produced products into their work, blurring the traditional distinction between art and kitsch. The Venturi and Scott Brown team deliberately blurred this same line in their works, such as *The National Football Hall of Fame* (1967), proposed for Rutgers University in New Brunswick, New Jersey: the hall was to be located behind a giant billboard beside a highway.[112] James Stirling and James Gowan's iconic postmodern Leicester Engineering Laboratory (1959–63) exemplifies the technique of assemblage, with its disparate building elements (theater, laboratory, tower, ramps, etc.) piled up around a staircase and elevator core, its ventilators referencing Le Corbusier's cult of the ocean liner.[113]

7. *Rhizomic assemblage*. Rhizomic assemblage differs from other assemblage in that it reintroduces the narrative path as an important element of the design process. There is still no emphasis on a single center or command position, still no place of total control. Instead there are multiple narratives that thread through the city, intersecting and bypassing each other as the case may be. The American architect John Hedjuk demonstrated the poetic potential of this approach in his *Berlin Mask* project (1983). Hedjuk imagined a city in which each actor constructed a symbolic "mask" or architectural structure that they then moved about the city, meeting and interacting with other actors. The characters associated with the masks were symbolic, deliberately mundane and stereotypical—priest, cobbler, etc.—but their interactions and interpenetrations were magical performances. The city ground-plane was a bounded, open area in which interactions took place, leaving behind a sculptural record in the resultant interlocked figures and masks that could always be recombined.[114]

John Hedjuk: Berlin Mask, 1983

Postmodern designers have interpreted the concept of the *rhizome* as a form of network that supports objects in space or as a background energy field that enables objects to function and that connects them to each other in extended, hidden networks. The term was made fashionable by Gilles Deleuze and Felix Guattari in *A Thousand Plateaus: Capitalism and Schizophrenia* (1987). An actual rhizome is a plant that takes many forms depending on its needs in a particular situation, below ground becoming a tuber to store energy gathered through a large networked root system, but above ground becoming a plant with stem and leaves for photosynthesis and flowers for pollination. Deleuze and Guattari use the botanic meaning of rhizome as a metaphor for any complex system of interactions in a decentralized network that responds to stimuli.[115]

Rhizomic assemblage mixes the concept of the narrative path of the individual with the networked or shared information of the group, forming a group consciousness from the collective experiences of individuals in communication with each other. Designers have used another of Deleuze and Guattari's concepts, the "layer," as a literal equivalent of a layer of information in their CAD drawing systems, a use not foreseen by the two philosophers, who sought to test every hypothesis through local knowledge and opposed the process of globalization via information systems as they understood it. This creative misunderstanding has produced some exciting applications of layering in the city that question the datum of the city sidewalk as the ground-plane of the city. All of a sudden, in Deconstructivist designs of the 1980s, platforms in midair or underground could be equally valid datums, as in Zaha Hadid's pioneering design for the Peak Competition (1981) or Bernard Tschumi's *Parc de la Villette* design, with its three layers (1982). (Both are discussed further below.)

The mixture of personal paths and narratives moving through a multilayered space, mixing and meeting in multiple nodes, makes the rhizomic assemblage a potent metaphor for designers in the polycentric city. It is especially appealing to those who reject the scenographic and historic qualities of *Collage City*, with its memory-driven sense of a Gestaltic whole hidden behind fragments. In an ideal rhizomic assemblage, which is theoretically generated from the bottom up (even if monitored through a top-down technological apparatus), there is no single dominant voice, just as Darwin saw no single designer in charge of evolution. But this lack of a central voice can be problematic as well as liberating. Rowe and Koetter, in the humanist tradition, inserted the prince or his equivalent to fill this gap. (In *Sim City* or in New York City, it is filled by the mayor and the city council.) Individual actors, in this vision of modified assemblage, are chiefly interested in their own territories; in *Sim City 1*, for example, only the mayor is charged with examining the relationships between fragments.

2.4.2 Rhizomic Assemblage and the Deconstruction of the City Section

Alvin Boyarsky: "Chicago à la Carte," 1970

Boyarsky: marina city, 1970

Deconstructivist architects also built on the fragmentary logic of *Collage City*, but without its emphasis on a sense of overall unity from the "splendid public terrace" and with an added emphasis on scenographic assemblage and networks. Alvin Boyarsky's article "Chicago à la Carte" (1970) proved prophetic not only in its analysis of the city in terms of layered infrastructure but in its interest in highly developed hybrid skyscraper nodes and a micro-urbanism of temporary booths and kiosk's.[116] This layered approach to the city and to movement through its layers and fragments became part of the teaching method of the Architectural Association School in London during the 1970s, linking many Deconstructivist practitioners who heard the Boyarsky "Chicago à la Carte" lecture (1970). Rem Koolhaas (an Architectural Association student and later teacher), in *Delirious New York* (1978), provides a Surrealist version of this approach, with the layers of the city beautifully exposed in the cover painting for the first edition. While the two great icons of New York, the Chrysler Building and the Empire State Building, are caught in the searchlight of the Rockefeller Center, under the grid of the city is revealed a vast subterranean world of pipes, service networks, tunnels, and subways, the supporting matrix of the city.

Deconstructivist architects developed the scenographic and Picturesque aspects of the *Collage City* formula as a system of activities and movements passing through multiple layers. James Stirling and James Gowan had already demonstrated the potential of this process in their aforementioned Leicester Laboratory Building (1959–63), which horrified many Modernists (e.g., Nicholas Pevsner).[117] In this design an approach ramp leads up to a small triangular platform (the roof of a podium below), from whence an access stair ascends into the auditorium and the tower above that. Beneath the tower, two suspended lecture halls are clad in red tile (a reference to Russian Constructivist schemes for Revolutionary Workers' Clubs). Movement in the building means a constant picturesque ascent and descent between the tower, the two auditoria, and the podium base. Stirling's later Neue Staatsgalerie in Stuttgart (1977–83) provided a horizontal equivalent of this scenographic path through layers in the pedestrian sequence through the terraced facade of the building, passing up through the terraced platforms, through the central, circular drum, and then out onto the surrounding hillside.[118]

Stirling's undermining of the centrally placed circular court (which had long been reminiscent of Leonardo's centrally placed, symbolic human figure) indicates a shift away from humanist collage to a system of montage and collage (anticipating rhizomic assemblage), where everything is equal, based on a network of flows and nodes with no privileged center. The empty drum functions as a memory cue to the neoclassical museum, with its central dome as in Karl Schinkel's Altes Museum in Berlin. But in this case, pedestrians can wander up through this drum while museum visitors look in upon them, reversing the usual inside–outside situation. Stirling recombined and reversed the arrangement of normal elements in a museum, conceptually decentering the composition despite the central location of the cylinder.

Layering the city section, decentering previously privileged hierarchies, and reversing normal codes have thus been some of the main trademarks of the Deconstructivist successors to *Collage City*.[119] Multiple scenographic and Picturesque paths passing through the multiple layers of fixed assemblages remained essential ingredients. Peter Eisenman's urban projects illustrate the development of this layered approach to the city, first glimpsed in Boyarsky's "Chicago à la Carte" but here used as a design methodology for the creation of a new, sectional public space. Eisenman's projects for Venice (1978, with red cubes) and Berlin (1980, sectional developments) began as formal, layered, grid-rotation exercises but became more complex when Eisenman reversed the normal code so that the voids of the street-grid network became solids (a code reversal similar to the *Uffizi Unité d'Habitation* confrontation in *Collage City*). These solids formed a system of thin, linear bar-like buildings across the landscape, a system of linear armatures that Eisenman soon learnt to tilt and manipulate for picturesque effect.[120]

Alvin Boyarsky: layered Chicago, 1970

Another example of such manipulation is Zaha Hadid's prizewinning but unbuilt *Peak Project* for Hong Kong (1981), which developed the idea of a new sectional public space that hung above the city on the mountaintop, looking down on the skyscrapers below. Hadid's project delaminated all the layers of a normal hotel program, reversing the vertical hierarchy. The public space could then be hollowed out in the center section of the building, allowing the approach road to pass through the middle. The approach along the ramp revealed the hotel as a scenographic assemblage above and below.

Boyarsky: Whacker Drive and Chicago River, 1970

Deconstructivist urban practice, as advanced by Zaha Hadid, Coop Himmelblau, or Daniel Libeskind, attacked both the Rationalists' emphasis on a single, privileged center *and* the Contextualists's reliance on the interpretation of fixed plans instead of dynamic sections. Libeskind's project for a housing block (1986) diagonally cantilevered over the Berlin Wall began to explore the new public space of the city opened up by Hadid's *Peak Project*, a theme that would be continued in his World Trade Center competition entry (2002).[121] Coop Himmelbau's unbuilt project for the French new town of Melun-Sénart (1987) pushed Hadid's "delamination" of elements around an empty center further; in it, he proposed that the public space of the town be formed by various urban elements floating in space one above another and linked by vertical circulation.[122] Studio Asymptote's project for the *Los Angeles Gateway* (1989) explored the poetics of a similar three-dimensional public space with movie and information screens in the city section.[123] Michael Sorkin's visionary project for an American new town (1987) of the same period proposed replacing the skyscraper-city downtown core with a central business district made from intersecting, almost-horizontal bar buildings piled up as in an Anthony Caro sculpture.[124] Brian McGrath's *Transparent Cities: A User's Guide* (1994) applied the concept of this three-dimensional public space to the layered analysis of the city, contrasting Rome and New York as a series of layers drawn as literal transparencies on Perspex sheets, allowing recombinations of layers and easily making the transition to layered CAD drawings.[125]

2.4.3 Rhizomic Assemblage and Landscape Urbanism: The Network City

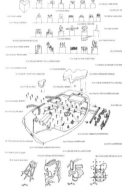

Bernard Tschumi: elements in La Villette Competition, Paris, 1982

Instead of privileging hierarchies focused on a single center like the Rationalists and Modernists, Deconstructivist designers sought the edge condition and periphery, reversing the normal code. They preferred open, multivalent systems with widely distributed centers of intelligence and a central void as an extended field punctuated or activated by multiple points or pavilions dedicated to specific activities. Thus, the French philosopher Jacques Derrida could describe Bernard Tschumi's *Parc de la Villette* (1982, now the largest park in Paris) as needing constant "maintenance"—not only in terms of the usual physical upkeep, but also in terms of supporting programs and activities.[126] La Villette, in Derrida's view, thus constituted a miniature model of the network city. Tschumi called his park an "event city," a prepared ground for the processes and fluid activities of urban actors in the decentered city of the future (recalling Archigram's "nomad city").[127] Tschumi had a longstanding interest in the choreography and notation of modern dance, which he used in his *Rituals* project (1978) to trace the narrative of a person's movements through a house, generating the house form around events and transitions.[128]

Unlike other parks in Paris, with their "keep off the grass" signs, in La Villette actors can pursue multiple paths and interests as on a British common (communally owned and shared open-air public space) or open heath. The space is open to multiple programs that can succeed each other, sometimes overlapping. There is no office of central control and the original plan was to keep adding new pavilions to the site for 20 years, each potentially triggering new possibilities. Parisian authorities were suspicious of this form of open planning, which derived from Cedric Price and Archigram's earlier ideas of flexibility and time allocations in the shared public space of the city. These ideas would also influence the concept of "performative urbanism" on a "commons," as advanced in the early twenty-first century by the Landscape Urbanist movement (associated with Jim Corner and his office Field Operations).

Franz Oswald and Peter Baccini, in *Netzstadt: Designing the Urban* (2003), provide a morphology of such performance platforms. They identify actors and their supporting networks, classifying a hierarchy of nodes, node figures, or patterns—their fields or boundaries, their structures, and their types of territory in the node field (water, forest, agriculture, settlement, infrastructure, fallow).[129] Local nodes with distinct building morphologies and typologies can be nested within nodal fields, providing a direct link to Collage City elements.

2.5 CONCLUSION

Urban design emerged as an innovative practice during a period of chaotic theoretical oscillations brought about by the collapse of Modernist master-planning. It was a method of bringing order to carefully delineated, special-district enclaves within the city. These enclaves became stationary but flexible coded assemblages. Urban designers created a closed system inside each enclave to shut out the chaos surrounding it. Gated communities or home-ownership associations in residential estates on the suburban periphery are an example of this equation of disorder with the outside world. The urban-design approach of the 1970s, as exemplified in the special district techniques of New York City, *Collage City*, or later suburban New Urbanism enclaves of the 1980s, proved a flexible way to handle a fragmented system of subcenters in the multicentered, postmodern city-region.

In the next chapter we will examine how all the seven "-ages" of the postmodern urban-design approach—decoupage, collage, bricolage, montage, photomontage, assemblage, and rhizomic assemblage—have, despite their differences, all shared and recombined a common group of urban elements. We will begin to classify these elements—armatures, enclaves, and heterotopias—and their associated urban equipment as a further step toward linking Lynch's three great "normative" models into a shifting, relational system of urban combinatorial possibilities.

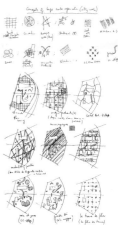

Bernard Tschumi: layers in La Villette Competition, Paris, 1982

The Deconstructivist layered city

Zaha Hadid, Peak Project
a) *Plans, 1981*
b) *Sections, 1981*
c) *Entry sequence, 1981*
d) *Axonometric of Hong Kong*

Hadid, Cardiff Opera House project, 1994–96
e) *Model*
f) *Model view*

a

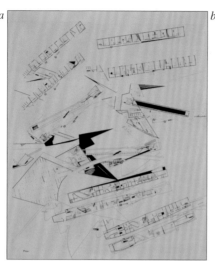

b

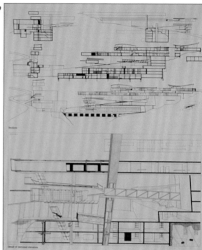

c

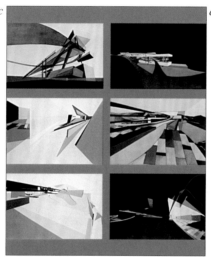

d

e

f

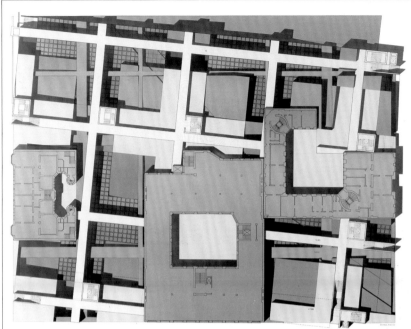

g

*The
Deconstructivist
layered city*

*Peter Eisenman, IBA
housing*
g) *Layered-garden
plan, 1978*

Bernard Tschumi
h) *La Villette,
layered axonometric,
1982*

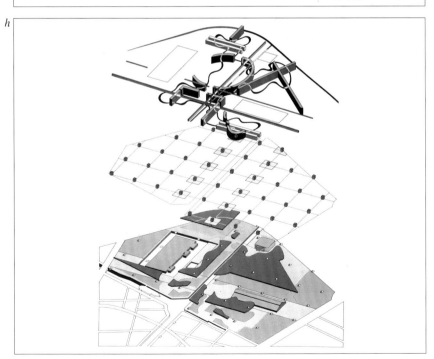

h

Chapter 3

Three Urban Elements

3.1 "ELEMENTS" IN URBAN DESIGN AND CITY THEORY

[A]n *element* means something that enters into a composition as a part of a constructed unity and fits into a formula; but this nomenclature also means a principle, the foundation of a theory that determines a discipline.
—Ernesto Rogers.[1]

Serlio's three stage sets have been a recurrent theme in this book. Here I turn to them again to illustrate the concept of the *urban element*, which is so closely linked to urban typology and morphology.

Each of Serlio's sets portrays a type of city, easily recognizable from Kostof's list of city typologies (Chapter 1). Every real city, generated by its actors as an assemblage for daily use, also operates as a semiological sign in the lexicon of city types and as a stage-set for a life-world. Serlio's Noble scene corresponds to the state city, an administrative center and setting for the public display of power. The Noble scene has been physically constructed for explicitly autocratic purposes, as in Serlio's scenography, and for putatively democratic purposes, as in Washington, DC In the Noble scene, the symbolic intermediaries of the state convey an impression of stability and permanence, even of eternity, with their obvious links to the ruins of the Roman Empire. In Serlio's scene, these intermediaries include Roman funerary monuments seen beyond the city gate, a Roman temple at the midpoint of the street (dwarfed by the new, roughly cubic palaces of princely Renaissance families), and the perspectival armature of the street itself.

The last is important because all the other architectural elements that might appear in such an assemblage can be combined and recombined within the perspectival framework of the street armature. They can also be arranged around an enclave such as a town square, as required, for example, by the "Law of the Indies" (the royal ordinance of 1573), which dictated the layout of colonial towns all over the Spanish Empire. The Law of the Indies required that the church (temple), governor's palace (with prison), and merchant's palaces all stand around a central square containing market stalls, a fountain, public stocks, and a gallows for public executions.[2]

By omitting some elements and substituting others, Serlio was able to transform the street armature of the Noble scene into the rural village and the mercantile city. His image of the latter—his Comic scene—is picturesque and irregular in its street alignment, with the church at the end of the street in partial ruin. There are small classical palaces mixed in with vernacular buildings (including a prominent brothel), but a Gothic merchant's shop/house halfway

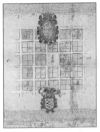

Foundation plan, for Mendoza, Argentina, 1561
RL Kagan, Urban Images of the Hispanic World, 1493–1793

Opposite *Paul Citroen: Metropolis Collage, 1922 (©2004 ARS NY / Beeldrecht, Amsterdam)*

down the street dominates the vista. Through careful references and combinations of symbolic elements, Serlio conjures up a city embedded in the great trading networks of the Mediterranean basin since the twelfth and thirteenth centuries.

Serlio's Satyric scene works yet another set of symbolic intermediaries: elements of an agrarian community housed close to the land, in cottages set along a tree-lined street that terminates in a tavern. Such rustic recombinations of elements in the landscape have had a great appeal in many periods, as exemplified by Fishman's suburban and exurban "bourgeois utopias."

Doug Suissman: symbolic skyline of Spanish and contemporary cities, LA Boulevards ca. 1989

Serlio saw himself as handling a palette of discrete urban elements within a scientific perspectival construct, following in the footsteps of Alberti's three-dimensional, combinatorial spatial matrix. He used the image of the street to illustrate how to construct a perspective drawing, and clearly stated that he was continuing a tradition taught to him by his teacher Peruzzi, who in turn had been trained by Raphael in his Renaissance "perspectival laboratory" in Urbino. European Rationalists in the nineteenth century (e.g., Durand, Haussmann, Cerdá, Stubben) saw themselves as modernizing this tradition; they explicitly believed that a city could be broken down into elements and that by analyzing these elements one could obtain a better understanding of the whole. As Choay has noted, they put on the "white coats" of doctors and laboratory technicians, analyzing the existing industrial city into its smallest components. This tradition continued in the work of the German Rationalists of the 1970s and 1980s, who also broke the city down into elements that could be combined and recombined. Robert Krier's *Urban Space* (1979) included a diagram of the city as composed of parts and layers that can be conjugated like a language to make regular and irregular squares, streets, boulevards, villas, parks.

Léon Krier's comic-book-style drawings of the 1970s and 1980s push this reductive and simplistic combinatory logic to an extreme, showing simultaneously the square, the houses, the church, the steeple, and the people (as in the children's nursery rhyme). The complexity of the nineteenth-century Rationalists' argument is here reduced to one-line equations that have great impact but yet are totally disconnected from the everyday world. The elements of the city are reduced to simple structural elements arranged in a simple, top-down hierarchy. (Krier shocked many by expressing his admiration for Hitler's plan for Berlin and the Communist Stalin Allee there).[3]

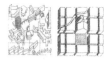

Léon Krier: modern and traditional European city morphologies, ca. 1976

New Urbanists in the 1980s and 1990s, although they endorsed democracy, also drew on this simple combinatorial clarity and typological logic in arranging their elements. Nonetheless, as in the old Spanish colonial towns, in the New Urbanists' visions a single church dominated the main public space and a village green surrounded by big houses with small houses tucked away in the back replaced the colonial square. The neighborhood shopping mall was magically converted into a network of village-street-like armatures, while mundane offices, industrial production, and sewage treatment plants never appeared in the drawings, banished to heterotopic elsewhere-realms. New

Urbanism's design codes created an orderly and disciplined hierarchy of elements within the enclave while simultaneously increasing the entropy of the world beyond their boundaries.[4]

There is thus a long tradition of research into urban elements in both Europe and America, a tradition both Rationalist and New Urbanist. But what, after all, *is* an "element"? Ernesto Rogers has given one view, quoted at the head of this chapter. The dictionary, more broadly, defines an *element* as "a basic constituent; substance incapable of being analyzed into any simpler form" (Penguin). Anne Vernez Moudon describes the European Rationalist tradition of analyzing cities into constitutive elements in her 1994 essay "Getting to Know the Built Landscape: Typomorphology."[5] Moudon writes that typomorphological studies,

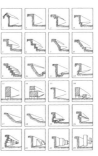

Robert Krier: facade, sectional variations, Urban Space *1976*

> reveal the physical and spatial structure of cities. They are typological and morphological because they describe urban form (morphology) based on the detailed classification of buildings and open spaces by type (typology). Typomorphology is the study of urban form derived from studies of typical spaces and structures.

Typical—type-fulfilling—spaces and structures thus constitute the fundamental elements of this Rationalist, combinatory approach. Moudon goes on to describe three European schools of morphological study based, respectively, in Venice, Italy; Birmingham, England; and Versailles, near Paris, France. In Birmingham, M. R. G. Conzens developed his "Planned Unit Development" analysis system in the 1930s, breaking down urban growth into incremental additions of large enclave units developed by land subdivision around street armatures. From the 1930s onwards, Conzens provided insight into the settlement patterns of medieval Ludlow and other English cities, inspiring others to study colonial settlement patterns throughout the British Empire and America.[6] In the 1960s and 1970s, Jean Castex and the Versailles School combined the British preoccupation with typology and land subdivision with an Italian analysis of morphologies as networks of solid and void spaces in the urban fabric in their study of Versailles as a new-town development.[7]

MRG Conzens: medieval planned unit development (PUD)

Architects from the Venetian School studied the combinatorial networks of *space types* and *built elements* in Italian cities for 60 years beginning in the 1930s. The concept of the room type, house type, block type, and street type were interrelated by a matrix, allowing the systematic study of medieval cities. In the 1960s, this methodology was applied to the systematic modernization and recombination of apartments within buildings and entire city blocks in Bologna without displacing the inhabitants.[8] Moudon notes:

> A typomorphological approach to defining type differs from other approaches in three ways. First, type in typomorphology combines the volumetric characteristics of built structures with their related open

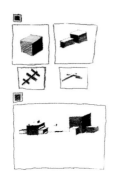

Paola Viganò: Constructivist elements, La Città Elementare, *1999*

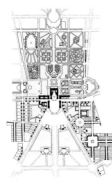

Versailles School: plan of city, axes and garden of Versailles, 1980

spaces to define a built landscape type. This approach is in opposition to the monumental, siteless typology of Durand, for instance. The element that links built spaces to open spaces is the lot or parcel, the basic cell of the urban fabric. Second, the inclusion of land and its subdivisions as a constituent element type makes land the link between the building scale and the city scale. Third, the built environment type is a morphogenetic, not morphological, unit because it is defined by time—the time of its conception, production, use or mutation.

Moudon sees the Venetian typomorphological approach as describing a combinatory system of elements inside a three-dimensional matrix, including the voids that surround any building in a "built landscape." This landscape is a site-specific, time-specific system that takes into account local circumstances, especially the lot and property subdivisions of the city.

Paola Viganò, in *La Città Elementare* (1999), also elaborates on this Venetian analytic tradition of a "built landscape," especially highlighting morphological code reversals and phase changes that produce sudden inversions, such as the "reverse city" that expands the city out into the surrounding region, the "city territory."[9] Viganò's "elementarism" enables us to link the closed urban-design elements of Rationalism, the "ensembles" of *Collage City*, with the assemblage of Lynch's Ecological City, which expands at a large scale across the landscape. Through an examination of elements and of *Collage City*'s code reversals, Viganò articulates the confrontation between two competing urban ecologies: that of the European Rationalists, with its streets and squares, and that of the suburban reverse city, with its large-scale voids, landscape elements, isolated pavilions, highways, and shopping centers, as described by Venturi, Scott Brown, and Izenour in *Learning from Las Vegas* (1972) and by many other American commentators.[10]

In constructing these layers, Viganò harks back to a formal tradition of elementarism in design that was present in the Beaux Arts School, especially in the work of Julien Guadet (*Elements in a Theory of Architecture*, 1902), one of Le Corbusier's heroes. Elementarism is the isolation of "elements" in a system as discrete objects that maintain constant forms, and the stressing of manipulation of the combinatorial and geometric relationships between such elements. Like Reyner Banham (*Theory of Design in the First Machine Age*, 1961), Viganò sees that Beaux Arts and Modernist architects both employed elementarism, making it nonsensical to set them in dualistic opposition. The difference between them is the product of a simple code reversal. Viganò proposes to frame the two systems of elements as layers in the "built landscape" of the city. Each is a part of the larger urban bricolage constructed by actors over time, a distinct trace of particular activities in a place at a particular time.

Viganò's layered elementarism is thus descended from Alberti's theory of architecture as a combinatorial matrix of potential elements or signs that can be manipulated, like a language, to make sentences. Indeed, Viganò explicitly references this illustrious rationalistic tradition, which began during the Renaissance and Enlightenment and continued in the Beaux Arts School and Modernism, including Russian Constructivism; Malevich's Suprematism; De Stijl; the work of contemporary Rationalists like Gregotti, Rossi, and the Krier brothers; and such Deconstructivist systems of composition as Tschumi's "mixage." Viganò lists a number of "manuals" describing the combinatorial techniques of elementarism, including those of Camillo Sitte, Stubben, Unwin (Howard's architect successor in the garden city movement), Gordon Cullen ("townscape"), Lynch, and the authors of *Collage City*, describing these as part of a great urban "continuity" (a term also used by Ernesto Rogers).

Venetian School: typomorphology, Bologna Study, 1973

Viganò highlights British town planner Frederick Gibberd's work in *Town Design* (1953, 1967) as unusual for encompassing both the old city's rules for combining elements and the new rules for suburban malls and industrial and housing estates being built in the British new towns. Anticipating Koetter and Rowe's Uffizi-*Unité d'Habitation* spatial code reversal of 1978, Gibberd defined the void of the "open air room" of the traditional city as "the reverse of the plastic body of a building," illustrating this concept with a "space body" drawing of the voids of Nancy's spatial sequence. The street walls of the space defined the void of the "space body," an idea developed by the Urban Design Group in New York in the 1960s as "street walls" and "view corridors." Gibberd also identified the street armature and enclave (precinct or cell) as the basic elements of the normative city.

Gibberd's ability to reverse urban codes allowed him to appreciate the reconfiguration of urban enclaves on the periphery as "precincts" and of groups of buildings as "environmental areas," patches of order in the periphery worthy of consideration by designers. The shopping center, for instance, represented a recombination of elements taken from downtown, department stores and specialty stores, and the street, all reconfigured inside a "precinct." Pedestrian precinct recombinations were also his preferred method for reconstructing the center of war-damaged European cities. He offered William Holford's enclave plan for reconstructing Paternoster Square beside St. Paul's Cathedral, London, to illustrate a "pedestrian precinct" (condemned, however, by the Prince of Wales for obstructing the cathedral dome with its towers, and now demolished). At the end of his career he attacked the megastructural trend of urban design and Peter Cook of Archigram's *Plug-In City* (1964).[11]

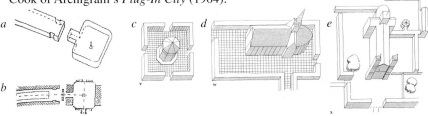

a–b) *Frederick Gibberd: "space body" diagrams, Nancy, France, Town Design, 1953*
c–e) *Gibberd: precinct enclave diagrams, Town Design, 1953*

Paola Viganò: Le Corbusier's modern elements, La Città Elementare, *1999*

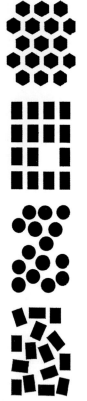

Christopher Tunnard and Boris Pushkarev: "scatter" patterns, Man-Made America, *1963*

Viganò develops the reverse-city concept of designing with the open "space body" between buildings and perceptively analyzes the emerging suburban system in terms of the minimalist art and sculpture that formed the subject matter of Rosalind E. Krauss's 1983 "expanded field of sculpture" essay (which discussed landscape artists such Robert Smithson).[12] Viganò finds many linear patterns in this new field: "seriality, rhythms, [and] repetitions" space isolated villas and object-buildings along routes of transportation and communication. She sees a continuity between the earlier theoreticians who explored the concept of the linear city (e.g., Leonidov and other creators of the Russian Constructivist disurbanization schemes) and the Pop studies of the Venturi, Scott Brown, and Izenour team on the linear Las Vegas Strip. Indeed, she credits that team's *Learning from Las Vegas* (1972) with the discovery of a seriality in Las Vegas, transferring this concept of spatial intervals and varied repetition from the work of conceptual sculptors like Donald Judd.[13]

To understand the new rules, Viganò goes back to Christopher Tunnard and Boris Pushkarev's "scatter" pattern diagrams of the city in the landscape (*Man-Made America*, 1963). She also traces the emergence of the sense of a new, abstract, isolated, "deep pattern" in the work of American authors like Lynch. She notes Lynch's identification of new patterns such as the linear industrial city, the net city, and the "ribbon" or finger city, with its new elements of parking, commercial centers, airports, and isolated houses in a "pavilion system" that stretches across the city-territory. Here the City as a Machine model rules, with its isolated pavilions and discrete elements scattered across the landscape.[14]

Within this city territory, Viganò characterized the big urban institutions—what the French would call "urban equipment"—as typological nodal systems employing standard industrial components. Le Corbusier had used the term "urban equipment" in his article "La Construction des Villes" (1910–15) to refer to the streets, squares, bridges, and so forth of the European urban tradition, which he proposed to recombine, following Howard, into garden cities.[15] Viganò shows how Corbusier, in his "Les trois établissements humains" (1946), extended this scientific tradition of classification to the new, isolated elements of the Modernist city. To illustrate his argument, Le Corbusier drew cartoons of the residential building typologies of slab and tower blocks, high-rise and low-rise factory buildings, and low-rise school and recreational facilities that he had imagined in the parkland landscape in the Ville Radieuse.

For Viganò, as for Rowe and Koetter, Le Corbusier's layout of the public space of the town center of St. Dié (1947) was an important breakthrough into a new mode of composition in the city-territory developing a new "deep pattern."[16] It was followed by the layout of the "campidoglio" of Chandigarh,[17] which employed the new system of "space-defining elements" (Rowe and Koetter's phrase, *Collage City*): esplanades, level changes, terraces, and overlooks manipulating the landscape at a heroic, monumental scale on the horizontal plane, creating a "fifth facade."[18] This was a new form of urban design, a "deep architecture" working at the scale of Lynch's city theory and city landscape. (Viganò notes that Kenneth Frampton also identified this new form in his article "In Search of the Modern Landscape," 1988.)[19]

The tradition of designing the "space body" or voids between buildings as a built landscape in itself is linked to the American Landscape Urbanism movement, discussed in the previous chapter as an outcome of *Collage City*'s publication in 1978. Viganò quotes the definition of "landscape elements" given by Richard T. T. Forman and Michel Godron in *Landscape Ecology* (1986). This book highlights their theory of "patches," a concept also employed by Lynch in his landscape theories (discussed in Chapter 1)[20] and similar to the more developed, contemporary "patch" dynamics theories of Monica Turner, Robert Gardner, and Robert O'Neil's *Landscape Ecology in Theory and Practice: Pattern and Process* (2001). In Europe, Viganò and the Venice School have many allies advocating the network city, in which the design of the voids between the buildings and of the journeys between them is as important as that of the buildings themselves. Here landscape patches within the patterns of a larger ecology interact with urban fragments that perform as built settings for actors managing events and flows within distinctly bounded, morphological fragments.[21]

Paola Viganò: diagram of Le Corbusier's 1947 St Dié plan, La Città Elementare, *1999*

By concentrating on the continuity of the connecting void-spaces in the built landscape, Viganò is able to see the city as a bricolage of patterns of activity constructed over time by actors with different goals, creating layers and patches of urban order. This expands considerably on the scope of *Collage City*. As we saw at the end of Chapter 2, Franz Oswald and Peter Baccini, in *Netzstadt: Designing the Urban* (2003), achieve a similar expansion of *Collage City* by mapping nodes and patches as fragmentary layers in a city-territory composed of the aquatic, agricultural, forest, urban (including infrastructures), and "fallow" (temporarily unused) ecologies of the Swiss landscape. Empowered by Geographic Information Systems (GIS), they calculate the energy flows of the various dissipative structures or patches of organization in these systems, giving the Net City concept a dynamic, interactive, informational, and ecological precision. Following Lynch, they measure the characteristic morphologies of these patches and systems in terms of "granulation" (density of land coverage) and "shredding" (patterns of void-spaces). Traditional morphological studies of plot size and building typology, massing, and construction are thus reframed in terms of the performance of catalytic actors creating patterns of energy and organization (described as "nodes" and "node fields").[22]

Paola Viganò: sectional analysis of the Chandigarh landscape, Città Elementare

Viganò argues that the unnamed tradition of "space body" design is concerned with the bricolage of urban space systems, the "disintegration and re-composition of urban space." She describes it as manipulating "city structures" and "urban materials." Urban materials, viewed from the "space body" perspective, tend to be physical but, recalling "symbolic intermediaries" in relationships between actor-designers, can be the voids or intervals inside or around almost anything that has to do with a city: buildings, typologies, blocks,

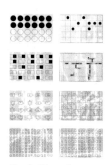

Paola Viganò: recombinatory tactics as games, La Città Elementare, *1999*

Paolo Viganò: interative interval or spacing diagram in the reverse city, Città Elementare *1999*

morphologies, streetscapes, sequences, mechanical and electronic support systems, the surrounding landscape and topography.[23]

In contrast to the rules of composition in the Beaux Arts and Modernist systems, Viganò's "deep pattern" of "space body" design and "pavilion system" spacing has only local, syntagmatic rules, no overall or "diachronic" order. Such rules are familiar from games like dominoes, where patterns are generated from local combinations of neighbors and vary with time, slowly building up larger patterns and shapes as the players take turns. The reverse city, likewise, has local rules and "space body" group codes that produce an unintended larger pattern such as chaotic American sprawl, with its strange distribution of functions, characterized by the availability of vast open spaces, local codes of combination, cheap fuel for transportation, and mass communications.[24]

In fact, Viganò proposes that there are *three* systems of "space body" combination in the new urban "territory." She compares these rules of combination to the rules that govern three distinct classes of traditional games. The first system of combination or set of rules (already mentioned above) is comparable to dominoes, where elements only touch along their edges, as in Choay's "syntagmatic system" or the old Islamic city. Here, patterns emerge from the players' discrete actions over time.[25] The second system of rules of combination and movement governs the play of the pieces and relationships between actors, as in chess or checkers: pieces do not touch, but actors move pieces that are abstractly related to each other across a network or grid. In the third system, rules govern a system of pieces that not only touch but physically interlock with each other to form an overall pattern or grouping, as in a jigsaw puzzle.[26] In this system, patterns of interlock remain syntagmatic because it is the character of local junctions that determine the viability of each move, yet these moves contribute to the coherence of a significant whole (literally, the big picture) that is bigger than any part.

Viganò's classification of combinatory and recombinatory tactics for actors is a useful starting point for looking at relationships between elements and actors in a layered bricolage. In any particular case, she says, the first thing to note about actors' tactics is whether they operate in static or mobile assemblages, forming sedentary systems or nomadic structures. The second point is that the spacing between elements inside a system (Viganò's "seriality") is important, whether the context is static or mobile. "Domino" codes imply edge-to-edge touching, with a system of local rules that govern the possibility of various arrangements or laminations; "chess" codes require pieces to move about on the overall grid as individuals without ever touching or combining, but the rules do allow a piece to take the place of another under some conditions; "jigsaw" codes imply both touching and coordination of parts within rules that govern the Gestalt or overall pattern of a larger informational system (the completed image).

Actors pay attention to whether elements are "touching" or "not touching" in combinatory systems. This is important both symbolically and practically.

"Touching" implies access and contact; "not touching" can imply separation and segregation. In the Archi Città, for instance, urban elements like walls and gates prevent touching and block network connections, creating nested hierarchies of enclaves (e.g., the imperial palace in Beijing). "Not touching" can also imply segregation of uses into separate enclaves as in the Cine Città, where the ideal is to separate every function but connect everyone equally. It can also mean "bypassing" places, as when high-speed channels of information in stretched armatures bypass enclaves not wealthy enough to connect in the postmodern city (see Graham and Marvin's *Splintering Urbanism*, 2001).[27] "Not touching" can also be a manifestation of invisible communication systems that link mobile actors, thus allowing disparate elements to compile into rhizomic assemblages in the Tele Città. Guy Debord's *Naked City* map of Paris (1956) illustrates the rules of noncontact between enclaves in an industrial society. Debord isolated every fragment, allowing connection only via a system of red arrows of desire.[28]

Guy Debord, "Naked City" Situationist diagram, 1956

Viganò highlights the role of an actor's choice of method for bonding elements and the construction of event structures as "bricolage" and "layering" in urban design.[29] We discussed bricolage in Chapter 2 as one of the seven "ages" of postmodernism, along with decoupage, collage, montage, assemblage, and rhizomic assemblage. Viganò, in *La Città Elementare*, defines the urban designer as a *bricoleur*, a person who works with what they find in a neighborhood, a city, or other territory and organizes elements in layers across different scales (from local events to regional infrastructures) and across time (with traces of old and new). The urban bricoleur transforms urban elements and materials by design to make open-space designs that include the individual and the scale of the mass infrastructure.[30]

Allowing elements to make contact with each other is part of the syntagmatic structure of the Archi Città, which is built stone on stone. Elements can touch, so that a prison, for instance, might be attached to a public house serving alcohol. "Touching" in the Cine Città, with its emphasis on movement and segregation, is carefully controlled in the style of cinematic montage and collage, with their emphasis on image, the displacement of actors, and scientific detachment. Luis Buñuel and Salvador Dali's symbolic cutting of an eyeball with a razor in the Surrealist film *Un Chien Andalou* (1928) violated all the Cine Città's taboos on touching while violently attacking vision itself, threatening blindness.

"Absolute New York," Ikea billboard, Lafayette Street, New York, 2001

Layering, overlapping, and transparency in the City as a Machine do not necessarily involve touch, as communication systems allow voice or visual control from a distance. In photomontage, for instance, images of disparate objects, displaced from their original locations, can be brought together through the photographic process without any of the objects being physically moved from their original locations. In the Tele Città, remote-communication systems allow inhabitants to stay at home and view everything remotely—a visual or informational omnipotence that sponsors, in reaction, an immense demand for the lost sensations of touch, taste, sound, smell, community, and interconnection. Community activities in festivals and rituals, sports events and parades, circuses and fairs, once provided an outlet for this sense of touch and shared, communal experience, but today a new class of milieux, from business centers to theme parks to downtown office centers and entertainment centers, has been invented to meet the sublimated demand for "touch." This aspect of the city also once sponsored the sleazy, heterotopic, "red light districts" of port cities, which have been reengineered for the media age as in Amsterdam sex entertainment centers or sublimated in manufactured fantasy worlds such as the "Paris, Paris" casino in Las Vegas.

Like Lynch, Rowe, and Koetter, Viganò maintains that urban actors and elements have ambiguous and complex relationships that can be analyzed through a layered, "space body" approach, as in collage. Rowe and Koetter's *Collage City* (1978) distinguished a whole category of heterotopic, "ambiguous" buildings that glued the city together, while in *A Theory of Good City Form* (1981) Lynch portrayed the city as woven together from disparate, linear elements of ideal "fast" and "slow" growth strands, creating an ambiguous, hybrid tartan. Below, I examine this ambiguous realm (already examined briefly at the end of Chapter 2) through an exploration of Picasso's wall sculpture *Guitar* (1912), which was originally fabricated in cardboard and now exists as a steel copy in the Museum of Modern Art, New York.[31]

Pablo Picasso: Guitar, 1912 (© Photo SCALA, Florence)

Guitar is a very ambiguous object. It is an instrument, but can obviously never be played. It is a sculpture, but hangs on the wall like a painting. And we recognize it as a "guitar" even though it is made of warped surfaces and is missing key components of a guitar's structure. The front surface of the soundbox, for instance, is cut away to reveal the interior and back. The curved walls of the soundbox form multiple receding edges whose S-shaped silhouette is perceived by our pattern-recognition system, giving a sense of depth and layering inside the soundbox. Our preliminary recognition of the guitar is confirmed because the fragmented soundbox touches and is attached to the "neck" in a recognizable fashion, cementing a basic relationship necessary for the recognition of the object. But there is no proper tuning apparatus on the head, just a symbolic scroll-like attachment, and the strings are not attached to the box at a bridge but flail uselessly in midair as if a ghost were playing them, as if they were vibrating to wild music in space. This bizarre instrument may have been created with memories of a specific place and event in mind. Peter Hall, in *Cities in Civilization* (1998), gives a wonderful photograph of Picasso and his friends at the Lapin Agile (Agile Rabbit) nightclub in Montmartre, where the nightclub's bearded owner sits on a barstool holding a guitar on his knees in the upright Spanish flamenco manner.[32]

Picasso: Guitar, detail of center-cylinder treatment (© Photo SCALA, Florence)

Guitar's soundbox contains another wonderful spatial invention, a hollow cylinder that comes up from the back plane of the box to where the front plane should be. The circumference of this open, circular tube presents itself as the missing circular opening of the soundboard, which would allow sound to escape from a real guitar. The circle is in the correct place, but as part of a solid figure in the void of the soundbox. Thus, all the visual cues for a guitar are present, but reversed and inverted so that void becomes solid and solid parts transparent. Inserting a hollow cylinder in the void of the soundbox plays with figure–ground, solid–void relations, creating novel spatial ambiguities and a new spatial poetic. Rowe, Slutsky, and Koetter admired similar moves by Le Corbusier in his villa projects of the 1920s, in which he created a new kind of visual, conceptual poetry. Both Picasso and Le Corbusier sought to suggestion a new poetic and psychic reality by removing all but the key parts of the mental models while at the same time playing with the Gestalt models that we all share.

Picasso's spatial and typological ambiguity anticipated the morphological and symbolic reversals of Gibberd's "space body" analysis, the Collage City's code inversions, and Viganò's reverse city. In representative collage, different layers and fragments are still coordinated by a repressed or obscured memory of the whole; that is, parts still refer to a whole, which serves as the ultimate reference point for the validity of all combinations. As in Picasso's *Guitar*, the arranged elements trigger the memory trace of the whole, so that actors can identify the subject despite the work's distortions and playful ambiguities. Using this methodology, Paul Citroen achieved the first collective portrait of the modern, dense city in a collage of photographic elements from New York and various European capitals ("Metropolis", 1922), creating an overwhelming sense of the psychic reality of the City as a Machine.[33]

James Stirling: worms-eye view of path and drum, Düsseldorf Museum, ca. 1975

The key to Picasso and Le Corbusier's collage approach was to see how much of the normative model they could remove, opening the traditional forms to Modernism while still retaining the overall Gestalt of a recognizable object or person. In the previous chapter, I discussed briefly the difference between collage, which retains this sense of the fractured Gestalt, and assemblage, which works from the qualities of the parts alone. I also reviewed how rhizomic assemblage incorporates the actor's movements and psychology, and treats the old parts of the city as elements, none more privileged than any other. In rhizomic assemblage, the city's parts are patches to be combined and recombined as a myriad of assemblages in people's everyday paths and social practices. Symbolic elements can be combined and prioritized by actors to show their dominance from the top down or bottom up. Each actor will experience the city differently, depending on what networks they inhabit and traverse; the design of any particular assemblage follows local rules and responds to local pressures from actors and flows through the larger network. Each actor constructs or reads their city from minimal cues, as we read Picasso's *Guitar*.

Stirling: thumbnail sketches of drum, Neue Staatsgalerie, Stuttgart, ca. 1977

Rhizomic assemblage combines the layered bricolage of the "space body" design approach with the psychological insights and goals of individual actors moving through and constructing structures in the city-territory. It can thus accommodate even the strange juxtapositions of the large "urban equipment" of postmodern sprawl that reduce to a minimum, like *Guitar*, the symbolic

Table 3.1. Basic Utility Elements and Agricultural-City Urban Elements

Organizational Structure	Enclave Typology	Armature Typology	Heterotopia Typology	Heterotopic Processes
Water-supply system *Energy sources:* *human labor,* *animals, wind,* *water, gravity*	Reservoirs Fountains Administrative/ maintenance works	Pipes Sluices Aqueducts	Pumps Water wheels Windmills	Solid- and liquid-waste disposal systems, dumps, incinerators, waste treatment plants, etc.
Land cultivation and subdivision system	Building lots and fields	Plowing, farming, road to market	Barn, silo systems Record system Court system	Waste products from agriculture (needed for fertilizer) Communication system Law enforcement (property)
Food-supply system Alcohol-supply system	Markets Granaries	Street market Vendors	Specialized market Bars/restaurants	Transport- and supply- systems Places of cultural entertainment

intermediaries required for the recognition of a city space. In the creation of malls and shopping centers, for instance, urban designers identified a set of patterns that worked in the early network city. They drew on a rich tradition and recombined existing elements in their experiments until they found a formula that worked. Other actors (e.g., local community groups and concerned citizens in historic preservation groups) found ways to influence design from the bottom up, using informal and nonconventional tactics. From all these different visions and interrelationships, patterns of activity and flow emerged. Emergence was partly bottom up and partly enforced, reinforced, or repressed from the top down (see discussion, below, of the mall as both enclave and armature).

It is worth recalling at this point that the actors in such a case are combining and recombining *urban elements* in their fixed collage or dynamic, rhizomic assemblage. In *Collage City*, Rowe and Koetter provide a list of seven urban elements (though they give no real methodology for their *combination*): (1) the armature-like "memorable street"; (2) the enclave-like "stabilizer" square; (3) another enclave-like element, the "potentially indeterminate set piece"; (4) an armature, "the splendid terrace"; (5) heterotopic "ambiguous or multivalent buildings"; (6) the heterotopic "nostalgia-producing" element; and (7) a distinct type of heterotopia, the "garden."

In *Good City Form*, Lynch provides a long list of urban elements that can be assembled into cities in terms of their "grain" and "texture," their porosity or resistance to movement systems, classifying them as "fast" or "slow." His first element (giving main headings only) is a territorial "framework" of armatures (star, grid, baroque networks, etc.); his second is the "central place" enclave settlement pattern (subdivided into single-, dual-, and multiple-center systems, including shopping malls); his third is a typological lexicon of "textures" (high slabs, towers in the green, dense walkups, ground-access walkups, courtyard houses, attached houses, freestanding houses, etc.); and his fourth is "open space" (enclave-like urban parks, squares and plazas, stretched-enclave-like regional parks and linear parks, playing fields, and wastelands). Lynch was concerned with the heterotopic recombination of the elements over time in his last category, including programmed "timing of use."

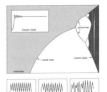

James Gleick; three-phase diagram leading to chaos or complex phase, Chaos, 1987

I now propose to develop my own list of urban elements and sub-elements that links to the Rationalist typomorphological system, with Viganò's reverse city in the background. For convenience I will use a narrative format, linking these elements and sub-elements sequentially to the Archi Città, Cine Città, and Tele Città models; in fact, these urban systems coexist, with each system emerging into dominance where particular actors gain power in particular places and times, constructing a dynamic urban bricolage of patches of order. The Cittàs are thus "dissipative structures" (see Chapter 1), forming and dissolving through time, not eternal, always moving with urban actors' preferences and resources.

In such an analysis I must first briefly note the necessity of a set of primary, infrastructural subsystems, that is, biological and ecological support systems for urban culture and urban elements in local patches. Actors construct mechanisms to facilitate or restrict flows necessary to human life, such as flows of water, food, and waste. It is not hard to imagine these patch installations as initially temporary, supporting seasonal activities on a "commons" or shared public area and later becoming permanent (much as Landscape Urbanists imagine their support systems today). Maintenance of these systems is essential, and organizations and institutions that persist from generation to generation are required to manage the components of their physical plant, such as the pumps, sluices, fountains, pipes, and reservoirs of the city water supply. Water also is implied in cleaning, bath houses, kitchens, and disposal of both solid and liquid waste, including human excrement (once used as fertilizer, rather than disposed of as a waste product). An idea of the complexity of these mechanisms can be formed from the utility set given in the video game *Sim City*. The basic utility set of *Sim City* also includes electric supply, telephones, cable systems, and media services. Even this is a very simplistic set of the sub-elements or *équipement urbain* needed to support a patch of urban order and its actors' activities (Table 3.1).

David Grahame Shane: Three phases with analogous urban patterns

Table 3.2 "Steady State" Classical and Postimperial Urban Elements

Organizational Structure	Enclave Typology	Armature Typology	Heterotopia Typology	Heterotopic Processes
Greek city-states	Agora Grid colony	Approach street Walls	Temple, theater Meeting house Courthouse Gates Ports	Ritual cleansing, sacrifices Slave labor, warfare, public games, fleets, tombs Religion Rubbish dumps Theater, art, literature
Roman Empire	Forum Walls	Imperial armature Grid colony	Bath house, public toilets, fountains, gymnasia Granaries Gates Reservoirs Aqueducts Walls	Ritual cleansing, sacrifices Slave labor, warfare, public games, fleets, tombs Religion Rubbish dumps Theater, art, literature
Viking settlements Islamic cities Medieval Europe	Market-square gates Mosque Cathedral	Main-street armature Souk Beach walls	Castle Mosque, cathedral Market admin. School, monastery, hospital	Prayer, ritual cleansing Slave labor, warfare, trade, religious art and literature, morality plays Burial grounds, dumps

Presuming that these infrastructural sub-elements are present and maintained at a scale appropriate to the city's growth, we can now proceed to list the sub-elements of a city in a "steady state" of incremental development. This implies that growth will occur at intervals in large parcels (i.e., in a "punctuated equilibrium" pattern) and as a self-organizing system of patches organized around a single node (following Von Thünen's central-place model). I presume that there is land for expansion and food and drinking water available to support the resident population.

In the "steady state," new urban organizations and sub-elements emerge and develop over time, structuring the city. These assemblages may be nomadic systems (e.g., invading armies or traders) or sedentary systems based on "capture and control" (living off farmers and agricultural surpluses). The Greek city-states, for instance, had armies, fleets, merchants, and traders (all "nomadic" in the sense used here) as well as basic agricultural infrastructures supporting life (all "sedentary"). The organization of the city-state was centered symbolically around the "space body" of the agora and its group of public institutions, creating a "democracy" that excluded the majority of inhabitants. Beside the army barracks and fleet facilities in the port, public institutions and *équipement urbain* emerged in the form of such urban sub-elements as civic meeting houses, courthouses, temples, and theaters, all initially heterotopic uses removed from everyday activity, addressed to the gods and having their own geometric order.

Plan of the Roman port and granaries along the main street, Ostia, Italy

Greek colonial cities, planned on a grid, placed all these sub-elements (temples, bath houses, gymnasia, schools, courthouses, etc.) around the agora, the central public space or enclave, as standard urban equipment. From here the geometric order of the core was extended to the entire city and male citizen-settlers, as equals, received equal lots of land (developed according to a courtyard housing typology). The Romans employed a similarly formulaic centering approach to colonial-city planning, one based both on the Greek grid and on their own military camps. In practice, like the Greeks, they varied the application with every site, but the city was again identified with a cluster of imperial symbols and urban sub-elements: temples, theaters, markets, arcaded street armatures, court-houses, gymnasia, public toilets and bath houses, and so on. In Rome itself, where all male citizens were entitled to food, a vast system of granaries and water supplies was developed to feed the one million people living there in 40 AD. Grain was imported from North Africa and Sicily. We know from the ruins of Pompeii that Roman street life was intense, with graffiti on the walls, storefronts opening on the main streets, and a red-light district close to the forum.[34]

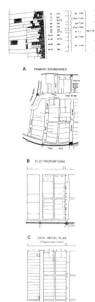

Our steady-state model has added several incremental patches or semi-cumulative layers of development since beginning as a simple agricultural settlement. Each layer or increment has its own set of urban sub-elements. There were *three* grids inside Pompeii's walls, excluding the original Sabian settlement enclave; even Roman colonial grid-towns, like Timgad (Algeria), added armatures at their gates (outward-extending roads lined with activity), if not further grid extensions. Nor did the collapse of Rome and the empire mean the end of steady-state incremental growth. Nomads came to inhabit the ruins and transform them, imposing their own linear organizational structures and so altering the centered patterns of the Roman urban sub-elements. Around the Mediterranean basin, Arab settlers and ex-Roman citizens transformed Roman grids and public open spaces into new private realms, namely, small-scale, private market stands and souks connected by new networks of paths to new attractors (e.g., mosques or cathedrals) built among the ruins and crypts of old monumental buildings.[35] In other cities, new towns literally inhabited the shells of the old Roman urban elements, creating heterotopic settlements. For example, the Roman arena at Arles was transformed into a fortified enclave, the theater of Marcellus in Rome was converted first into apartments and then into a Jewish ghetto, and Diocletian's palace at Split was transformed into a small grid town (much as American New Urbanists would superimpose a village structure on modern malls).[36]

MRG Conzens: land measurement and subdivision in medieval planned units of development

Table 3.3 "Steady-State" Renaissance and Baroque Urban Elements

Organizational Structure	Enclave Typology	Armature Typology	Heterotopia Typology	Heterotopic processes
State capitals Sedentary systems	State offices Public square	Parade streets Boulevards Road systems	State palaces Churches Almshouses Hospitals Prisons	Public institutions Carriage systems, repair shops and factories, justice system and "transportation" of convicts, armies
Trading ports Nomad systems	Docks and warehouses	Sea lanes Canals	Shop/houses Hotels, markets Factory mines	Shipping systems, repair yards, transfer points, communication systems, navigation systems
Colonial installations Agrarian systems	Walls/forts Central square Docks	Promenade street Grids	State palace, cathedral, prison, market	Import/ export flows Mining camps, raw-materials- extraction systems

MRG Conzens: composite plan of medieval Thame, England

Nomads had their own systems of organization, as M. R. G. Conzens showed in his investigation of the "planned unit development" techniques used by the Normans along their border with Wales, traced by later scholarship to Viking settlements (e.g., John Bradley's study of Viking settlements in Ireland).[37] The Viking trading network stretched from China to America, with trading posts established as temporary, not agricultural, settlements.[38] In Waterford, wooden houses formed the armature of the main street, which was sited on a peninsula so that boats could be moored or beached at the back of each house's garden area. A meeting hall faced the most sheltered anchorage and a market stood on the opposite side of the peninsula. Churches were only added later, off the main street. In Cork, the Norman expansion of the town repeated this same pattern first established by the Vikings across the river from the original fortress.

At this point, our steady-state model has added several nomadic interventions to the original Chinese, Indian, Greek, or Roman colonial grid at the core, creating a bricolage of patches. New urban sub-elements have emerged in the shape of Islamic or Christian institutions, as well as new, larger trading organizations handling the markets and their trading networks, not to mention new utility and agricultural infrastructure systems to support the activity of the urban enclave. These new sub-elements are listed in Table 3.2, representing a second level of steady-state, large-scale incremental development.

Table 3.4 Industrial Systems: "Binary" Urban Elements

Organizational Structure	Enclave Typology	Armature Typology	Heterotopia Typology	Heterotopic Processes
Industrial systems SPLIT Sedentary systems Consumption Production	Factory, office, housing Mass housing	Railway, Wall St., etc. Boulevards Alleyways	Arcades/ department stores Theaters, cinema, museums Stock market and commodity market	Mass communications Photography, biography, film studios Vaudeville circuits
Trading ports Nomad systems SPLIT	Stations, docks and warehouses	Railway, streetcars, telegraph	World's Fair Grand hotels Bordellos	Consumption/production Advertising/press/comm. Travel, shipping, tourism
Sedentary systems SPLIT Colonial installations Agrarian systems	European city Central square Vernaculars Plantation	Promenade street Grids Road /railway	State palace Court, prison, school, hospital Opera, theater "Native" camps	Import/export flows, docks Mining camps, raw-materials-extraction systems Monoculture crops

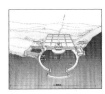

Bramante: reconstruction of civitas vecchia, Rome (from Bruschi Bramante architetto, 1969)

I have already reviewed the "paradigm shift" from medieval to Renaissance in Chapter 2. Following Choay, I have pointed to the three-dimensional spatial matrix that was introduced by Brunelleschi in the guise of perspectival construction and scenography, championed by his student Alberti. Given the example of More's Utopia and of the Urbino panels with their building typologies, it is not hard to list the Renaissance and Baroque urban sub-elements that surrounded the great public squares and avenues of the ideal European city. This grid model and its sub-elements correspond to the schema contained in the Spanish Law of the Indies, which became the mandatory norm across South America and throughout the Spanish empire. Urban sub-elements in this urban fragment included the governor's palace, church, merchants' houses, arcades and stores surrounding the central square, and the public symbols at its center: gallows, fountain, stocks.

In the wake of this paradigm shift, the European merchant princes' drive to colonize the world, establishing colonial towns and formalizing a global trading system, created a network with tension between center and periphery. European ports acted as "sorting machines" for the flows of the various trading networks that operated first along national and later on a global scale. These ports grew in importance and eclipsed the previous national centers. Their hinterland stretched across Europe and around the coast of Africa to Asia and India, and across the Atlantic to North and South America.

Table 3.5 Modern Urban Elements (CIAM)

Organizational Structure	Enclave Typology	Armature Typology	Heterotopia Typology	Heterotopic processes
Modern industrial systems Dual-centered	Housing Work Admin./industry Leisure	Transport Communications Vertical compression Horizontal stretch	Hospitals, schools, asylum Housing block	"Sorting machines" Banking Mass communications: photography, film studios, television and radio
Industrial systems Dual-centered	Factory Department store Office	Production Lines/strip malls Disney	Skyscrapers Superblocks Megastructures	Consumption/production Advertising/press/ communications Central planning/banking
Colonial installations Agrarian systems Dual-centered	Airport, port Central square New towns Suburbs	Promenade-street grids Neighborhood center Highways	Governor's palace, courts, prison, Markets, Malls	Import/export- flows control Mechanical farming Mining camps, raw-materials extraction-systems

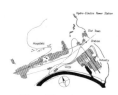

Tony Garnier: diagram of the Cité Industrielle, 1911–18 (from D Wiebenson, "Les Nouvelles Conditions du Projet Urbain" 1969)

As trade flows intensified, so did specialization of actors at the opposite ends of trade routes, amplifying the differences between sub-elements in metropolis and colony. Factory systems developed to take advantage of the scale of the global trade, producing specialized agglomerations of industry that grew very fast and at terrible human and ecological cost. Sales systems developed to market the new products, exacerbating the gap between rich and poor, leisure and work. Steam displaced sail, and merchant bankers developed specialized enclaves of command and control in such places as Throgmorton Street (in the financial core of the City of London) and Wall Street (in New York).

Conspicuous consumption and the display of wealth drove the creation of new sub-elements in one part of town, while penny-pinching and brutal labor practices drove the creation of new elements in the other part. Boulevards, department stores, arcades, monumental public buildings, opera houses, and theaters all marked the ascent of the bourgeoisie. Slum conditions, long factory hours, child labor, industrial pollution, cholera, and poverty were the fate of the poor. Colonial settlements reflected this duality with their own split between grandiose elements of imperial culture and the impoverished vernacular elements of "native" inhabitants.

Cerdá, in the European Rationalist tradition discussed earlier, attempted to simplify and reform the messy and slum-ridden industrial city of the laissez-faire,

Table 3.6 Postmodern Urban Elements

Organizational Structure	Enclave Typology	Armature Typology	Heterotopia Typology	Heterotopic processes
Postmodern systems (multicenter net)	Gated enclave Big-box retail Special district Festival market Atrium	Las Vegas Strip Miracle mile LA City Walk Strip malls Galleria	Theme parks Entertainment district Megamalls Hybrid homes/offices Vast barrios	Splintering urbanism Mass tourism Mass entertainment Shopping/leisure Self-built housing
Modern industrial (binary system)	Housing Work Administration/industry Leisure	Transport Communications Vertical stretch Horizontal stretch	Hospital, prison, school, asylum Housing block Rural urbanization	"Sorting machines" Mass communications: photography, film studios, television, and radio
Neocolonial Installations Agrarian system (single-center system)	Gated enclaves Airport, port Central square Precincts	Malls Promenades Street grids Highways	Theme parks State palace, courts, prison Plantations	Tourist attractions Import/export flows Mining camps, raw- materials-extraction systems

free-market approach through government regulation. He, and other designers, sought a new harmony with Nature and developed isolated building forms, pavilion systems, to achieve this objective. All the industrial sub-elements of the city that had created chaos before—steel mills, cotton mills, factories, and workshops—would be segregated as new patches of order, cleaned up, modernized, integrated into an organic whole, at peace with nature. With this goal in mind, Le Corbusier applied CIAM's principle of the segregation of the four functions (housing, work, leisure, and transport plus miscellaneous), as determined in the 1933 Athens Charter, in his Ville Radieuse project of the same year. He even conceived of new urban sub-elements to house the four functions. Some of these sub-elements have indeed come into being, such as large slab blocks of housing, highways in the park, and skyscraper office towers clustered in the central business district.

Le Corbusier: Town-center detail, City of Three Million, *1922 (© FLC ADAGP, Paris and DACS, London, 2005)*

Other sub-elements imagined by Le Corbusier, however, did not appear, like the station-plus-airport hybrid shown at the center of his central business district, or shopping centers in the parkland without adequate parking (in his *City for Three Million*, 1922). Viganò finds other examples of morphological experiment and bricolage in this period: in Russia, for example, the Constructivists experimented with a wide range of Modernist communal and highly individualized "pavilion"-type urban elements, rejecting the street wall.

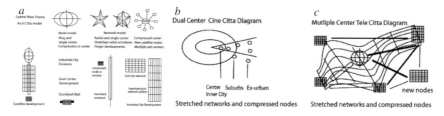

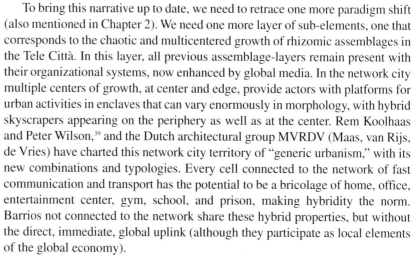

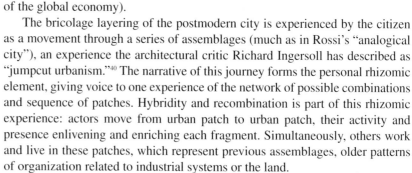

a) *Radial, linear and ring city patterns*
b) *Ring city patterns with satellite rings*
c) *Network cities*

Hellmuth, Obata, and Kassabaum: Axonometric of Galleria shopping center, Houston, TX, 1967–2005

(Berlage's plan for Amsterdam South, however, retained it.) Still other bricolage elements appeared that were not foreseen by the Modernists, like the modern shopping mall and hybrid towers (e.g., Belgiojoso, Peressutti and Rogers's Torre Velasca in Milan, 1958, or Skidmore, Owings and Merrill's John Hancock Tower in Chicago, 1969). The pioneering Los Angeles mall designers Gruen and Beckett began in the 1950s to explore a more generic, combinatory territory in their mixed-use malls at the edge or center of town, opening the way for peripheral megamalls like Houston's Galleria (Hellmuth, Obata, and Kassabaum, 1967).

To bring this narrative up to date, we need to retrace one more paradigm shift (also mentioned in Chapter 2). We need one more layer of sub-elements, one that corresponds to the chaotic and multicentered growth of rhizomic assemblages in the Tele Città. In this layer, all previous assemblage-layers remain present with their organizational systems, now enhanced by global media. In the network city multiple centers of growth, at center and edge, provide actors with platforms for urban activities in enclaves that can vary enormously in morphology, with hybrid skyscrapers appearing on the periphery as well as at the center. Rem Koolhaas and Peter Wilson,[39] and the Dutch architectural group MVRDV (Maas, van Rijs, de Vries) have charted this network city territory of "generic urbanism," with its new combinations and typologies. Every cell connected to the network of fast communication and transport has the potential to be a bricolage of home, office, entertainment center, gym, school, and prison, making hybridity the norm. Barrios not connected to the network share these hybrid properties, but without the direct, immediate, global uplink (although they participate as local elements of the global economy).

The bricolage layering of the postmodern city is experienced by the citizen as a movement through a series of assemblages (much as in Rossi's "analogical city"), an experience the architectural critic Richard Ingersoll has described as "jumpcut urbanism."[40] The narrative of this journey forms the personal rhizomic element, giving voice to one experience of the network of possible combinations and sequence of patches. Hybridity and recombination is part of this rhizomic experience: actors move from urban patch to urban patch, their activity and presence enlivening and enriching each fragment. Simultaneously, others work and live in these patches, which represent previous assemblages, older patterns of organization related to industrial systems or the land.

It is no surprise that there is an enormous range of urban sub-elements, given our definition of urbanism and the city as a network of actors with urban events and platforms within it. Above, I have attempted to track six relatively stable patterns of urban development in the history of Western European and American cities. Namely, in the Archi Città, steady-state formation I noted three stages, the premodern, medieval, and Renaissance and baroque, all around a single center; in the Cine Città there was the binary dynamic of rich and poor, messy industrial city and reformist, Modern city; and finally the net city, with its multiple centers and hybrids. This progression from single centers to dual or split centers and thence to multiple centers is simple enough, a three-stage development from a "steady-state" pattern around one core to a binary system with growth alternating between separated cores to a multithreaded system with pulses of growth occurring at multiple, hybrid centers.

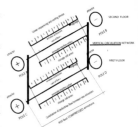

Standard armature (high street)

These three stages or models of city growth correspond to the Archi Città, Cine Città, and Tele Città (which I will denote, in urban shorthand, by the numerals 1, 2, and 3). The Archi Città includes urban equipment or recombinatory sub-elements from the steady-state growth model described above, and its most characteristic or fundamental element is the enclave. The Cine Città includes urban equipment or recombinatory sub-elements from the binary growth model and is based on the armature and twin attractors. The Tele Città includes urban equipment or recombinatory sub-elements from the postmodern, multicentered network city, and features hybrid assemblages as nodes.

Compressed armature (mall)

In the remainder of this chapter, each major organizational element will be denoted in shorthand by its first letter: E = enclave, A = armature, and H = heterotopia. An enclave associated with city model 1, the Archi Città, would be denoted E1. In addition, I will describe an urban element as "compressed" if it is taller or has a smaller footprint than is normal for its category, and will describe an urban element as "stretched" if it is taller or longer than usual or associated with accelerated urban transport or communications that alter the traveler's perception of space and time. (Examples: A three-story mall is "compressed"; a limited-access highway, on which you travel 20 or more miles in 20 minutes instead of 1 mile, as on foot, is "stretched.") Elements may also be horizontal or vertical in their orientation.

In the next two sections I will examine in more detail two basic urban "patch" elements, the enclave and the armature, as recombinant assemblages before moving on to the third, the heterotopia. I view these two elements in terms of their "space body" characteristics. The enclave centers flows in a space, the armature facilitates flow along a channel. I will categorize some of the forms taken by these elements and link them both to Lynch's normative models and to the humanist urban-design tradition represented by *Collage City*. In the fourth and final chapter, we will return to the heterotopia and look at patterns of relationships between city elements and city models. We will examine how actors make recombinations and the role of heterotopias as special "shifter" elements, that is, assemblages that help make the complex transition of a living city from one model to another possible.

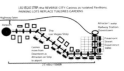

Stretched armature (Las Vegas)

3.2 ENCLAVE: A PRELIMINARY DEFINITION

When we describe a city we habitually break it down into conceptual fragments: neighborhoods, districts, places of special interest or character. This mode of description is so normal it forms the basis of many successful guidebooks, such as the Michelin or Eye Witness guides. This fragmentary vision found a place in the work of the avant-garde Situationist group in the 1950s, especially in Guy Debord's *Naked City* map of Paris. Debord cut the map of Paris into a series of "atmospheric" fragments connected only by red arrows of desire that look straight out of Paul Klee.[41]

Kevin Lynch: diagram of walled garden enclave City of Faith, A Theory of Good City Form, *1981*

It is the basic argument of this book that *all* great cities are necessarily built around such specialized districts, plan units, or enclaves as centering devices for flow systems. These centering devices have performed different functions at different periods and in different urban systems. The square in front of the cathedral is different from the square in front of the factory or department store, and all are different from a square in Disneyland. Each is the product of incremental growth patterns that proceed in a "punctuated equilibrium" style, that is, in small spurts of activity that accumulate over time. All enclaves center, slow down, and store urban flows and energies, forming temporary node structures. The emergence of enclaves and of enclave recognition is fundamental to the urbanization and settlement process.

Traditional urban histories have concentrated on enclaves, especially the historic squares in European cities (e.g., Paul Zucker's *Town and Square*, 1959, or A. E. J. Morris's excellent *History of Urban Form*, 1972), marking the square as the apex of European urbanism. This notion is echoed in America by contemporary New Urbanists. This traditional history traces the European square from the Greek agora and Roman forum to the medieval cathedral or market square, then to such triumphs of the Renaissance as Brunelleschi's initiation of the Piazza della S. S. Annunziata (1421), Michelangelo's Capitoline Hill project (1537), to miscellaneous baroque squares, and finally to the squares of the nineteenth century, such as Haussmann's construction of the Place de la Republique (1868–70). Readers desiring more information on this distinguished history are referred to Morris or to Edmund Bacon's *The Design of Cities* (1967), with its splendid maps and details. Here, however, we are concerned with the evolution of the enclave through the three phases outlined above and its global iteration in other cultures and in colonies, not only with its high points in European history.

Michelangelo: approach stair to Capitoline Hill Rome, 1537

One British dictionary defines *enclave* as "an outlying territory belonging to one country and lying wholly within the territory of another" (Penguin English Dictionary, 1979). Webster's Collegiate Dictionary (for American English) offers "a distinct territorial, cultural, or social unit enclosed within, or as if within, foreign territory." The word *enclave* is derived from the same root as the verb "to cleave," to cut, break, or split off. Enclaves are bits of land metaphorically split off from their parent block and displaced to a "foreign" location; they have an internal coherence that refers to a distant place, one beyond their immediate surroundings. Preserving this reference in hostile surroundings requires an interior order capable of compensating for displacement and exterior "chaos" or contradiction. Further, because territorial enclaves are by definition cut off from a home territory, their inhabitants often long for links to that "home." The presence of enclaves in a city breeds a fragmentary quality.

It is not hard to connect these definitions with individual features and larger life-worlds actually found in cities. We can all think of territorial enclaves that exist inside larger cities: the Forbidden City in Beijing, the Vatican in Rome, the United Nations in New York, embassy compounds everywhere. All these are distinct territories literally embedded in the body of a larger urban entity. Symbolically, "home" for both the Forbidden City and the Vatican is heaven, while for the United Nations it is a transnational ideal of peace, a kind of secular heaven.

Plan of Capitoline Hill project (courtesy of the University of Toronto Urban Precedents website)

We may note several points further about enclaves: (1) They have distinct interior spatial and social orders that help distinguish them from their surroundings. (2) Special attractors lying within them give them their peculiar characteristics; they relate to an ideal or distant community through a system of displacements. (3) They have perimeters or boundaries that define the limits of their interior spatial orders, which are organized around their special, central attractors. (4) Gates perforate these perimeters, connecting to transportation and communication channels that admit outsiders and allow insiders to access the larger urban complex and points beyond. (5) They are places of rest and stasis. (6) They may contain various urban typomorphologies within their perimeters but are often dominated by the repetition of one typological pattern. (7) They have gate-keepers and systematic, internal codes that serve to restrict the territory's social and functional order to specific people and uses. Designated actors enforce restrictions, which may take the form of functional codes and prohibitions or of restrictive building codes to exclude designated uses or people. Inhabitants, property owners, landlords, developers, street gangs, city regulations, or courts may enforce these codes and control access by various groups.

To summarize: an enclave is a self-organizing, self-centering, and self-regulating system created by urban actors, often governed by a rigid hierarchy with set boundaries. It serves to slow down and concentrate nomadic flows using a variety of techniques, from perimeter walls and gatekeepers to formal, geometric devices in the plan of the settlement. Urban actors have employed enclaves since the advent of cities, from ancient Egypt to the grandiose urban visions of Mussolini and Stalin, the network city, and beyond. The enclave is also an incremental unit of city growth. In my notation an enclave is designated by the letter "E."

Diagram of the enclave as a self-centering system

Below, I make some broad distinctions between enclaves in various city models and urban design strategies, citing examples where possible; I find it convenient to distinguish between a normative model "E", a compressed model

"]E[", and a stretched model "–E–". In addition, heavy media influence and concentration is indicated by an "m." Adding to this the Città numbers given at the end of the last section, I will designate Archi Città enclaves "E1," Cine Città enclaves "E2," and Tele Città enclaves "E3." Curly brackets around an element indicate it is in a dense urban fabric, downtown in a historic district; for instance, a courtyard house would be {E1}.

I have already mentioned the enclave's attributes, namely a closed perimeter (often walls, with a main gateway); guardians; a single, self-referential center; a system of codes and hierarchies built about a holy spot that defines the good (or at least a great good) in life. Examples range from the Roman residential districts in Pompeii, made up of courtyard villas (E1), to the normative enclaves of streetcar suburbs, that is, row houses or suburban developments of pavilionized, residential villas comprising a "bourgeois utopia" on the edge of the city (E2). We have also examined how single-function industrial enclaves were stretched as industrial zones along railway tracks to take advantage of space-time acceleration in the railway corridor (–E2–).

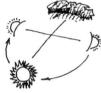

One can observe compression, too, in small, tight-knit, specialized industrial enclaves such as the "Diamond district" in Antwerp, or London's Hatton Garden (]E2[). These highly specialized industrial districts often become heterotopias in relation to their surrounding cities, anticipating aspects of the postmodern enclave in their fortification and linkage to global communications. And we have seen as an example of postmodern enclaves (E3) the "pedestrian pocket" neighborhoods of the New Urbanists, which depend heavily on global communication systems for their appeal. Strict codes control these wired communities, with their scenographic emphasis on place-making elements such as essentially decorative open porches (attached to centrally air-conditioned houses).

My Archi Città enclave category, E1, is based on streets and on street-wall continuity, which forms a street-based matrix throughout the enclave using the "space body" of streets and squares to direct flows and constrict passage. This pattern of urban centering has a long tradition stretching back to preclassical antiquity in the City of Faith and continuing to the built structures of the European Archi Città. Generally, a central geometric point is defined in the landscape and four primary axes are extended outward from this center of the (local) world. (In medieval European thought, only one city—Jerusalem—had the privilege of being *the* center of *the* world.) These axes extend out to the horizon and often correspond to the cardinal points of the compass, to sunset and sunrise, or to features of the night sky. In Chapter 1 we have already noted the cosmic orientation of these single-center systems, especially in the City of Faith.

In *The Idea of the City* (1976), Joseph Rykwert examines in great detail the workings of a particular E1 single-center enclave system, the Roman system for creating a new town. This system was not so different from geomancy systems in China or India, all of which Lynch referred to as "cosmic" diagrams. First, augurs came to the site of the intended settlement to divine its suitability. They slaughtered animals that had grazed on the site to search for impurities and bad omens. If the signs were favorable, they harnessed white oxen to a sacred plow and cut a furrow to mark the boundary of the city, the future site of its walls. Gates were built at the four cardinal points of the compass to perforate the sacred perimeter. The augurs lifted the plow as they crossed the future sites of these gates, since these would be a source of pollution, letting in strangers and infecting the purity of the E1 enclosure. At the intersection of the four cardinal axes, the augurs placed the forum, the symbolic center of the new city, an enclave within an enclave. Here, temples to imperial and local deities would rise as enclaves within an enclave within an enclave. At the symbolic center of the city the augurs dug a hole, a *centrum mundi* or world-center, into which new citizens had to cast objects associated with their old home as symbols of their commitment to the new city.

An E1 enclave such as a Roman colony or military camp has only one point of focus; Roman public monuments are gathered about a central, public square that is surrounded by a private building fabric. Height limits frequently controlled the vertical dimension of buildings, creating a vertical hierarchy in which religious or civic monuments overlooked the private fabric. The theme of E1 enclave nesting is illustrated by the structure of Pompeii, which, as Etienne describes, archeologists have found consisted of a series of enclaves. At the core of the city a tiny, irregular Sabian encampment predated the Romans. This encampment, with its own bath house, remained embedded in the center of the Roman town proper, which grew as a series of three increasingly regular grid additions, each a separate unit, and was eventually surrounded by a defensive wall. There was a theater district located on a hill, a commercial area at the foot of the hill, a red-light district nearby, and a peripheral sports campus.[42]

Medieval European and Islamic cities also abounded in specialized E1

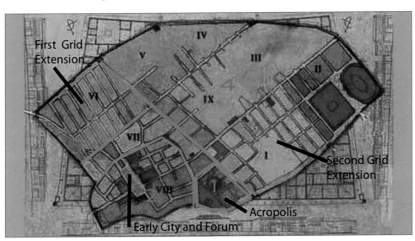

Plan of Roman Pompeii as a nested system of enclaves

Richard Sennett:
plan of Venice with
enclaves and ghetto
Flesh and Stone,
1994

enclaves within their walls, ranging from cathedrals or mosques (with their associated schools and bath houses, markets and monasteries) to precincts occupied by specialized guilds or merchant organizations, often from foreign countries. Istanbul, the great trading metropolis of the Silk Route, had many such precincts for foreign and local merchants, as did its rival Venice, which also segregated its merchants by nationalities and its Jews in a ghetto (an E1>H1 switch; heterotopias will be discussed extensively in the next chapter). Richard Sennett dedicates a chapter to the "fear of touching" as the source of the Venetian regulations in *Flesh and Stone: The body and the City in Western Civilization* (1994).[43] Nor are such fears confined to the medieval period, as A. J. Christopher's *The Atlas of Apartheid* (1994) demonstrates in its history of the "Group Areas Act" in South Africa in the twentieth century.[44]

The dictionary definitions of "enclave" emphasize territory and nationality, reflecting nineteenth-century experiences of nation-state formation in Europe and wars over ethnic enclaves or territorial claims. Indeed, land and land-ownership are fundamental to the making and marking of E1 enclaves. In our look at typomorphology in the previous section, we have already encountered M. R. G. Conzens's "plan units," which related urban development directly to the agricultural land subdivisions that underlie the modern city. Conzens was thus able to map with great accuracy the transformation of the city field by field, unit by unit, and fragment by fragment from agricultural use to urban or suburban activity (an E1>E2 switch).[45]

In England, urban historians could map this transformation with great accuracy because of the extensive landownership records in public records that are now available to scholars. John Summerson applied this method in *Georgian London* (1946), studying the plan units of the great estates based on previous agricultural divisions (E1>E2).[46] H. J. Dyos, in his study of the south London suburb of Camberwell, applied the same approach to each landowner's development, plotting the less orderly transformation of a rural village into a subcenter of the greater London metropolitan network (without the self-organizing patterns imposed by the great landlords of central London).[47] Dyos found that the presence of the estate organization and tradition in central London made all the difference to the overall pattern of development. And we have already linked Portugali's description of cellular automata in *Self-Organization and the City* to such self-organizing systems, which are based on landownership enclaves with specialized feedback loops that maintain and repeat a basic fractal pattern in a series of related assemblages.

Summerson: View
north over Covent
Garden, London, ca.
1632, Inigo Jones
1966

The history of the great estates in London illustrates enclaves as self-organizing systems and cellular automata producing a fractal system that can maintain and repair itself (in this case, for over two centuries). The Covent Garden development in London in 1632 began this Archi Città enclave (E1) tradition in Renaissance London, with a single, closed center on the periphery of the city. This was transformed in subsequent centuries into a system of large,

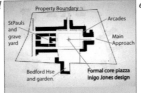

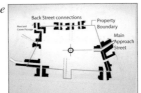

a) *Inigo Jones: St. Paul's, Covent Garden, ca. 1632 (rebuilt several times)*
b) *Jones: Covent Garden central plaza, ca. 1632*
c) *Covent Garden analysis—peripheral development, empty center, 1971*
d) *Covent Garden analysis—formal center of design, 1971*
e) *Covent Garden analysis—peripheral connections from center, 1971*
f) *Restored interior of Covent Garden Market as a festival mall, 2004*
g) *Exterior of Charles Fowler's cast iron fruit and vegetable market insert 1830s*
h) *Plan of Covent Garden with market building inserted 1830s, (courtesy of University of Toronto)*

interrelated urban enclaves (E2), growing ever westward and competing with the old center of London.[48]

As an attractor within the original E1 development, the king required the Earl of Bedford to construct a church facing the open, central square or piazza, connecting this project to utopian Renaissance constructs that were later applied in British colonies in America, such as New Haven and Philadelphia, as well as in the Spanish colonial Laws of the Indies. The emplacement of this ideal, Renaissance, E1 central-square design helped register the Covent Garden enclave as a distinct urban image of the larger body of London.

Through the Bedford Estate Office, the earl and his descendants created a bureaucratic administration that controlled activity within the enclave. The office acted as a mechanism of code enforcement and feedback within the estate, which thus acted as a self-organizing cellular automaton with built-in feedback (i.e., the office) to repair and maintain its structure. As Portugali noted in *Self-Organization and the City*, such cellular structures form "fractal" (self-similar) systems within the city network. Since the earl and his descendants retained the ground lease, the Bedford Estate Office regulated construction in the enclave in perpetuity, only leasing the land to house owners for 100-year periods. The office attempted to restrict prostitution when the area became the theater and red-light district of London in the eighteenth century, and in the nineteenth century it intervened to rationalize the fruit and vegetable market that grew up in the empty space of the central square. The insertion of Charles Fowler's steel, glass, and stone Covent Garden Market structure in 1830 marked the end of the

David Grahame Shane: great estates and London street improvements, 1971

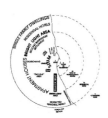

Robert Park and Ernest Burgess: Chicago School diagram of migration in the industrial city, ca. 1922, The City Reader, 1996

office's long struggle to maintain the fiction of a respectable, monofunctional residential area (E2) and its recognition of the estate's heterotopic, mixed-use, industrial-and-market functions (an E2>H2 shift).[49]

In general, however, enclaves in the modern, industrial city are polarized into monofunctional enclaves of production, consumption, and storage (E2) linked by "supplementary systems" of communication (Choay's phrase). This specialization and segregation is in part due to actors who require specialized services, setting in motion the agglomeration of businesses in specialized enclaves, but is also the result of city regulations restricting uses. The result has been the City as a Machine as described by Lynch, with its multiple, monofunctional enclaves (E2) connected by transport and communication channels. Delanda has described this kind of urban organization (e.g., European port city serving a colonial empire) as a "sorting machine," because in it actors continually categorize and sort urban material. Segregation of uses creates an ecological system of flows and patches, of enclaves whose characters and relationships change over time with successive occupants and altering flows.[50]

American sociologists Ernest Burgess and Robert Park, researching the social structure of the industrial city of Chicago in the 1920s, developed the canonical definition of the Modernist urban enclave (E2) system. Burgess wrote of the "growth of the city . . . as a process of distribution . . . which shifts and sorts and relocates individuals and groups by residence and occupation," a process which "gave form and character to the city."[51] Park described the city as an ecological system of urban enclaves where ethnic or racial minorities created self-contained ghettos to facilitate their own survival. Different groups have moved in "succession" through this process as American cities have expanded; here "succession" is borrowed from ecology, where it describes the colonization of a given territory by successive waves of plant and animal species, each of which prepares the way for the next. Industrial cities' growth-rings record these waves of immigrant succession (to mix our biological metaphors), which push "concentration and decentralization" in particular enclaves. Burgess said that "disturbances in the metabolism" are caused by any sudden rise in the flow of people into a city, such as a sudden inflow of new immigrants from Europe or the American South:

> [N]ormally the processes of disorganization and organization may be thought of as in reciprocal relationship to each other, and as cooperating and moving in an equilibrium of social order toward an end vaguely or definitely regarded as progressive.[52]

Under pressure from a new flow of immigrants, the self-organization patterns of the neighborhood E2 enclaves break down and became disorganized; such "disorganization" is "normal," the prelude to that "reorganization" that "is the lot of newcomers to the city."[53]

Abrahamson further argues that postmodern E3 urban enclaves are no longer as economically independent as in the past; their connections are regional and even global, and their self-definitions are now cast in cultural and institutional rather than geographic terms, being formed through all-important symbolic intermediaries linked via the media to our conscious and unconscious desires. Enclaves, he notes, form around attractors or magnets, symbolic intermediaries that draw specific settlers to a certain spot. Among these are the typical urban sub-elements that we identified earlier: markets, cultural centers, specialty restaurants or food shops, places to meet friends, places of worship, immigration lawyers' offices, travel agents, cinemas. All these symbolic intermediaries act as attractors, giving E3 immigrant enclaves their peculiar characteristics. They relate to an ideal or displaced life in a distant or imaginary "homeland," supplying images of urban settings or landscapes from a distant city or state, importing food and lifestyle choices associated with the homeland to the new platform. When such elements are inserted into a pioneering, all-American, regional planning community like Radburn, New Jersey (planned by Clarence Stein in the 1930s, with cul-de-sacs to protect pedestrians), the result can be somewhat surreal. On a recent visit, everyone in the peaceful communal gardens under the 50-year-old oak trees was reading newspapers in Russian. While Burgess saw such enclaves as typified by the inner city, Abrahamson argues that we now have them throughout the urban region, as demonstrated by Soja's maps of Los Angeles (1989) or John Hull Mollenkopf's 2,000 census maps of the New York City region.[73]

John H Mollenkopf: census analysis of immigrant areas in New York City 1993

Soja and Mollenkopf studied the formation of immigrant enclaves in postmodern cities of the North America, namely Los Angeles and New York. The same process, however, can be seen at work in the formation of the barrios and ranchos of South American cities or the inhabitant-built shanty towns of Africa (e.g., in Lagos or Cairo). In *The Structure of the Ordinary* (1998), N. John Habraken, like John Turner, shows how shanty-towns run on basic rules about land subdivision that constitute an informal land control system. Typically, such rules begin with the claims of the first squatters and later allow the sale to later immigrants of plots that were first settled without legal title. Halbraken illustrates the enormous scale of these informal, bottom-up, stretched-enclave (–E3–) formations in his study of Mexico City.[74] Here the displaced immigrants recreate the grids, row houses, or courtyard typologies of the villages from which they came, modified by their limited resources. The ubiquity of satellite dishes and antennas attests to the new immigrants' possibilities in houses that may have no running water, sewage disposal, or even legal address (services much harder to construct or tap into than satellite radio or the electrical grid).

Inside E3 enclaves in the Tele Città, the displacement of urban elements and images from elsewhere is normal. The typomorphologies of past systems—the Archi Città and the Cine Città—become symbolic intermediaries meaningful to actor-designers negotiating their place in the flows of the informational city.

Favela heliopolis, Rio de Janeiro hillside, 2004 (from P Neitzke and E Blum, eds. Favela Metropolis: Berichte und Projekte aus Rio de Janeiro und São Paulo Bauwelt Fundamente, *Vol. 130, Birkhäuser: Basel, 2004*

This process is more than the superficial pastiche of postmodernism that it was accused of being by its critics; it is a psychological image-transference process endemic to the system that acts as a compensatory memory device, reassuring displaced persons who feel far from home. For Portugali, these old images would be "enslaved systems" held within the dominant order of the informational city or network city.[75] The ability to read these "enslaved systems" in novel ways is a skill necessary for the survival of immigrants in the Tele Città, as the displacement of images plays an important role in the complexity of the multilayered network city. The codes of each E3 enclave are psychologically and visually linked both locally and globally, forming part of the network of the Tele Città.

Actors in each E3 enclave are theoretically free to follow their own logic in the Tele Città, from the scale of the individual house up to communal milieux. The postmodern single-family house has, accordingly, become a more complex enclave, not limited to the normative image of the monofunctional suburban home. This is in accord with the "scrambled egg" structure of the Tele Città. Giant corporations (e.g., Hewlett Packard, Disney, Apple) have been founded in garages and then moved to corporate campuses. Proliferating home offices, home factories, home leisure centers, home gyms, and the like all break the monocultural stereotype. Immigrant communities are now added to this mixture. The Venturi and Scott Brown partnership and Archigram teams pointed out in the early 1970s that the *theme* of each individual house (E3) has become important, its imagery announcing the freedom and individuality of the owner.[76]

The apparent freedom of each owner is what contributes to the Tele Città's chaotic image. Each element in the Tele Città "scrambled egg" competes for survival within the larger network; the skill of the actor-designer in constructing the image-space of an E3 enclave as an attractor will be one reason for the success of that enclave in a world of media "illusions." Another will be the actor-designer's ability to build an organization to maintain the enclave, creating cellular automata to reinforce self-organizational pattern-making. These organizations, as in the case of the Bedford Estate office mentioned earlier, sometimes depend on police powers, creating a world of "discipline" in Foucault's sense, that is, of security and surveillance. But as the "hyper-ghetto" demonstrates, this process of image creation is highly unpredictable. Anti normative "ghetto"-style elements, for instance, can have appeal for segments of the population not yet integrated into the Tele Città (e.g., teenagers) or as spectacle (thrills for TV-watching suburbanites).

Staircase in favela heliopolis, Rio de Janeiro, 2004 (Blum and Neitzke, Favela Metropolis)

Our preliminary definition of the enclave has expanded from the single-center, E1 enclave of the Archi Città to binary polarization of E2 enclaves in the Cine Città to multicellular proliferation of E3 enclaves in the Tele Città. Classification remains ambiguous, provisional; enclaves that were heterotopic in one system can shift value and become normative in another, and vice versa. We will examine this phenomenon further in the next chapter.

Table 3.7 Urban Elements: Three Enclave Codes

Enclaves and Features	Urban Equipment	Examples (see also case studies)
E1 = Singular center: agora, forum, main square, or plaza *Steady state*: repetitive units; inside the city *Variations*: {]E1[} = compressed, inside city; castle/cathedral/palace; –E1– = stretched on edge of city; parade grounds, palace parks, fairgrounds	Boundaries, gates, fountains, temples, markets *Normative*: main square	E1 = Pompeii A1 = main square, Beijing
E2 = Binary center: normal enclaves, specialized city squares; courtyards stretched outside the city or cut inside *Variations*: {]E2[} = compressed in city; –E2– = stretched outside city or cut in; {–E2–} = vertical enclave	*Compressed*: Department store/mall *Stretched*: Railway yards, docks, parks, green belts, atria	Printemps, Paris London Dock1900 New York Pocket Parks London City Council Plan 1947 Marriot, New York
E3 = Multiple center + m *Normative*: main square, Beijing E1 + media = E3 subcenters *Compressed and stretched*: skyscraper downtown,]E2[and –E2–; {–E2–} + m = E3 *Themed variations*:]E3[= multithemed, compressed inside enclave; –E3– = stretched scenographic enclaves, linear parks, etc.	Multilands *Themed*: enclave entertainment district, theme park, historic district, special district	Orlando, 2000 (New Urbanism): E1 + m = A3 E2 + m = A3 E3, {E3}, –E3–

Urban elements codes: x = normative; {x} = compressed ; –x– = stretched; {–x–} = stretched in city; m = media influence.

We have also seen that E3 enclaves form at a variety of scales in the Tele Città. At a micro scale, millions of private homes take on a new complexity of use and form novel linkages to global communication systems. Home, business, recreation, and utilities can be mixed in one unit and spread evenly across the landscape in the "scrambled egg" of the Tele Città system. And as noted earlier, there are many local varieties of these network cities beyond the American model, as in the Flemish diamond and the Veneto grids in Europe or the Latin-American, African, and Asian versions of the network city. In *Pet Architecture* (2001), Yoshiharu Tsukamoto Architectural Lab at the Tokyo Institute of Technology and Atelier Bow-Wow demonstrate how this hybrid "micro-urbanism" has the power to colonize even the smallest, leftover sites in the city.

Left *Foster and Partners: View to the National Gallery, Trafalgar Square, London, 2004*
Right *Political rally in Trafalgar Square, London, 2004*

Networks of E3 micro-enclaves act as reservoirs and support systems for those great global centers (e.g., Mexico City, Tokyo, southeast England, London, Belgium, Holland, Los Angeles, or the northeast corridor in the US), whose scale and density are unprecedented in history. In *Made in Tokyo* (2001), Momoyo Kaijima, Junzo Kuroda, and Yoshiharu Tsukamoto further illustrate how pervasive the hybrid mixing of programs has become in the middle range of urban projects in Asia, especially when these are connected with new transportation systems (e.g., railways and highways). In the case of Tokyo, these hybrid building elements serve to form macro-enclaves, new subcenters planned inside the great global center based on railways. In fact, this is a familiar story, as we saw in the case of Tokyo and its 1964 subcenters plan and in Houston, with the "nonplan" evolution of the Galleria as the "new downtown" for automobiles.

Many enclaves in the various network cities function as network nodes and markers, including a new or rehabilitated public space that symbolizes that sector of the network and so gives a sense of place to the surrounding environs. For example, the old core of Venice with its canals, drawing 12 million tourists annually, functions as a symbolic core for the surrounding population of 1.5 million in the Po delta, a network city surrounding the old port. Old Amsterdam functions in a similar way for its sector of the Dutch ring city (Randstadt). Piazza San Marco in Venice or the Dam (central square) in Amsterdam take on a new life under these circumstances. Following Barcelona's lead for the 1982 Olympics, European cities have intervened to recondition and rehabilitate their central squares as new public life-worlds, living rooms where individuals can be made comfortable. Previously, individuals had been merged into the mass for formal political demonstrations or protest rallies, military or state-controlled parades in the Cine Città; now they are herded together to enjoy the spectacular repackaging of their cultural heritage as historically themed places where they can (ultimately) spend money. Jan Gehl and Lars Gemzøe, in *New City Spaces* (2001), provide an excellent survey of these new public spaces which recondition the central areas of the European city for individual use, leisure and pleasure, tourism, shopping, eating, drinking, and walking without the worry, noise, and fumes of cars.[77] They describe nine different approaches to the creation of such spaces in nine different European cities and give case studies of

39 streets and squares, mainly from Europe but also including examples from Melbourne, Australia; Tsukuba, Japan; and Riyadh, Saudi Arabia.

The result of this paradigm shift has been a general move to limit automobile access to such symbolic enclaves and to make them comfortable for old people, children, women, and minorities (including immigrants) not previously counted as part of the "public." While retaining their symbolic function for political protests organized from the bottom up (e.g., the huge anti-Iraq war demonstration in London's Hyde Park in 2003), these public spaces have also taken on a new, small-scale humanity. Foster's scheme for pedestrianizing Trafalgar Square in London (2002), for instance, diverted traffic and provided a café and public toilets, as well as a grand set of stairs on the north side that face south (perfect for sitting in the sun) and lead up to the terrace in front of the National Gallery.[78] In Lyons, the rehabilitation of the central squares of the city (e.g., Place des Terreaux, 1994) included elaborate schemes for lighting the squares and fountains at night, giving the center a new lease of life in the cool summer evenings.[79] In Copenhagen, cafés and café tables have invaded pedestrianized squares (e.g., Sankt Hans Torv Square, 1995) so that they become like Italian piazzas in the summer.[80] In America, street markets and farmers' markets have been introduced to revive central areas under the auspices of the New-York-based Project for Public Spaces.[81] The Green Market in Union Square, New York, for instance, is a great attractor, with high-quality produce brought to the market by local farmers. Traditionally, this square had also been a place of public demonstrations—there was a long peace vigil here and many spontaneous shrines on the south end of the square after the terrorist 11 September, 2001 attacks on the World Trade Center—but this political-enclave role has now shifted to nearby Washington Square in the Village, away from the city's major traffic arteries.[82]

The switch from single-cell enclaves to binary enclaves and then to polycentric E3 constellations of new public enclaves requires hybrid heterotopias as shifter elements to make such transitions possible. Many enclaves begin as heterotopic H2 or H3 experiments, where novel combinations of elements are tried, and then, if successful, become normative enclaves. Lynch built such experimental spaces into his vision of a "place utopia" in *Good City*

Far left *The terrorist attack on the World Trade Center, New York, September 2001*
Left *Clouds from collapse of the World Trade Center, New York September 2001*
Right *Peace rally, Union Square, New York, September 2001*

Enclaves

Campo, main square, Siena, Italy:
a) *Plan and section (courtesy of University of Toronto)*
b) *Campo (photo courtesy of Professor S Milovanovic-Bertram, University of Texas)*

Place des Vosges, Paris:
c) *Plan and section (courtesy of University of Toronto)*
d 1) *Panorama of gardens, 2004*
d 2) *View of arcades, 2004*
d 3) *View of house facades, 2004*

Bedford Square, London:
e) *Plan (courtesy of University of Toronto)*
f) *View of square, 2004*

Rockefeller Center, New York:
g) *Plan and section (courtesy of University of Toronto)*
h) *Plaza with ice skating, Christmas 2004*

a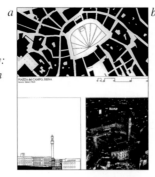

b

c

d 1

d 2

d 3

e

f

g

h

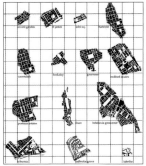

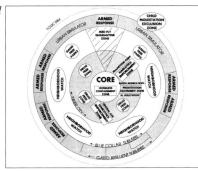

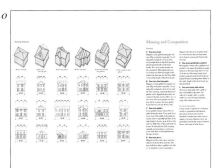

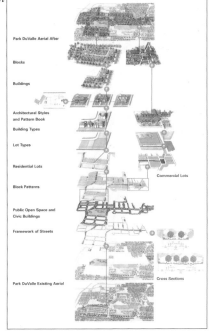

Armatures

i) *David Grahame Shane: analysis of great estates and street improvements, London, 1971*

j) *Shane: scale-jump over 250 years, great estates, London, 1971*

k 1) *Ebenezer Howard:* Garden Cities *diagram, 1897*

k 2) *Robert Park and Ernest Burgess, Chicago enclaves and ecology diagram, 1923*

k 3) *Aerial view of Sun City, AZ*

k 4) *Postwar tract-housing "pod', Long Island, NY, 1950s*

l) *Mike Davis: "The Ecology of Fear," paranoia-enclave diagram, 1998*

m) *Urban Design Associates: urban assembly kit drawing, ca. 2003*

n) *Urban Design Associates:* Liberty Pattern Book, *ca. 2003*

o) *Urban Design Associates:* Liberty Pattern Book, *ca. 2003*

Giorgio Vasari: Uffizi, Florence 1565, (view to the north), 2004

Kevin Lynch: City of Faith armature diagram A Theory of Good City Form *1981*

David Grahame Shane: Armature diagram

Form.[83] In a complementary process, disused enclaves from the Archi Città and Cine Città have come to life again in the Tele Città as heterotopic elements. As a result, the self-organizing patterns of the Tele Città often appear chaotic from the perspective of earlier systems. In the next section we will examine the role of armatures in relationship to enclaves and to each other; in the next chapter we will review the third urban element, the heterotopia.

3.3 *ARMATURE*: A PRELIMINARY DEFINITION

We do not normally speak of cities in terms of "armatures." Yet every village main street, downtown shopping street, suburban "miracle mile," or mall works as an armature. These linear urban assemblages bring people together in an axial space to form relationships, to make commercial transactions, be entertained, or to take part in ceremonial or casual communal activities. In the case of either a main street or a mall, despite their obvious differences, the basically *linear* arrangement of the armature defines a space of flow and of sequential experience. Gibberd's "space body" drawing, cited earlier, depicted the void component of the great example of this sort of axis at Nancy, France. These normative armatures act as containers for the activities and spatial practices of urban actors on foot.

The basic linear, urban armature links the sub-elements of the city, its urban magnets or attractors; these may be cathedrals, department stores, city halls, markets, theaters, or multiplex cinema complexes, or indeed anything or anybody that draws people to a particular site or place.

The account of the street armature that follows is based on the normal and classical description of the history of the European street, but develops certain features of this history in order to relate the armature to Lynch's three models. The scenographic history of the street armature has been well presented many times, as for instance by Siegfried Giedion in *Space, Time and Architecture* (1941) or by A. E. J. Morris in *History of Urban Form* (1972). It is briefly mentioned here to round out our picture of the armature; readers are referred to these authors for a fuller treatment.

A classical history of the armature would begin with the unsuccessful attempts of Brunelleschi to build a perspectival street in Florence (despite his initiation of the Piazza della S. S. Annunziata north of the Duomo in 1421) and proceed to Bramante's success in Rome, followed by Michelangelo's Via Pia on the Quirinale (already mentioned in our discussion of the stretching of the armature in the baroque), ending the Renaissance history with the Uffizi (begun in 1566) which compressed all these lessons into one state-based formula at the command of the Prince. It would trace the migration of this concept or model north via Nancy and Paris in France to Holland (where canals and brick buildings were introduced) and to Britain (e.g., Covent Garden). The transformation of the Uffizi armature into Napoleon's Rue de Rivoli (1807) and the military parade streets of the nineteenth-century European nation-states (e.g., Unter den Linden in Berlin, the Mall in London, the Champs Elysées in Paris) is part both of the history of the stretching of the armature and of the scenographic history of the European street. These state streets became the great boulevards of Haussmann's Paris and of the Ring Strasse installations of the German Rationalist planners in the 1850s and 1860s, filled with trees and cafés.

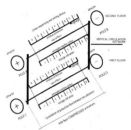

Armatures are linear systems for sorting sub-elements in the city and arranging them in sequence (actual house or lot numbers were only added with the advent of to-the-door postal service in the nineteenth century); each armature forms a recognizable topological module aligned between distinctive poles. Urban actors have used systems of armatures in recurring, fractal-like patterns for organizing urban flow spaces from Roman colonies to Viking settlements, from medieval towns to modern malls.

David Grahame Shane: compressed-armature diagram (mall)

Extending the notation outlined earlier, I highlight three different armature patterns in the three city models, namely, A1, A2, and A3. A1 is the 600-foot (200-meter), normative Archi Città pedestrian armature; A2, which develops in the Cine Città, takes two forms, reflecting the binary nature of the industrial system with its split between production and consumption, stasis and flow. Armatures are either *compressed*, and their sorting capacity increased, by high-rise density (e.g., in arcades), or they are *stretched* by new transportation or communication technologies, giving rise to the linear city (as in Ivan Leonidov's design for Magnitogorsk, 1930). What I term the "compression" of the glass-enclosed shopping mall or skyscraper (a *vertical* A2) increases the organizational capacity of the armature by expanding its structure to multiple levels, intensifying its power by upping its density. In contrast, the strip or stretched armature (–A2–) may be a mile or a mile and a half long, as in the "miracle mile" of so many suburban shopping strips or the archetypal Las Vegas Strip. Stretching increases the power of the armature to act as a linear sorting device by adapting it to the scale of the car and driver. Modern communications systems also enlarge the "attractor basin" of the merchants on the strip in scale with the range of the automobile.

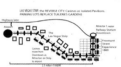

Shane: stretched-armature diagram (Las Vegas Strip)

Armatures of the third type, hybrid A3 armatures, are distinguished by their visual imagery, which registers itself in the multicentered mediascape of the city. I have already remarked on the power of attraction exercised in some enclaves by the scenography of the A3 armature, as in theme parks, festival markets, New Urbanist developments, and megamalls (e.g., the Galleria in Houston or the remodeled casinos of the Las Vegas Strip of the 1990s). Thanks to Gruen and Maitland, we can see that the traditional, normative, 600-foot A1 armature has survived as an organizing device into the twentieth century in the mall formula of the reverse city, where it is adapted to the utilitarian E2 mall and the scenographic E3 theme park.

Barry Maitland: 600-foot armature modules in city plans, Shopping Mall Planning and Design, *1985*

Webster's defines an *armature* as "a framework used by a sculptor to support a figure being modeled in a plastic material; a framework." Modernist sculptors

Alberto Giacometti:
Wheeled Figure,
sculptural armature
(Kunsthaus, Zurich)

such as Giacometti sometimes reveal the armature supporting a figure, or even reverse the classical code by shaping the armature to *be* a figure; in either case, the sculptural armature is a strong, skeletal structure or network composed of basically linear elements and supporting a larger, figural representation. It has its own geometry and strength, which both lend support to and receive it from the figural element. The "body" of the city can thus be imagined as possessing an armature or framework that supports it. Lynch stressed *conceptual* armatures, those shared, communal, organizational, mental structures by which the city's inhabitants map it and its paths.

In classical cities, streets often formed the key armatures. For example, an orderly street architecture of repetitive elements formed armatures along the sides of Greek public spaces. The 600-foot armature of the stoa form defined the uphill side of the irregular, sloping agora in Athens, a place of business and assembly that also doubled as the grandstand for the sacred running track of the stade on the downhill side (also about 600 feet long), bringing order to the space. Koetter and Rowe mention the stade as an example of a "potentially infinite urban set piece"; here, Athenian athletes competed to enter the Olympics. The Olympic stadium also included a 600-foot track dimension (giving rise to the 200-meter track event of the modern Olympics).

The A1 armature and running track were also deemed necessary urban equipment for Greek colonial settlements. Planned Greek colonial foundations that were laid out on a grid, like Miletus, also included this 600-foot dimension. In Miletus, the stoa on the agora was a little shorter, while a wide public street leading down to the port was, once again, about 600 feet long.[84] By a coincidence, the 600-foot armature reappears in the highly irregular Roman Forum, stretching as a processional way from the orators' platform in front of the temple of Concord at the foot of the Capitoline Hill to the basilica of Constantine and temple of Venus. The temple of Venus stood beside the arch of Titus, the triumphal arch at the end of the Via Sacra ("sacred way") leading around the Palatine Hill to the Tiber.[85]

In his seminal study of the armature in the later Roman Empire, William MacDonald cites as his inspiration the work of the German Rationalist Robert Krier in the 1970s.[86] Krier's insight into the traditional street as the organizing idea of the European city caused MacDonald to realize that a similar organizing device, with a 600-foot module, had been used throughout the Roman Empire from North Africa to Germany, from Spain to Syria, and around the Mediterranean trading basin. MacDonald gives the canonical definition of an A1 urban armature in his writings on the urban practices of the late Roman Empire: Roman towns were organized around a linear, elastic armature that tied all the disparate urban sub-elements (market, temple, theater, etc.) together into an identifiable image or urban signature. "Armatures," MacDonald writes, "consist of main streets, squares, and essential public buildings linked together across cities and towns from gate to gate, with junctions and entranceways predominantly articulated."[87]

The armature acts as a linear sorting device, sequencing urban sub-elements along its length. The position of sub-elements (e.g., temples or bath houses) along A1 armatures was different in each Roman city. Pictures of the urban skylines of Roman towns show institutional sequencing along the town's armatures, with large public buildings standing out above the lower, residential fabric. The image of the city was thus controlled by a simple, linear code that sequenced events along the main street. MacDonald describes how travelers would know which city they were approaching from the particular sequence of public buildings on the skyline, and how paintings would enshrine this sequence in a silhouette of the skyline.[88] Choay analogically describes such linear, sequential coding as *syntagmatic*, that is, produced by rules working on a neighbor-to-neighbor basis along the spatial sequence. (The word's original meaning is "pertaining to a relationship among linguistic elements that occur sequentially in the chain of speech or writing," Random House Unabridged Dictionary, 1987.)

Left *Rue de Rivoli, Paris, 1804, (view to the Place de la Concorde, 1990s)* **Right** *Rue de Rivoli, shopping arcades, 1990s*

MacDonald also emphasizes the flow of the A1 armature and "flight" of the eye in classical cities, echoing Gordon Cullen (see Chapter 2). MacDonald shows how, in the case of the ancient city of Palmyra, the architecture of the A1 armature—arcades, gateways and midpoint markers—played an important part in the mechanics of urban sequence. This Roman town was built in the desert between two rival oasis settlements. Its central armature was divided into three sections of about 600 feet each, with the transitions between each segment marked by sub-elements: a portal, statuary in a circular junction, gates covering a hinge-like junction. A system of sub-elements along this "space body" axis articulated the structure of the town. Linear, colonnaded arcades were important to the architecture of this armature, creating continuity and giving shade. Fountains were also important, providing a local air-conditioning effect as well as a rich soundscape contrasting with the silence of the surrounding desert. These architectural environmental-conditioning devices, along with various imperial inscriptions (e.g., those engraved on the colonnades), marked the power of the empire and of trade in opposition to the dry heat of the desert.

MacDonald argues that the sequence of the A1 armature was elastic in Roman towns; urban sub-elements could be asymmetrically placed, irregular, and highly localized without destroying the overall pattern of the armature:

> [Armatures] pass unimpeded through their towns; vary in configuration and numbers of parts within the frame of an empire-wide conceptual order; are not derived overall from city planning, largely because they are emphatically three-dimensional; are composed of public structures only; are perceived as Roman chiefly because of an appropriate architecture; were formed gradually by addition and extension.[89]

William MacDonald: axonometric drawing of Palmyra armature, The Architecture of the Roman Empire 11, *1986*

Further, the design of the continuous arcade architecture of the Palmyra armature contextualized sub-element buildings, such as temples or bath houses, that might otherwise have been left as freestanding objects. The continuity of the sequence made the architecture of the armature a distinct linear space, structuring the fabric of the city. And as MacDonald also shows, A1 armatures could be extended incrementally with new linear additions. The classic Roman colonial settlement of Timgad in Algeria, for example, originally operated as a grid-town enclave organized around a dominant main-street armature; this was subsequently projected beyond the walls in two separate linear A1 extensions.

The perspectival axis (A1) at Palmyra must have been visually striking and perhaps, in an otherwise nonperspectival world, strange. The straight armature of the long colonnaded street captured the space in an axial system with a single vanishing point, yet the normative Roman representation of space in visual art, like the Chinese, employed a parallel system of perspective with no single vanishing point. In paintings, Romans showed the front of a building flat with one side reducing back to indicate depth, layering these structures to show relative distance. Pompeiian wall paintings show this system of perspective at work, as do the pictures of the trades that identified particular stores (bakery, goldsmith's, etc).[90]

Roman street Pompeii, (photograph courtesy of John Zheng)

In MacDonald's examples, the linear flow-space of the street armature becomes the image–space of the empire, impacting on the consciousness of all urban actors who pass through it. An A1 spatial schema was imprinted upon those actors by the force and language of the sub-elements expressing imperial power, that is, the arcades, commemorative columns, fountains, and temples that formed the architecture of this armature. Cities competed with each other for the most elaborate displays in such spaces. The image–space of the street was thus tied to the state apparatus of imperial power, establishing a clear link between the illusion-codes of the A1 armature and power, discipline, and authority in the city. "Disciplinary" concerns of the state dominated in the architecture of this design, imposing a public order on a "platform" supported by rules and regulations about public behavior, security, and police power.[91]

From the ruins of Palmyra we might imagine a cold, impersonal, imperial power at work, creating a cool armature amidst the heat of the desert. The ruins of Pompeii tell a different story: imperial street life as a riot of colors, with graffiti everywhere using pictograms and symbols to address illiterate slaves and agricultural workers. We also know from Pompeii's ruins the price of bread, the methods of weighing and working gold and silver, and the activities in the brothels and the bath houses on the armature. While Pompeii had its forum by the center of the old Etruscan foundation, it grew through the addition of A1 armatures surrounded by residential grids (first a small, slightly irregular grid, then a much larger, regular grid). The main-street armature of this last extension led from the historic center and theater district out to the new walls and gate, where a sports and bath complex served as a new urban attractor. Along this A1 armature were aligned shops, with side streets leading to houses. There were paved sidewalks for pedestrians, awnings for shade, wheeled vehicles moving along ruts worn in the stone roadbed, and rainwater draining down the center of the street. Drinking water was supplied to wealthy houses directly by underground pipes, to the general public by public fountains. There was an underground sewage system. While the sequence of the Roman armature was variable, the length of each visual segment was usually around 600 feet.[92]

Spiro Kostof: Diagrams showing the development from the Roman grid to medieval and Islamic city plans, The City Shaped, *1991*

The practice of organizing cities around a normative A1 armature was gradually transformed from the bottom up after the fall of the Roman Empire, as Spiro Kostof has documented in *The City Shaped* (1991). Urban actors in the Roman Empire valued the public, open spaces of the city—the forum, circuses, and sub-elements like gymnasium and theaters—as communal spaces of display and power. Later actors—Goths or Vikings, Arabs or Ottomans—filled in these public spaces, the architecture of which had no meaning for their social and spatial practices. This privatization of previous public spaces took many forms, varying with the new urban actors.[93]

Kostof also shows how the Roman A1 armature tradition was recombined in medieval Islamic societies with new sub-elements. Here the courtyard-house typology of the Romans survived, although the Roman street grid did not, the latter being replaced with a cul-de-sac system of courtyard houses working within the jurisprudence of the Koran. New street armatures emerged that followed contours, curving and flexing with the topography. Water lines and drainage were often associated with these armatures, which sometimes followed earlier agricultural irrigation patterns. These rhizomic armatures worked within a tree-like network hierarchy, with small private cul-de-sacs leading to small streets that gave in turn onto larger armatures fronted with a continuous architecture of small shops and traders' kiosks. In Europe, a similar cul-de-sac system also broke down the Roman grid blocks into private clan spaces, but with row houses as the basic housing morphology.[94]

Islamic souk or market armature, Stephano Bianca, Urban Form in the Islamic World, *2000*

In the Islamic world, the arched bays of store fronts created an architectural continuity, as the colonnade did in the Roman imperial armature. The architecture of this armature was extended into a roof of canvas or wood to give shade and protection from the weather. These armatures led to the great mosques, which were associated with great markets, the latter housed in covered

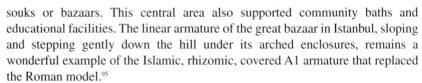

souks or bazaars. This central area also supported community baths and educational facilities. The linear armature of the great bazaar in Istanbul, sloping and stepping gently down the hill under its arched enclosures, remains a wonderful example of the Islamic, rhizomic, covered A1 armature that replaced the Roman model.[95]

Where Roman spatial practice in the colonies emphasized the public, imperial space of the armature, medieval European and Islamic streets emphasized the private and the local. The A1 armature still extended as an elastic element through the town plan, but its nature and quality changed radically. M. R. G. Conzens identified an armature based on a normative main-street or high-street structure as the basis of the "plan unit" in the medieval city. Later scholars linked the institution of the high street to Viking settlement patterns in Ireland and across Europe. In his exemplary study of the British castle town of Ludlow, Conzens showed how the establishment of the castle as a defensive enclave led to the planning of an armature as an approach street leading to its gate, Castle Street, which ended in Castle Square. This medieval A1 main-street armature, which in its initial form was approximately 600 feet long, recombined sub-elements such as town halls and market structures along its axial space, as well as a church hidden behind the houses lining one side of the main axis of approach to the castle.[96]

Terry R Slater: Village armature, plan of medieval Thame, England, from M R G Conzens "Starting Again," in Built Form of Western Cities, *1990*

Conzens found that six armature-based units, in addition to the Castle Street armature, formed the city in increments. There were also two plan-unit developments of small side-street grids at right angles to Castle Street. These side streets conformed to the 600-foot module, establishing long, thin blocks at right angles to the main street. The topography of the sloping site then began to restrict development in this area; more-irregular plan units later filled in the hillside below the castle. Where Castle Street met other streets to form a crossroads and cattle market (the Bull Ring), a "market colonization" area developed. Each later street extended about 300 feet out from the road junction.

In the medieval period, the new urban actors organized their sub-elements (churches, mosques, castles, ports, markets) around village main-street armatures. These armatures cut across old Roman grids where necessary, connecting the new attractors. The town of Trier, Germany, illustrates this reorientation clearly, with a diagonal path connecting new cathedral shrines and markets across the ruined Roman city. These new networks of village main streets developed their own specializations. In *La Rue au Moyen Age* (1984), Jean-Pierre Leguay describes how specialized street armatures developed in medieval cities for the production of shoes, clothes, gold, and silver, as well as for specialized markets for meat, fish, and other goods. On these streets production took place within the merchant's or craftsman's row house, using apprentices as labor, often in houses like those portrayed by Serlio in his Comic scene.

Hampstead high street, London, looking south from Heath, 2004

In Europe, merchants built their row houses and shops in the public spaces of the old markets and forums. These structures stepped out over the street to provide protection from the elements. An open sewer ran along the center of the street, and water was drawn from wells or pumps in the street. Signs proliferated and store-fronts folded down to provide a counter space. At night their closure presented a hard, uninviting face to the night watchmen who patrolled the city—and to potential thieves.[97]

Choay stressed that these medieval village main streets were syntagmatic, that is, did not form around grand, geometric vistas; they were formed, rather, by local considerations, as neighbors set up businesses and homes in reaction to each other along the axis of the street. There was no sense of the overall perspective of the street, as in Roman armature design. Each house and store was articulated in relation to its neighbors in a private world of relationships and small-scale property negotiations. These medieval A1 armatures did not provide formal perspective vistas in what Kostof has called the "grand manner" of the classical scenographic tradition, even if they did frame their termini (the attractors at each end of the street axis).

This chaotic, picturesque, pedestrian-oriented, 600-foot armature system, eventually portrayed by Serlio in his Comic scene, did not disappear with the Renaissance or the Enlightenment but continued into the Industrial Revolution and modern city as the dynamic, local "high street" of the village or neighborhood. Normative 600-foot village main streets survive in the centers of great metropolitan constellations such as London, New York, and San Francisco. Using metropolitan London as a test case, it is possible to argue that the dictionary definition of the city as a hierarchical network was structured around a hierarchy of village main-street A1 armatures, whether legacies from earlier villages, impromptu suburban expansions, or purpose-built. In north London, for instance, Hampstead and Kentish Town high streets were once local village high streets. These were transformed in the industrial revolution into A2 armatures in a metropolitan network. Camden Town high street, because of its location at a hub of roads and railway junctions serving north London, took on a regional role, yet has always been more local than the self-proclaimed "high street of London," Victorian Oxford Street, with its compressed A2 armatures, vertical shopping arcades and department stores like Selfridges or John Lewis.[98]

Each A2 armature has its place in the network of distribution and consumption in the city. At the head of this high street hierarchy in London sits Regent Street, mentioned in our earlier discussion of the scenographic street. This planned street armature was proclaimed the "shopping street of Europe" in the early 1800s, making it Europe's high street for middle-class consumption and display. Both Oxford and Regent Streets are made up of several 600-foot segments, creating an extended network serving regional needs. The much smaller 600-foot-long Upper Bond Street had served the niche market of the superwealthy for a century by 1800, making it and the Burlington Arcade perhaps the pinnacle of this plan-unit armature and of the village-street hierarchy in London. Similar hierarchical networks of village main-street armatures can be

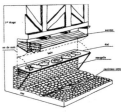

Medieval street architecture and section, Normandy, France, Jean-Pierre Leguay, La Rue au Moyen Age, *1984*

Medieval street overhangs, Venice 2004

Throgmorton Street, London, ca. 1900

found in other European cities or in American cities, such as New York or Boston, that grew to incorporate outlying settlements. The fashionable Rue St. Honore is a striking specimen in western Paris. Fifth Avenue in New York is the most obvious American example, at the top of an urban hierarchy contained in a grid. Every American city once had its Main Street in its downtown shopping district, with its heterotopic department stores as an attractors.[99]

Our London example also demonstrates how these 600-foot, village main-street pedestrian A1 armatures were adapted to the specialized functions of the Industrial Revolution and to its split between production and consumption. At the heart of the British imperial and capitalist system lay the City of London, a separate administrative and judicial enclave embedded within greater London and exempt from many taxes and regulations applied elsewhere. At the core of the City, once a Roman grid, lay Threadneedle Street, a tiny, diagonal, medieval village street that became home to the bankers who ran the British Empire and emerging global economy around 1900. This 30-foot-wide village-street armature formed the basis of a highly compressed and interconnected financial community where all the main actors would know each other personally, possibly meeting in the street on their business. Indeed, the London stock market began in the 1700s as a curbside street activity under a tree, before moving into a coffee house and then into a hall in a neighboring block. Much the same story might be told of the New York stock exchange, starting on the curb under a tree in the small Dutch village-street of Broad Street at the junction of Wall Street in New York, or of the Tokyo exchange, which originated in the narrow streets of the purpose-built Maranouchi neighborhood in Tokyo. Around these "village" street armatures gathered the banks, stock exchanges, insurance markets, and other financial and control functions of the great capitalist enterprises, establishing a distinct, compressed armature (]A2[) as a milieu or node for urban actors at the heart of a global financial network.[100]

Compressed, village-street-like armatures also formed the basis for high-density places of consumption in wealthy London and Paris in the 1780s and 1790s. These glass-covered, interior-street armatures cut through the land-ownership of the city block, creating their own, private, safe, sheltered, village-street-like shopping environments. Known as *arcades* in London (e.g., the Burlington Arcade), *passages* in Paris, *passagen* in Berlin, and *gallerias* in Italy, they came to symbolize modernity across Europe. J. F. Geist's exemplary study of this typology, *Arcades* (1983), traces the dissemination of this new urban sub-element across the globe. Geist elaborates on the section and architecture of these intense armatures, with their vast shows of cast iron and plate glass derived from Paxton's Crystal Palace (1851). In "Paris: Capital of the Nineteenth Century" (1935), Walter Benjamin saw these compressed armatures (]A2[) as part of the emergence of a new global trading system, with its new patterns of consumption, marketing, and advertising (including the mechanical reproduction of works of art), creating a new, inauthentic, urban world best seen on display in the armatures of the city. (He borrowed this idea from André Breton of the Surrealists, particularly his description of the Passage de l'Opera just before its demolition in his *Paris Peasant*, 1926).[101]

Industrial production could also be compressed along street-like A2 armatures in specialized, high-density buildings in the city. The high cost of machinery and power plants encouraged industry, once past its domestic, village-scale stage of development, to concentrate in multistory factory enclaves. The economy of sharing specialized services encouraged further agglomeration in specific industrial districts, like the now-fashionable SoHo area, with its cast-iron facades, in New York. Manchester, Birmingham, London, New York, Hong Kong, and many other industrial centers developed compressed, multistory factory districts, like the "garment district" in New York. Henry Ford's application of the linear logic of industrial production to production itself created the assembly line, further hastening the concentration of industry in compressed, multistory "daylight" factories (exemplified by Albert Kahn's design of Ford's Highland Park Plant, 1909, which Le Corbusier shows in *Towards a New Architecture*, 1927).[102]

Albert Kahn; Ford Highland Park plant, Detroit, MI, 1909

Cerdá's Rationalist studies of the industrial city had not predicted the apparently anachronistic revival of]A2[compressed armatures as centers for command and control of the economy, specialized manufacturing, and consumption. He concentrated on the logic of flows in industrialized societies and the necessity of the *stretched* street armature (–A2–) for communications and transportation, accurately describing the logic of the elaboration of the stretched –A2– armature in section and the amplification of its width that took place in Paris under Haussmann and Alphand in the 1850s. Water-supply and waste-disposal systems were incorporated in this section. The water supply could also be used by the fire department to fight fires and the sanitation

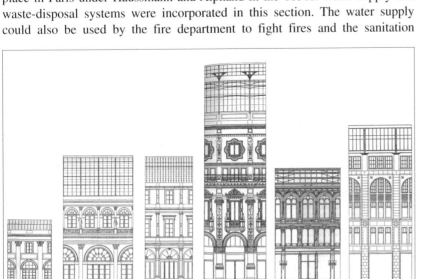

J FGeist: elevations from arcades, illustrating scale-jump over 50 years, Arcades, 1983

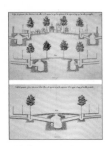

Ildefons Cerdá: sectional study of avenues, 1855

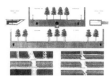

Adolphe Alphand: plan and section of Parisian boulevard, 1870

Louis Sullivan: study of set-back system for Chicago skyscrapers, 1890

department to clean the streets. In addition, water could support gardening and protect trees in times of drought. Cerdá also showed gas-supply lines for cooking, heating, and lighting and telegraph and telephone lines in the street section. By 1900, designers had added electric subways to this section, as in the Aldwych–Kingsway line, London (begun 1904).[103]

Cerdá segregated traffic by function and speed in his A2 armature, the fastest lanes being reserved for the bourgeoisie in their carriages, with wagons and freight in the slow lanes. Separate side roads serviced the housing along the main streets, and in the most elaborate of his street sections he provided pedestrian promenades in park-like settings. These stretched, multilane, –A2– armatures grew to be over 200 feet wide (e.g., in Paris, where Haussman widened the existing Champs Elysées to 230 feet from 116–135 feet and created the 400-foot-wide Avenue Foch, originally Avenue de Bois de Boulogne, in 1854). Olmsted applied the same logic in parkway systems such as Ocean Parkway (1870–72) in Brooklyn, stretching many miles down to the sea with its park-like settings in wide median strips.[104]

Later Rationalists continued the development of this sectional analysis of the stretched –A2– armature, compressing the section into narrower widths and loading it with new transportation and communication systems, increasing its capacity. Eugène Hénard, Haussmann's successor as city planner for Paris, in 1910 analyzed the history of the Parisian boulevard, showing the armature of the past, present, and future. The future boulevard included long-distance railways sunk deep in the street section, with local systems above that linked into building sub-basement to get trash and deliver coal. Above this was the street surface, with glass-covered sidewalks and streetcars running down the center of the street. Gas lamps illuminated the street at night and buildings with conservatories and gardens on their roofs rose to 10 or 12 stories along the street walls. Airplanes landed on the roofs and came down by elevator to street level or to be garaged in the basement. Cars used the same elevator and garage system. Besides gas, water, electricity, telephone, and telegraph channels in the street section, salt water was provided for air-conditioning and oxygen for rooftop recovery chambers filled with plants designed to counteract the stress and polluted air of the future, industrial city.[105]

The rational study of the street armature in section led to extreme hypotheses of hyperdense street armatures. As early as 1890, Louis Sullivan in Chicago proposed a system of set-backs to allow light into the street between skyscrapers.[106] King's view of New York as a hypermodern metropolis with deep canyon streets between skyscrapers was popular before the First World War.[107] The 1916 New York zoning code provided for set-backs as envisioned by Sullivan, but based on the Parisian system of controlling the set-backs in relation to the street width to allow light and air into hyperdense streets.[108] The tiny colored drawings of Italian Futurist Antonio Sant'Elia (1910s) explored the dream of a superdense, multilevel –A2– street armature with rooftop airports and

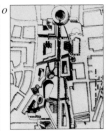

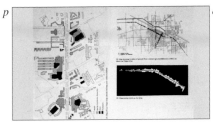

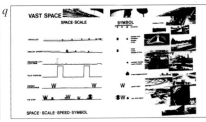

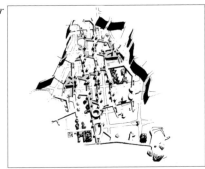

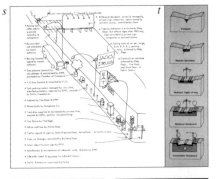

Armatures

l) *Proposal for railway viaduct over Thames*
m) *Le Corbusier: detail of highways,* City for Three Million, *1922,*
n) *View of Stalin Allee, East Berlin, 1972*
o) *Robert Krier: Stuttgart street plan, 1976*
p, q) *Venturi et alia: analysis of the strip and open space (*Learning from Las Vegas *1972)*
r) *Smithsons: Berlin plan with "finger buildings," 1958*
s) *Kevin Lynch: Micro-urban devices for street control*
t) *Doug Suissman: Los Angeles boulevard evolution ca. 1989*
u 1, 2) *Middle levels of escalators, Hong Kong*
v) *Venetian canal under repair, 2003*
w) *Bernard Tschumi: bridge building, Lausanne*

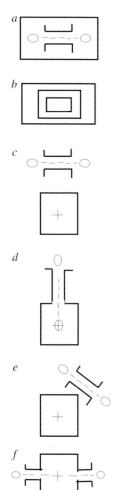

a

b

c

d

e

f

Armature and enclave
combinations:
a) *Armature in
enclave*
b) *Nested enclaves*
c) *Armature outside
enclave*
d) *Axial alignment,
armature–enclave*
e) *Armature bypasses
enclave*
f) *Armature bisects
enclave*

Armatures served to differentiate Roman cities and to organize the productive flows of the industrial and port cities of Europe in their hour of triumph; recently they have acquired a secondary role as linear structures carrying scenographic images in privileged enclaves (malls, artfully designed neighborhoods, etc.). These images, in their turn, provide essential orientation in the postmodern city of multiple centers, each identified by images carried in the media. In the next section, before moving on to our last urban element, the heterotopia, in the next chapter, we will briefly examine how urban actors have built normative urban models using various combinations of enclaves and armatures.

3.4 ARMATURE AND ENCLAVE COMBINATIONS IN NORMATIVE CITY MODELS

Urban actors have combined armatures and enclaves to make various models of the city. In Chapter 1 we examined the conceptual worlds inhabited by various classes of actors: the warrior-priests of the Archi Città, the engineer-bankers of the Cine Città, and the eco-citizens of the Tele Città. We associated each Città with one of Krugman's self-organizing economic models: a single center in the agrarian economy, two or a few satellite cities in the industrial economy, and a large number of edge-cities in the informational economy. Each dominant actor has their preferred model, and each model implies a chosen ranking and combination of urban elements and sub-elements. The two sections above have outlined the organization of sub-elements around self-centering and linear organizational patterns; I will concentrate further on the combination of these two patterns in this section, before going on, in the next chapter, to study the role of heterotopias in stabilizing and transforming the dominant models proposed by Lynch.

The enclave dominates as the organizing principle of the Archi Città, with its single center and agrarian economy operating as described in Von Thünen's Central Place theory. In this model, an E1 main square dominates the layout of the town with a hierarchy of smaller squares supporting its role as a central meeting place (as mandated in the Spanish colonies by the Law of the Indies). The governor's palace, prison, cathedral, and courts gather around this square, and merchants' houses and the market locate there. This "central place" nests inside a hierarchy of other enclaves (e.g., the Forbidden City of ancient Beijing), creating a patch of order, a rigid urban pattern and formal arrangement that can easily be enforced by urban actors.

Within this formal arrangement, the dominant actors' emphasis on stasis, hierarchy, and a single center means that A1 armatures often serve as subservient axes of approach to the holy enclaves of the Archi Città. These axial armatures gain their importance from their connection to the dominant center of power. They lead flows to the dominant center. These axes may be irregular or curved, as in the medieval Islamic or European cities. They can be located inside an enclave or city, leading to the central square, or outside, leading to a gate or port.

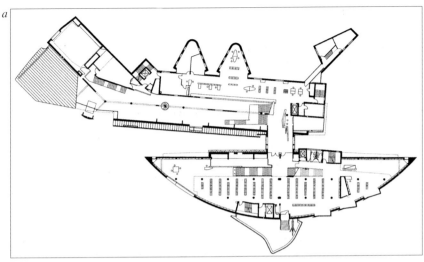

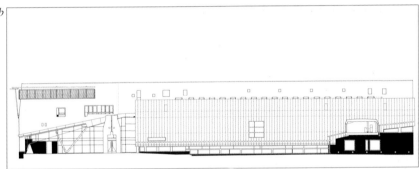

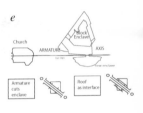

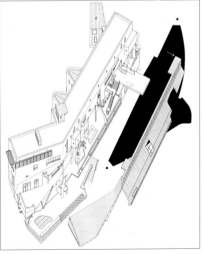

Bolles+Wilson:
Münster Library,
1993
a) *Plan*
b) *Elevation*
c) *View down street*
d) *Axonometric*
e) *Diagram of site-*
plan analysis

Table 3.9 Three Normative Models with Recombinations of Urban Elements

City Type and Features	Urban Equipment	Examples/Elements
Archi Città= E/A + H. Enclaves dominate armatures, system must have heterotopic space. *Nesting enclaves*: E1 = singular center: agora, forum, main square, or plaza *Steady state*: repetitive units; inside the city *Variations*: {]E1[} = compressed, inside city; castle/cathedral/palace; –E1– = stretched on edge of city; parade grounds, palace parks, fairgrounds *Armatures approach to enclave from outside*: A1 = singular or imperial main street armature connecting two oases *Steady state*: repetitive units *Armature approach from inside enclave*: inside the city; 600 feet (200 m) long. *Variations*: {A1} = compressed in city; –A1– = stretched on edge of city *Armatures connecting enclaves*	Main square, walls, gates, temples, markets Main street, arcades, gates, fountains, temples, markets High street, single streets	E1 = Pompeii A1 = main square, Beijing A1 = Palmyra A1 = main Street London Covent Garden area Timgad/Ludlow
Cine Città = A/E + H. Armature dominates system. *Stretched armatures connect enclaves in system/grid*: –A2– *Compressed armatures inside enclaves*: {A2} *Stretched armatures forming fingers of growth*: –A2– *Stretched armatures cutting through enclaves*: {–A2–} *Stretched armatures bypassing enclaves*: –A2– *Stretched armatures direct-linking enclaves*: –A2– *Enclaves blocking stretched armatures*	Highway grid Arcades, malls Railway/highway/strip Railway, boulevard, highway	Machine city, LA Paris, Houston Copenhagen plan Paris, South Bronx Regent Street Soho, London Upper West Side, New York London/Tokyo
Tele Città = H/A + E. Heterotopias dominate system; see Ch. 4. *Compressed armature/enclave*: Multiple + m = A3, a 600-foot scenographic armature *Compressed enclave/armature*: house + m = E3; housing + A1 + m = A3/E3 *Compressed and stretched*: skyscraper downtown, A2 + E2 + A3 + m = A3/E3 *Themed variations*: {A3} = themed, compressed inside enclave E *Rhizomic/pictographic routes*: –A3–= scenographic route outside or between E3 enclaves	Themed space/ district Gated enclosure/ historic district Entertainment District/ Business Improvement District Themed armature Themed street armature	Orlando 2000 New urbanism Times Square New York Main Street Disneyland Disney World highway

Urban elements codes: x = normative; {x} = compressed ; –x– = stretched; {–x–} = stretched in city; m = media influence code of the surrounding urban fabric so that it was completely open, transparent, and absorbent, a tabula rasa, empty landscape or parkland capable of holding the city elements in specialized building typologies at a new, enormous scale, like that of the ocean liner. In Table 3.9 I give the formula for the Cine Città as A (armature) dominating E (enclave), A/E, with H (heterotopia) serving in a subservient position. Thus, the Cine Città = A/E + H.

Although we have not yet examined the heterotopia in detail, it is so essential to an understanding of the Tele Città that I include the Tele Città in Table 3.9 for completeness. I have already noted the prevalence in the Tele Città of heterotopic functions in the basic housing cell (which often serves simultaneously as home, office, entertainment center, gym, and garden center) and have argued for the heterotopic, adaptive reuse of preexisting city elements (e.g., A1 armatures or E1 enclaves) as A3 or E3 image assemblages. Koetter and Rowe's "great street" armatures and "stabilizer" enclaves thus become part of the Tele Città's stock of illusory images. Actors can then use these assemblages as part of their mental mapping of the city.

I would like to end by reviewing briefly an important combinatorial tradition that is central to the history of urbanism and treats the bricolage of armatures and enclaves within a local patch of order or urban fragment. This combinatorial tradition of street and square can be traced from the Archi Città through the Cine Città and on to the Tele Città as a clear example of the catalytic role of urban actors and the transformations they have achieved. (I mentioned this combinatorial history of axial armature and central square earlier in this chapter, referring readers to Paul Zucker's *Town and Square*, A. E. J. Morris's *History of Urban Form*, and Edmund Bacon's *The Design of Cities*.) Such axial street-and-square arrangements are exemplified in the City of Faith model by the plazas located before temples in Aztec towns or by the long, central avenue leading to the Forbidden City in Beijing. In the Italian Renaissance, they occur also in Brunelleschi's scheme for the area to the north of the Florence cathedral and in Michelango's stretched and distorted armature in his approach stair to the Capitoline Hill (1537) and the hilltop plaza (with the new town hall and illusionistic paving in the form of a dome) in Rome. Inigo Jones employed the same axial armature approach and enclave layout for his plan of Covent Garden in London in 1632.

The axial approach street combined with a closed square reappeared in the Cine Città as a typical solution for the plaza before a large monumental or governmental building, as well as the preferred solution for the meeting of the old city with the railway station, as in countless European towns (e.g., the Milan or Helsinki central stations). There were several projects to make terminal squares in New York in the early 1900s prior to the construction of Grand Central station, with its internal atrium. Grand Central was envisioned with a skyscraper as a vertical marker and further vertical emphasis at the end of Park Avenue. Eliel Saarinen made a plan for Chicago's Grant Park in 1922 that envisioned a sunken highway and boulevard terminating in a skyscraper over a central station east of the Loop, with a giant plaza in front surrounded by museums and cultural institutions. Le Corbusier's *City for Three Million* of the same date had the same basic schema of approach street and central station capped by skyscrapers.[137] This tradition extended from the Beaux Arts into Art Deco design, as in the axial arrangement of the RCA Building in Rockefeller Center at the end of the pedestrian approach street and sunken square with unenclosed ice-skating rink.

This axial combination of public square enclave and approach armature has survived (albeit vestigially) in the Tele Città in the arrangements of postmodern malls and in the placement of towers on squares at the ends of approach axes. There is a disconnection, however, between the distant tower and the space at its base, as with Johnson and Burgee's Transco Tower (1983), attached to the Galleria mall in Houston, whose rotating spotlight acts as a giant, solitary beacon at night that can be seen from the highway and from the airport across town. The fountain at the side of the tower functions much like the skating rink at the Rockefeller Center (approached by car, in this case) and is a favorite place for wedding photos. Foster's Shanghai Bank Tower (1986) in Hong Kong commands the main square and its approach by water from Kowloon in a more traditional way, although much of the movement around the ferry terminal is underground or in sheds.

This disconnection of the armature-and-enclave combination from the surrounding urban fabric in the postmodern city has allowed urban actors to reformulate the street and square as a new form of layered, urban bricolage within the mall. I have already described the role of scenographic armatures and enclaves as powerful attractors inside enclaves in the Tele Città, as in megamalls, theme parks, gated communities, and New Urbanist schemes. I have also noted the prevalence of armature-and-enclave combinations as urban fragments in the great tourist-attractor enclaves such as Disney World, with their proliferation of subcenters. Armatures and enclaves as scenographic attractors become the mixing places of the Tele Città, deliberately designed to mix people without necessitating contact. Each attractor operates as a hybrid at several levels, allowing each actor to choose their level of comfort and exclusivity—for an appropriate price—making heterotopias the dominant urban form of the Tele Città. In a system of rhizomic assemblage, there is no necessity for disparate parties to meet as they follow their separate routes through the city's armatures and enclaves, passing each other by on the sidewalks of the city.

The mnemonic formula for the Tele Città should, ideally, indicate its inclusion of both previous cittàs as media content. For the sake of simplicity, however, I have concentrated on the role of the heterotopia, to illustrate the shift in actors' values. In the Tele Città H (heterotopia) dominates both E (enclave) and A (armature); thus, the Tele Città = H/(A + E).

Finally, to show that urban actors continue to manipulate the enclave-and-armature combination in creative ways in the postmodern situation of the Tele

Città, I cite the Bolles-Wilson Münster City Library project (1987–93) as an exemplary model of an urban-design project that works at multiple scales—as part of an informational net city, as part of a regional hub from the Cine Città, and at the level of an architectural detail in a recreated City of Faith (Munster was rebuilt as a historic, Gothic city after being bombed flat by the Allies in the Second World War). The library was defined by Foucault as a heterotopia of deviance, my heterotopia of discipline (H2). It was a repository of knowledge (and therefore of power) in the nineteenth century. In this case, the library also has a digital presence. The designers reinforce the idea of the city block as an enclave and at the same time cut a new armature across it (aligned with an old church spire). This cut is an extraordinary space, partially formed by pulling the copper roof down the facade and echoed on the inside by the organization of cascading stairs on either side of the armature.[138]

In Table 3.9 I list the combinations of enclave and armature (with associated sub-elements) that serve as organizing elements for each of the three normative città models. In each case there is a shifting balance between the enclave and armature in the composition created by urban actors. For the first set of actors enclaves dominate; for the second set, armatures are primary; the third connects the enclave and armature equally but disconnects them from the surrounding urban fabric. The porosity of the enclave varies in each case with this shifting balance, as flow structures cut and shred the closed urban fabric of the City of Faith to create the industrial city. Finally, the enclave-and-armature combination becomes a three-dimensional construct inside a totally sealed enclave, paradoxically more porous and open to a larger network of actors than ever before in the megamalls and theme parks of the global city.

As so far presented, these three models are not only utopian but *static*. This is unrealistic and must be modified. In the next chapter, I will discuss the heterotopia as the crucial urban element that enables the city to maintain itself stably and urban actors to shift from one urban model to another or to hybridize the models. The concept of the heterotopia thus provides a dynamic bridge between city theory, city models, and urban design.

Enclaves and armatures

Piazza San Marco, Venice:
a) *Plan (courtesy of University of Toronto)*
b) *Armature from water, 2003*
c) *Approach armature, 2003*

Bath, United Kingdom:
d) *Plan and section (courtesy of University of Toronto)*
e) *Approach to the Circus, 1990s*
f) *The Circus, 1990s*
g) *The Royal Crescent, 1990s*

Rockefeller Center, New York:
h) *Plan and section (courtesy of University of Toronto)*
i) *Plaza enclave*
j) *Armature to Fifth Avenue*
k) *Armature to plaza*

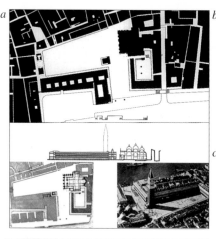

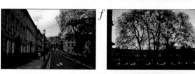
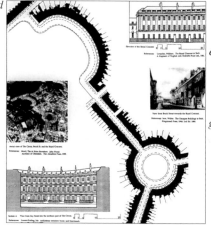

but after the end of the eighteenth century was moved "outside the borders of cities" because of the fear of infection and illness. The heterotopic site of the cemetery still existed inside the urban system, but its form and location were changed and the normal codes of the Archi Città inverted.[8] In the Cine Città the cemetery became "the other city," a frightening, separate place, the city of the dead (set in the suburbs).

Foucault's third principle of "heterotopology" is that a heterotopia can juxtapose "in a single real place several spaces, several sites that are in themselves incompatible." He gives as an example of these "contradictory sites" the theater or the cinema, places that can "bring a whole series of places that are foreign to one another" on stage or screen one after another. In the premodern world, Persian gardens and carpets also had this ability to bring together disparate scenes and seasons from the sacred cosmology. For Foucault the Persian rug was a "sort of mobile garden."[9]

His fourth principle concerned how heterotopias linked to precise "slices in time," making "heterochronies." There are heterotopic sites of "indefinitely accumulating time," like museums (which began in the seventeenth century as personal collections and expressions) and libraries. Foucault links the transformation of these personal museums and libraries to the modern desire to record human progress and gather information. He opposes these modern heterotopic sites, with their infinite time scale, to the temporary fairs and popular festivals that are absolutely of-the-moment in the "marvelous empty" fairgrounds on the edge of the city. These sites became active temporarily twice a year, filled with "heteroclite objects; wrestlers, snake women, fortune-tellers, and so forth."[10]

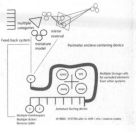

David Grahame Shane: "mirror" control systems in heterotopias

Foucault's fifth principle is that heterotopias, like all other enclaves, have gates and walls that "presuppose a system of opening and closing, that both isolates them and makes them penetrable." Heterotopias are not usually freely accessible to the public. Actors may have to undergo a ritual cleansing upon entry (as into a bath house, Islamic *hamman*, or Scandinavian sauna), or perhaps entry is "compulsory, as in the case of the barracks or the prison." Free access to a heterotopia is "in fact only an illusion: we think we enter where we are, by the very fact that we enter, excluded." Foucault gives as an example of such a heterotopia the guest room at the back of a Brazilian farmhouse, where travelers are free to spend the night. Although guests can enter freely, they are also excluded from the family realm of the farm. American motels—which Foucault mistakenly thought (in the 1960s) were fast disappearing from American society—fall into this category, too.[11]

Foucault's sixth and final principle of heterotopology is that heterotopias function inside urban systems either as sites of freedom and "illusion" or as sites of "compensation" and discipline. In sites of "illusion," the mirror function of the heterotopia comes into play. Foucault imagines that such heterotopias will reveal the normative sites "within which human life is partitioned, as still more

Heterotopia Bruno de Meulder: Jesuit colony in Belgian Congo, ca. 1900, "Mavula: An African Heterotopia in Kwango, 1895–1911, 1998

illusory." As an example he gives "those famous brothels of which we are now deprived," referring to those nineteenth-century Parisian brothels licensed by the state in which rooms were redecorated and staff wore appropriate costumes for the satisfaction of customers' fantasies. In contrast, sites of "compensation" are real spaces as "perfect, meticulous, as well arranged as ours is messy, ill constructed and jumbled." The European colonial settlements in America or the Jesuit colonies in South America were examples of such sites, where the form of the cross dominated all planning and the church bell regulated all activities.[12]

Foucault ends his essay by talking about the ship as the heterotopia "par excellence." The boat is intermediate between the colony and the brothel, those two "extreme types" of heterotopia. It is an instrument of economic development, "a floating piece of space, a place without a place, that exists by itself, that is closed in on itself and at the same time given over the infinity of the sea and that, from port to port, from tack to tack, from brothel to brothel, it goes as far as the colonies in search of the most precious treasures they conceal in their gardens." This description could be applied to almost any vehicular form of transport, including trains and cars. (Foucault does also refer to railway carriages and convoys in traffic as "sites" in this article.)

Foucault's article is an enormous source of inspiration, but also difficult and illogical. Which heterotopias mirror the medieval "tree" system of organization, with its "localization" and "emplacement," and which mirror the modern "grid" system, where the "heterotopias of deviance" appear, destroying the earlier "heterotopias of crisis"? How do sites of compensation and discipline fit into this picture? Which heterotopias participate in the third, "serial" model Foucault outlines in the article, where an apparently self-organizing system of actors in complex relationships forms a network of "sites"? What role do sites of freedom and "illusion" play in these systems? What is the relationship between heterotopias and economic development that is hinted at in the reference to ships?

Many scholars have attempted to answer these questions; I will briefly review how selected scholars have interpreted Foucault's article in terms of city theory, architecture, and urban systems. Françoise Choay included heterotopias in her 1969 article "Urbanism and Semiology," four years after Foucault's article. Choay saw projects like city walls, cathedrals, and castles in the medieval city as heterotopic (their role and structure in sharp contrast to the normative, syntagmatic, neighbor-to-neighbor relationships of houses) and diachronic (taking more than one generation to complete).[13]

Another Parisian scholar, Georges Teyssot, associated with the Venice School and Manfredo Tafuri, has created a bridge between the Venetian typological analysis of city institutions and Foucault's focus on the role of institutions in the creation of professional and scientific knowledge. In his article "Heterotopias and the History of Spaces," Teyssot traces the Rationalistic transformation of French hospital typologies under the control of the emerging professional class of doctors who studied illness and madness (basing his work on Foucault's *Madness and Civilization*, 1972). He also extended this analysis to Modernist public housing typologies.[14]

Robin Evans, in *The Fabrication of Virtue* (1982), describes his research on the reformation of English prisons that led to the creation of Bentham's Panopticon. Evans conducted this research in parallel to, but independent of, Foucault (it was first published in the *Architectural Association Quarterly* in 1971).[15] Foucault read and praised Evans's work, which gives a detailed account of the prison in the premodern period. Foucault himself calls the premodern prison a "crisis heterotopia." Evans describes how premodern prisons were still integrated into society as special places of treatment (what I would call H1 heterotopias). He describes prisons that were adaptations of Venetian palaces, with courtyards; prisons in English row houses, with yards; even prisons accommodated in the rooms above castellated city gates in towers (with a bar or tap room for prisoners). Many prisoners moved temporarily into prisons with their families to try to pay off their debts, and their friends came to see them.[16]

Bruno de Meulder: mining camp in the Belgian Congo, ca. 1900, "Mavula: An African Heterotopia in Kwango, 1895–1911," 1998

Evans also describes how prison living conditions appalled reformers like John Howard in the eighteenth century. Reformers highlighted the survival of medieval dungeons in castle prisons, with torture chambers and cramped cells for solitary confinement. Bentham's jail offered living conditions that were far superior, including voice tubes for communication to jailers, air conditioning, heating, running water, and a toilet in each cell. This heterotopia of deviance and discipline (what I would call an H2 heterotopia) deliberately isolated prisoners in order to reform them, that is, induce them to conform to the industrial norm of modern society. Evans demonstrates that this drive to segregate and isolate inmates backfired as more and more categories of prisoners had to be isolated, making the system unworkable (while other reformers questioned both its efficacy and its humanity).[17]

Following Foucault's seminal article, many scholars focused on heterotopias of "deviance and discipline," generally neglecting the heterotopias of "illusion." Among the exceptions were scholars of Walter Benjamin (1892–1940) such as Susan Buck-Morss (*The Dialectics of Seeing: Walter Benjamin and the Arcades Project*, 1991). Benjamin made the connection between the Industrial Revolution and its systems of production and consumption as joined with supplementary communication systems (e.g., marketing). Benjamin understood arcades, department stores, and boulevards as places of "illusion" and of consumption.[18] Following this logic, Kevin Hetherington (*The Badlands of Modernity: Heterotopia and Social Ordering*, 1997) interprets Foucault's heterotopology broadly to include "places of alternative social ordering," such as factories at the start of the Industrial Revolution or the shopping arcades and department stores that distributed the goods manufactured in this global system of exchanges.[19] Later scholars, such as Margaret Crawford, updated this concept of shopping and "illusion" as an "alternative social ordering" and its organization around shopping-mall armatures in her essay on Jon Jerde's mall designs in *You Are Here: The Jerde Partnership International* (1999).[20] Despite the prominence of the illusory side of such commercial heterotopias and the potential for ambiguous double-coding, many critics still emphasize these shopping malls as sites of "deviance" and discipline (H2). Michael Sorkin and his co-authors of *Variations on a Theme Park* (1992) share this critique of heterotopic, privately owned "public" space.

The proliferation of heterotopias in postmodern cities formed the focus of Edward Soja's study of the urban geography of Los Angeles in *Postmodern Geographies* (1989). Soja begins with a section on the importance of his discovery of Foucault and his concept of the heterotopia as a distinct spatial unit. This spatial emphasis freed Soja from the mathematical models and abstract city theories then current in Modernist city planning; it gave him a methodology to focus on specific places and specific actors in the city, highlighting specific flows and spaces so that he could produce maps showing the closing of "rust-belt" industrial factories in central Los Angeles while "sun-belt" banking and finance corridors opened between Santa Monica and downtown. It also gave him a methodology for isolating enclaves in the city and focusing on the relationships between actors in different heterotopic enclaves.[21]

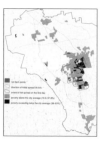

Charles Jencks: diagram of the 1992 Rodney King riots, Los Angeles, Heteropolis, *1993*

Soja's work was popularized after the largest civil uprising in American history in the Rodney King riots of 1992 by Charles Jencks in his *Heteropolis* (1993).[22] The "heteropolis" theme entered mainstream academic discourse, forming the subject for the American Collegiate Schools of Architecture conference in Los Angeles in 2001. By this time, marketing experts had learned to place their products, whether new cigarettes or vodkas, in heterotopias of "illusion" such as nightclubs and cafés, in an attempt to manipulate the mainstream market through fashion leaders.[23] By 2002, heterotopias were one of the themes selected for *Documenta X* in Kassel, Germany, a trend-setting art show for dealers, buyers and critics.[24]

Benjamin Genocchio is one of the rare scholars to have stressed the "illusion" side of Foucault's analysis of heterotopias. In doing so, he reexamined the relationship between utopias and heterotopias. In a series of articles during the 1990s,[25] Genocchio stressed Foucault's connection between utopias and heterotopias, throwing a stronger light on the "illusory" utopian image; he also stressed the dangers of the frozen, mechanical, and panoptic dimension of the "illusory" utopian project, echoing Walter Benjamin and Tafuri.[26] He contrasted this project's emphasis on internal order with the messiness of ordinary life and living as described by Foucault. He illustrates this contrast by citing an Australian video project (Denis del Favero's *Undercover* project in Wynyard metro station, Sydney, 1992) that sought to undermine illusions of central control and order, allowing an interstitial, heterotopic space of freedom to open up for a short time. The project installed a surveillance system in a pedestrian subway that displayed subversive images referring to Australia's past and the fate of its aboriginal occupants. The municipality later closed down the installation—which it had commissioned—after critical feedback from the press.[27]

Recent research has extended the heterotopia concept to postcolonial studies and to the mass immigration that has produced the multicultural mixture of the postmodern megalopolis. Bruno de Meulder has investigated nineteenth-century Jesuit heterotopic colonial establishments in the Congo that were very similar to Foucault's Brazilian examples.[28] Hilde Heynen, Meulder's colleague at Leuven University, and the American scholar Zeynep Celik together edited a special issue of the *Journal of Architectural Education* that studied the heterotopic settlements of immigrants in many different cultural situations, these ranged from internal immigrants on the edge of Ankara, Turkey, overlooking the city's racetrack to global immigrants building store-front mosques in Western cities like New York.[29] These and other scholars have explored and expanded Foucault's initial and confusing concept. My goal in this section is to sort and categorize Foucault's disorganized thoughts about heterotopias and to bring them into relationship with the categories of the enclave and the armature.

Foucault began by describing three different urban systems of organization and by distinguishing between places of rest and flow. He then concentrated on places of rest (enclaves) and began to compare places that really exist to unreal places and hybrid sites that reflect both utopian aspirations and their real surroundings, in miniature and multiple cells. In addition, he described how these sites are controlled by actors, are more or less open to the public, and can take different forms depending on their relationship to their surroundings. Foucault distinguished between crisis heterotopias of primitive societies and heterotopias of deviance—both with slow-changing or rigid internal orders— and heterotopias of illusion, with their rapidly changing, flexible and fluid internal orders. For brevity I denote crisis heterotopias as H1, heterotopias of deviance as H2, and heterotopias of illusion as H3.

Vito Acconci and Steven Holl: Storefront for Art and Architecture, New York, 1993

Much of the confusion about heterotopias arises because they are, in fact, complex enclaves and enclaves are everywhere in the city. Nonheterotopic enclaves tend to house a singular, predominant function (e.g., housing estate or office park); heterotopias are distinguished by additional features and functions such as further interior enclaves and armatures managing multiple flows. Heterotopias do, however, resemble other enclaves in having boundaries and gates, interior codes, and gatekeepers who enforce those codes.

Modern industrial societies create many parallel, separate worlds or enclaves for specific, segregated inhabitants. The crucial distinguishing features are always the three "M's": the *mirror-function*, which reverses the surrounding codes; the *multiple pockets* within the heterotopic enclave, which facilitate mixture and change; and a utopic "simulation" that reflects in *miniature* the entire surrounding system, with its codes altered or reversed. Built into this mirroring system is also a concept of the "site" and its relationships in time, implying that any heterotopia will be a dissipative structure dependent on a particular organization of society at a particular time. Thus Bentham dreamt of

*Heterotopia 1
Axonometric of
hidden Catholic
chapel in Amsterdam
row house, Dorling-
Kindersley,*
Eyewitness Travel
Guide to
Amsterdam, *1995*

a compensatory machine enforcing an extremely rigid discipline in the extremely fluid situation of the early industrial revolution, just as New Urbanists do now in an age of globalization.

The fast-disappearing "heterotopias of crisis" (H1) that Foucault noted in 1964 usually stood as institutions inside the city's syntagmatic and small-scale fabric, like the cemetery beside the church at the "heart of the city." The rise of the "heterotopia of deviance" (H2) formed the center of Foucault's life study, with its "compensatory" discipline used by state or private agents of modernization (e.g., doctors in clinics or hospitals). Foucault was less interested in "heterotopias of illusion" (H3), seeing them as places of escape from the tyranny of production via fantasies of freedom. A more developed interpretation of heterotopias of illusion stresses how their capacity to contain flexible, illusory spaces has aided actors in marketing and differentiating their sites in a highly mediated (media-rich) world. Differentiation, disjunction, and the rapid displacement of images are key elements of heterotopias of illusion, reacting against the universal connectivity and universal relationships of the postmodern, network city.

The biggest source of confusion about heterotopias is their role in facilitating and monitoring change. My intention in numbering the three types of heterotopias is to indicate these paradigm shifts as heterotopias shift from inside the fabric of the city to outside, and then to multiple centers. Heterotopia of type 1 (H1) are associated with Lynch's City of Faith; they accommodate change within the fabric of the city, often behind innocuous facades that hide their true content. Heterotopias of type 2 (H2) are associated with the great drive to modernize European society, when urban functions often shifted outside the city in order to develop new, specialized morphologies and typologies in the open space of the suburban network. Heterotopias of type 3 (H3) are associated with Lynch's Ecological City and reflect the shift from processing material goods to processing symbolic information in communication systems. These numbers also indicate a shift from being dominated by immediate responses to crises, to "disciplinary" codes designed to provide stability, to informational codes processing images and "illusions." Elements of the city that operate in the gray zone of shifting forms wreak havoc on the normative categories of scientific and stable systems.

The multiplicity of small enclaves nested inside the heterotopia enables the structure to handle shifting balances and change within a stable environment. Change is contained in the miniaturized model of the contextual system. The norm in such a nested system is flexible, changing from level to level. Portugali, as we saw in the previous chapter, argues that the dominant norm at any one time can "enslave" other systems and determine the overall characteristic of the whole enclave or platform for that moment.[30] This is also true within a heterotopia, which may (indeed, usually does) contain multiple, contending norms, but with the difference that actor-designers can easily monitor and compare rates of change between cells. Actors in close proximity to each other are more aware of each other, of competing norms and their shifts. Thus, as

*Heterotopia 1
Palladio: Teatro
Olympico, Vicenza,
1580*

actors' preferences change over time the multicellular heterotopia has the capacity not only to change its dominant system of organization but to allow actors to choose consciously among alternatives, to know themselves as agents, to respond from the bottom up.

I would like to end this section by briefly describing an extraordinary example of an urban heterotopia that illustrates many of the themes of this introductory analysis. In *City of Darkness* (1993), Greg Girard and Ian Lambot describe the Walled City of Kowloon, which existed for a time as an enclave within the body of Hong Kong.[31] It was a city in miniature, with multiple compartments that became more complex over time. It both mirrored and inverted the normative codes of Hong Kong, where landownership is so important. Like Hong Kong it developed on the vertical axis, but unlike Hong Kong no one owned the land. And unlike the tower blocks prevalent around it, the Walled City developed as a single superblock of incredible density and complexity.

Jeremy Bentham: section of Panopticon prison, 1820s

The Walled City arose after the Second World War on the site of an old military camp inside what was then the British colony of Hong Kong. The campsite officially belonged to China, which had no way of reaching it, as it was surrounded by foreign territory. By the same token, however, British colonial jurisdiction could not be applied inside the camp's boundaries. As a result, the campsite fell between jurisdictions, neither British nor (effectively) Chinese. In the period of housing shortages and massive immigration after the Chinese Revolution in 1947, many immigrants arrived and illegally squatted on the land, building houses. As immigration pressures continued, these houses and compounds, built around courtyards, were extended vertically, mirroring the skyscraper solution applied elsewhere in Hong Kong because of the land shortage.

The result was a matrix of vertical housing blocks with many irregular horizontal corridors making connections between buildings at various levels. Commercial and service establishments grew up along these corridors and in the courts to serve the population. In addition, the complex, being outside of both British and Chinese law, became an attractive headquarters for gangster elements, which were impossible to find within its maze-like structure. The Walled City was thus "other," detached from its host society; it housed displaced refugees and immigrants who created their own institutions and organizations. Its form also mirrored the skyscraper code of the surrounding society, where land was scarce. The complex was a product of an industrialized society, yet the immigrants' social organization was preindustrial, grounded in the site. Like an ocean liner, it sailed to another realm; its three-dimensional matrix and organization were self-contained and fell between the cracks of international law.

Facade of the Walled City of Kowloon, Hong Kong, 1990s (photograph Ian Lambot from City of Darkness *available at www.watermark publications.com)*

The British authorities demolished the Walled City, in consultation with China, before returning the colony. Once it was demolished the Walled City took on a new life as myth, inspiring many reproductions (e.g., in cyberpunk literature) as a noncorporate, irrational data haven, a heterotopia par excellence,

Right *Walled City of Kowloon aerial view (photograph Greg Girard)*
Below *Facade (photograph Ian Lambot) Photographs from* City of Darkness *available at www.watermark publications.com*

a place of cybernetic freedom lodged in the body of corporate cyberspace.

The Walled City had many of the features of an Archi Città ghetto, including a traditional, low-rise village shrine and temple (H1) dating from before 1947 at its center.[32] It was contained within a finite space and compressed by population inflow. Its courtyard structures originally mirrored vernacular traditions, but became transformed into skyscraper blocks.[33] At the same time, it was an industrial enclave (H2), the product of a massive influx of immigrants seeking work in the Cine Città. The Walled City contained factories and small industrial plants, shops, and places devoted to leisure and pleasure. The rooftop of the complex played a special role; here children could fly kites and play games. The Walled City was also a temporary dissipative structure in the flows of Hong Kong, fated to return to Chinese control. Media images of the Walled City portrayed it as a slum and center for criminals. Several movies (e.g., Tsui Hark's *Time and Tide*, 2000) have exploited its three-dimensional, maze-like quality. The Walled City thus entered the living rooms of the Tele Città audience branded as a doomed, negative, heterotopic element employed for the service of fantasy or illusion (H3).

This heterotopia existed for 50 years before being destroyed to create a park. It was unusual in that it was generated from the bottom up, outside of but still reflecting the normative rules and regulations of the jurisdictions around it. Its hybrid skyscraper/superblock format also reflected and transformed the building typologies of the surrounding city of Hong Kong. The avant-garde Dutch group MVRDV highlighted the utopic design element of the complex, pointing to its superdense, three-dimensional spatial matrix as a long-dreamt-of urban-industrial ideal (as in King's *Dream of New York*, 1915).[34] The Walled City was an exceptionally dense development even for Hong Kong; yet in some ways this heterotopia made Hong Kong possible, handling certain difficult needs (e.g., large numbers of migrants) and helping to make the normal development and stable systems of Hong Kong possible.

The Walled City of Kowloon was a complex and multilayered structure, containing many heterotopic sites in strange locations and combinations within itself. In the next section we will examine the *internal* combinatory logic of crisis heterotopias and heterotopias of deviance before moving on to study rhizomic assemblage in heterotopias of illusion. We will end the chapter by looking at the role of the heterotopia in relation to the three normative models proposed by Lynch. How do heterotopias act as catalysts and instruments of change that facilitate shifts between the three normative urban models?

Water supply in corridor, Walled City of Kowloon (photograph Greg Girard from City of Darkness *available at www.watermark publications.com)*

Rooftop playground and antennae, Walled City of Kowloon (photograph Greg Girard)

4.2 RECOMBINATION IN HETEROTOPIAS OF CRISIS AND DEVIANCE

Moses King's Dream of New York, 1915 (courtesy of Avery Architectural and Fine Arts Library, Columbia University)

In the previous section, I distinguished three types of heterotopias based loosely on Foucault's pioneering 1964 article "Of Other Spaces." I selected these three types—the crisis heterotopia, the heterotopia of deviance, and the heterotopia of illusion—as best fitting my purpose of describing how heterotopias contain the rejected elements necessary to construct an urban system. In each of Lynch's three normative urban models there should be, at least as a first approximation, three mirroring structures where exceptions congregate. All three will be heterotopic, but each will formally reflect the system that it belongs to and from which it is excluded. That is, each urban system will maintain characteristic places of reverse logic whose existence is necessary for the consistency of its own logic. These places will in some way invert the dominant code of their surroundings, containing those people, objects, or processes deemed "other" by the dominant actors. The Walled City of Kowloon in Hong Kong is clearly such a place.

Alternatively, we might consider the three spatial systems described by Foucault in his 1964 article. The first of these is concerned with "emplacement," the second with "extensions," and the third with relationships between "sites." On this basis alone we might expect three heterotopic structures: one that deals with displacement in a system of emplacement, one that deals with compression in a system of extension, and one that deals with deliberate disjunction, voluntary servitude, and disconnection (mirroring and inverting a larger system concerned with the illusion of freedom and connective relationships between "sites"). We might expect these three types of heterotopia to differ from each other as much as their contextual systems do.

Foucault's three spatial systems are based on a series of code inversions and recombinations. That is, the structure of each of these spatial systems involves a reversal or violation of the logic of the previous system, a major paradigm shift. (Such a shift might be achieved in incremental jumps, not necessarily all at once.) The "hierarchical ensemble" of the medieval city, for instance, involved "localization" and enclosure in the enclave system of "emplacements"; the heterotopia of crisis was an essential stabilizing factor. Then this system was split apart and new hybrids developed that were based on codes of "deviance" and "illusion." Heterotopias of deviance emerged to accelerate this change; the old enclaves were "dissolved" in the open, nonhierarchical, infinite, grid space of Galileo, where everything was in movement, flowing along stretched and compressed armatures. Time replaced space as the principle of coordination. Then heterotopias of illusion helped reverse the codes of the heterotopia of deviance, so that instead of rigid rules, segregation, and sorting, the relationships between actors in networks become more fluid and open, making connections between "sites." Heterotopias of illusion accelerated this process, reemphasizing place as "site." Such heterotopias intensify and handle exceptional peaks and spikes in the drive for accelerated virtual connections, allowing further dispersal;

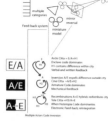

David Grahame Shane: Conceptual modeling and code-inversion diagram

they are places of disconnection and disjunction, temporarily interrupting and amplifying the network of flows in our systems of communication and transport.

Many other urban critics have identified model shifts and code reversals such as those Foucault describes. His shifts are like the code inversions involved in the reverse city as described by Viganò in the La *Città Elementare* (1999), expanding on Koetter and Rowe's *Collage City* (1978). Where Foucault differs is his emphasis on particular places and actors as agents of the changes taking place in the larger society and his stress on the role of the "mirror" in forming a sense of identity in the midst of flows. Each type of heterotopia plays a specific role in accelerating, slowing, or handling change in his three spatial systems.

These three heterotopic sites (crisis, discipline, illusion) share a basically multicellular organizational structure. Foucault's six points, discussed above, outline the points of this organization clearly. The heterotopia's interior will reflect the surrounding system's overall organization in miniature, but with code inversions. These spaces will deal with "slices" of time in various ways and using multiple sorting devices, both sequencing armatures (as in theaters and cinemas) and place-making enclaves (as in museums). All heterotopias are controlled enclave-spaces with gates and walls, more or less open to their surroundings, but the form of a heterotopia will vary from system to system and from place to place and will often involve the adaptive reuse of structures built for other purposes.

Within their boundaries, crisis heterotopias (H1, my first category) tend not to be very efficient about sorting their inhabitants. They rely on arcane, magical formulas. They allow heterotopic mixtures that would be disapproved of by modern medical or educational science. Foucault lists as actors within crisis heterotopias a strange mix of people who are weak or temporarily at a disadvantage, including children, "adolescents, menstruating women, pregnant women, [the] elderly." In the heterotopia of crisis the logic of combination remains local and syntagmatic, centered on a single focus or authority. It relies on comparisons to immediate neighbors, on touch and feel, on physical contact, on the interpretation of symptoms as metaphysical signs.

In *Madness and Civilization* (1961, revised 1972), Foucault marvels at the criteria used to classify and assign sick people and prisoners to their cells in premodern French hospitals and prisons: people known to the king would get special treatment in one place, people lapsing from good families would go to another place, the poor (as always) would have yet another place, and so on. Lepers and lunatics known to the king might end up in the same room, which made little medical sense but satisfied a social and regal logic that saw the king as the center of the world.

For Foucault, all heterotopias have a "compensatory" side, which enforces codes and disciplines within the space, and also an "illusory" side that retains traces of the utopian goals the managers of the space hold in high esteem and that justify their codes. In crisis heterotopias, the "compensatory" and "illusory"

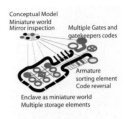

Conceptual Model
Miniature world
Mirror inspection

Multiple Gates and gatekeepers codes

Armature
sorting element
Code reversal

Enclave as miniature world
Multiple storage elements

Heterotopia provides
Multiple Mix and match
potential for Actors
in special enclave setting

David Grahame Shane: multiple actors in conceptual modeling and media space

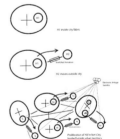

Shane: changing position of heterotopias in the city

mixed without difficulty, creating a blended, hybrid logic that is foreign, in retrospect, to modernity. Foucault cites the Islamic *hamman*, a ritual bath house where being cleansed included a spiritual dimension, as another example of a heterotopia of illusion. Many religions have had rituals and bath houses through which converts can pass and thereby renew their faith, as in Jewish ritual bath houses or the Christian baptistery.

In his introduction to *Madness and Civilization*, Foucault describes his interest in Jorge Luis Borges's imaginary logics (attributed to ancient Chinese philosophers), which Borges compared to "laundry lists" that made no connected sense. The sequential, logical form of the list itself carried over as a rational, continuous, modern system, creating a strange hybrid. Names on the list still abut each other and keep the formal continuity of the sequential logic, but the content of each cell makes no sense, scientific or common. More proximity and sequence give no sense of a clear order or system of associations. The situation was similar to the visual representation of the city in premodern perspectival systems, where each cell had its own reference frame and was rotated in relationship to its neighbors, with no overall logic. In terms of writing our urban equations we can say that the crisis heterotopia (H1) is composed of a mixture of deviance-suppression codes (D) as well as of utopic illusion codes (I), resulting in the expression $H1 = (D + I)$. (The parentheses indicate that the heterotopia is contained within the fabric of the city.)

*Heteropia 1
Venetian palace as a
prison*

In this system, the combinatorial key was that variations were contained within the basic cellular units of the urban system, that is, the housing cells at the base of the nesting hierarchy of the city. These were sealed units, houses on a domestic scale that could accommodate change within the fabric of the city. From the outside they might even appear as normal domestic units, with doors and windows in their facades like actual dwellings. However, their internal organization, as in the case of the Venetian prison in the palazzo cited by Evans,[35] would be completely altered to accommodate a heterotopic system. There would be multiple spatial subdivisions and specialized areas to separate flows and sort people, things, and objects to their appropriate locations. In times of crisis (e.g., during a plague) almost any house could be converted into a crisis heterotopia,

Heteropia 1
Left *Section of Felix Meritas School, Amsterdam*
Right *Palladio, Teatro Olympico, Vicenza, 1580*

as the authorities would seal the sick people into their house to die and come to collect the bodies at night. At different times there were domestic-scale sick houses, prison houses, work houses, bath houses, and public houses. The "public house" has survived in Britain as the ultimate crisis heterotopia, the "pub," the center of social life for villages and working-class areas for several centuries.[36]

The combinatorial system within these domestic-scaled heterotopic cells depended on touch, on bonding things edge-to-edge, on working in a "jigsaw" system, as described by Viganò in *La Città Elementare* (1999). As in a jigsaw, all the pieces fitted into a larger pattern or whole image of the City of Faith. "Compensatory" and "illusory" codes mixed to achieve this goal. In the crisis heterotopia, these goals were compressed and miniaturized within the space of a single domestic cell, not unlike houses in seventeenth-century Amsterdam with hidden (because illegal) Catholic chapels or modern-day urban storefront churches or mosques in immigrant areas in America. The edge-to-edge bonding of elements in this system helped maintain the syntagmatic system of the medieval city and the continuity of the street facade.[37]

Crisis heterotopias thus did not especially stand out in the premodern city but rather were woven into its texture, often taking the outward form of a courtyard house, row house, or apartment. Examples include the medieval almshouses built for widows in the heart of cities such as Amsterdam or in Louvain and still occupied today as originally intended. Here individual houses, each a heterotopia of crisis, were gathered around a communal space and administered collectively as a charity by the Church. Belgian and Dutch almshouses miniaturized the normative row house (portrayed by Vermeer) to accommodate widows without families. Code reversals here involved the common ownership of property instead of individual ownership; the absence of children, work and families; and the privacy, peace, and isolation of the block interior, with only a few openings to the street and these guarded by gates and doorkeepers.

Alberti writing in *On the Art of Building in Ten Books*[38] notes that every house was a small city, an observation that fits neatly with Foucault's concept of the crisis heterotopia as a multifaceted enclave. Alberti was thinking perhaps of the multifamily occupation of merchant and princely Renaissance palaces, with

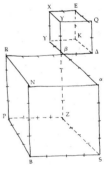

George L Hersey: nesting cubes, Pythagorean Palaces, *1976*

Plan of Oxford high street

their miniaturization and mirroring of the multiplicity of the city. Multiple, complex programs were woven together inside the three-dimensional spatial matrix of the palace, conceived as instantiating the ideal Platonic form of the cube. The gatehouse and courtyard gave onto storehouses around the perimeter of the ground floor; on the next floor the piano nobile contained public reception rooms and perhaps a ballroom, private offices, living rooms, libraries, bedrooms, and bathrooms; family members' apartments were above and servants' bedrooms in the attics. Feeding and running such a village community inside the compressed three-dimensional matrix of a single building required a special steward (who also maintained the fabric of the building itself). Accommodating the sick or insane inside this communal building envelope did not pose a problem unless too many people entered this category.[39]

The cubic mass of the Renaissance palace represented an extreme case of the domestic crisis heterotopia. These heterotopias were inflated to a new scale by the wealth and power of merchant-princes in the Renaissance city-states. Their geometry was informed by Renaissance ideas about central-point perspective; harmonic proportions relating to a geometric, cubic whole; numerology; and iconographic references to ancient Rome. Magical theories about number cohabited with modern, rationalistic mathematical calculations. The ideal beauty remained a self-closing system nested inside another such system, part of a series ascending up to heaven from earth or from heaven down to earth.[40]

Regardless of their particular form, crisis heterotopias are sacred or forbidden places reserved for individuals who are in a state of crisis in relation to the society in which they live. In crisis heterotopias, actors miniaturize their specialized equipment, the symbolic intermediaries used to negotiate with other actors. The multiple uses that mirror the larger city are often accommodated within one domestic-scale cell, even within a single room. In the old system of "emplacement," the specialized equipment required for multiple uses was highly mobile, reflecting a code reversal. Museums began as "wonder cabinets" inside scholars' houses; offices began as highly specialized desks with multiple compartments for businessmen's use (an origin commemorated in the French for office, *bureau*, also meaning a desk). Some desks could be folded and carried from place to place, becoming mobile offices.

Actors creating crisis heterotopias did not necessarily need new buildings; they might easily adapt domestic or other buildings to their uses as they sought to establish small-scale and local-niche operations linked to cosmic, magical, and mythical networks. Crisis heterotopias therefore often observe Foucault's second principle by occupying sites or forms built for other purposes under different regimes.[41]

The pattern of gathering and agglomerating small-scale heterotopias of crisis in guarded courtyard enclaves, as in the Dutch and Belgian widows' almshouses, can be seen in many cultures. In many cases, houses containing people with specialized knowledge or skills act as self-organizing attractors within the larger

Oxford quadrangle and houses

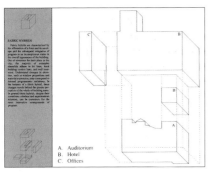

A. Auditorium
B. Hotel
C. Offices

to construct a closed, compressed, centrally controlled world that could be overseen by a single person. This reversed the predominant code of dispersal that was already spurred on by the acceleration of transportation and communications in stretched armatures, described so acutely later by Cerdá in his *Theory of Urbanization* (1867). The Panopticon—an ultracompressed miniature city within a larger, increasingly dispersed city—thus reversed the dispersal code. A hidden central controller or clock was assumed at the heart of the system, to keep this miniature City as a Machine coordinated and running. Yet the Panopticon was a reflection as well as a reversal. Bentham took the organizational codes and conceptual sorting devices of the port city and compressed these devices into the professional disciplinary apparatus of his Panopticon.

The skyscraper, also invented in the nineteenth century, rivals the Panopticon as an influential Modernist heterotopia of deviance. The skyscraper has an enormous capacity to sort and segregate along its vertical armature. The Modernist history of the skyscraper is almost entirely written in terms of monofunctional office buildings, which appear as the norm;[48] Few critics have pursued how mixed-use heterotopias of deviance were assembled in skyscrapers in the Cine Città or have systematically examined the combinatorial relationships between the urban elements in these complex, three-dimensional structures. An exception is Joseph Fenton, who identifies three combinatorial codes in hybrid buildings in his *Hybrid Buildings Pamphlet Architecture #11:* (1985). Each of these codes represents a different set of relationships between elements defined in terms of Modernist, single-function programs. Fenton's first class of combination is Fabric Hybrids. In Fabric Hybrids, the street-and-block system of the city dominates, forcing all disparate elements to lie within the perimeter of the typical block, as in the Renaissance palace example given earlier. At a large scale, these Fabric Hybrids may be seen as descendants of earlier crisis heterotopias, working syntagmatically within the cellular fabric of the city.

Fenton provides many examples of dense urban institutions packed with different uses inside the Fabric Hybrid typology, derived from the row house or courtyard morphology. In one frequent heterotopic combination, a theater sits below offices, residences, or hotels, reversing the puzzle pieces of the Theatre

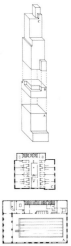

Fenton: Fabric
Building analysis—
Downtown Athletic
Club, New York,
Hybrid Buildings

Feydeau of pre-revolutionary Paris. Sullivan and Adler's Auditorium Building (1887–89) in Chicago's Loop is one such, with the theater in the base, a hotel wrapped around and above it, and offices climbing up to one side. A bar capped the small hotel's tower section, where Sullivan and the young Frank Lloyd Wright would take refreshments after work. Sullivan's partner Adler wrote that the complexity of "these overlappings and interpenetrations form a Chinese puzzle."[49]The Fabric Hybrid system operates within the framework of the classical cubic-palace typology descended from the Renaissance palaces that developed within the proportional grid of the perspectival system. Elements in this system make contact with their neighbors, sharing walls, doors, entrances, and courtyards. All elements must be cubic and fit within the low-rise building mass, which is oriented to the width of street armatures and square enclaves. Cellular elements are stacked on top of each other to fill out the building envelope. Vertical circulation gives access or passes by each floor, depending on programmatic requirements. Separate staircases and entrances can lead to different sectors of the building. Different sectors of the building can be combined or recombined as required. The three-dimensional perspectival matrix I discussed in connection with Brunelleschi was essential to this sorting and packing of elements in a closely bound space. Cutaway sectional perspectives, as drawn by Leonardo, showed a building's overall form and its interior, sectional organization simultaneously. Renaissance courtyard- and palace-type buildings belong to this combinatory tradition, becoming converted in the nineteenth century to club houses, foreign offices, department stores, and apartment buildings with complex, heterotopic programs inside compressed three-dimensional matrices.[50]

Fenton's second combinatorial "hybrid building" typology is the Graft, in which long surfaces of elements are laid against each other so that one is laminated against the other. His diagram shows several, vertical, interlocking blocks of different geometries being pressed against each other, but blocks can also be grafted horizontally, forming layers of different programs. Each block represents a single program that runs parallel to another program up or across the building section. The programs may, but need not, share their vertical circulation. Each block can change without affecting the others.

Fenton shows several examples of Graft buildings with specialized building elements forming enclaves within the building. In the Graft system of bonding, the various building elements are expressed on the exterior, rather than conforming to a block-and-building envelope established by urban codes as in the Fabric Hybrid. The functional elements can be read distinctly from the outside, following the Modernist dictum that "form follows function."

Fenton cites as Graft buildings such classic modern American buildings as Howe and Lescaze's Philadelphia Savings Bank Tower (1932), because of its stacked, separately expressed functions. Here street-level stores support a two-story banking hall, with offices in a 30-story tower above. (This Deco building now houses a fashionable hotel.) The Carew Tower in Cincinnati, Ohio, designed by Ahlschlager, Delano, and Aldrich in 1931, combined department stores, a retail arcade, offices, a hotel, a restaurant, a ballroom and a parking garage, each with separate vertical massing and entrances. In Frank Lloyd Wright's H. C. Price Company Tower in Bartlesville, Oklahoma (1953), three segments of the building were offices, while the fourth segment was occupied by an apartment with a separate elevator. A variation on this Graft bonding technique might be seen in Ken Yeang's grafting in the late 1980s of multistory ecoterraces and gardens into the sections of towers to relieve air-conditioning loads in Malaysia.[51] Norman Foster's Deutsche Bank Tower in Frankfurt (1995) represents a further development of this concept. Here the fourth segment was a garden or terrace on every floor. A terrace spiraled upward around the core, occupying different segments as it climbed the building and so giving a multistory garden to every section of the tower in turn.[52] Daniel Libeskind's 1,776-foot tower in his early design for the World Trade Center site used the lower portions of a tall TV and radio antenna as a similar ecogarden grafted onto a lower tower, giving every floor gardens and public spaces.[53]

Daniel Libeskind: innovative design study for the World Trade Center site, 2003

Links between the vertical blocks in a Graft system of bonding can occur at every floor, as in the Price Tower, or at intervals, as in Yeang's multistory eco-terraces. At 500 Park Avenue, New York, Polshek Partnership Architects grafted their residential, stone-faced tower onto the back of the original low metal-and-glass Pepsi-Cola office building by SOM (Skidmore, Owings, and Merrill; 1960). The new residential tower had a separate entrance, a new entrance being made for the old office tower.[54]

Another possibility in Graft systems is the "sky lobby" connector, in which hotel guests enter by elevator to the 20th floor, bypassing the offices below, as in the Hotel Century Southern Tower in Tokyo's Shinjuku subcenter (built over a

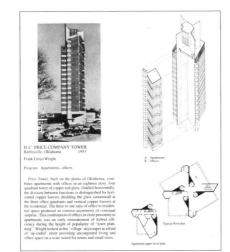

Left *Joseph Fenton: Graft Building diagram,* Hybrid Buildings Pamphlet Architecture 11, *1985*
Middle *Graft Building: Frank Lloyd Wright, Price Tower, Bartlesville, AZ, 1953*
Right *Fenton: Monolith Building diagram* Hybrid Buildings

railway station, 1997–98). In this case, the link to the hotel lobby is on the exterior of the building in a glass elevator, offering an exhilarating ride up to the hotel lobby, with its bar overlooking Mount Fuji in the smoggy sunset. In some cases there may be no links at all, as in buildings that give separate elevators in a core to each of the segments, with separate street entrances and addresses (Odaku G Building Design Team, Nikken Sekkei and Japanese Railway Eastern Design Corporation, 1997–98).

Fenton cites the Downtown Athletic Club building in New York (Starrett and Van Vleck, Duncan Hunter, 1931–32) as a Graft building because of its stacking of functions and set back form.[55] Rem Koolhaas, in *Delirious New York* (1978), has also commented on the extraordinary, illogical, collagist combinations made possible by the skyscraper format in the Downtown Athletic Club. Segregated functions were stacked with a rigid logic, the largest and heaviest blocks being placed at the bottom of the building. This multifaceted athletic facility built around the vertical armature of the elevator reversed normative codes for suburban sports facilities, which are usually built in rural locations and based on horizontal, stretched-enclave layouts.

Koolhaas praised the Downtown Athletic Club as a surreal, "delirious," hypermodern combination of sports-related functions. Much to Koolhaas's delight, one could enter the building, take the elevator, and arrive at a squash court, a bowling alley, a miniature golf course, a swimming pool, an indoor tennis court, a bar or restaurant, or hotel rooms, all on different floors. The building incorporated all the elements of a miniature city within its section, rendering it, like Foucault's ocean liner, a modern heterotopia of deviance.[56]

Koolhaas pointed out that the strict Modernist code, evolved for work purposes, was here inverted for leisure. He noted the absurd combinations possible when the logic of Modernism is subjected to nonfunctional, nonlinear, semilogical sequences of instructions devoted to pleasure. He was, however, oblivious of the social origins of the Downtown Athletic Club in the exclusion of Catholics, Jews, and African Americans from the White, Anglo-Saxon, Protestant (WASP) athletic clubs in midtown and from the university athletic clubs of the 1920s and 19s30s. The city's dominant urban actors excluded those perceived as new immigrants, deviants, and generally "other." Those excluded, while often making money and achieving success in business, still needed their own heterotopia of illusion (H3) for gymnastic activities. They therefore created the Downtown Athletic Club as their refuge, transforming the skyscraper—Modernist symbol of efficiency and business (H2)—into a place of pleasure, leisure, and physical exercise, reversing its usual logic.

The Downtown Athletic Club endured as a dissipative structure for only two generations, as the other clubs accepted the former outcasts in the 1970s and even accepted female members starting in the 1980s.[57] In its declining years, the club derived most of its income from the television rights of the Heisman Trophy for best American college football player. This important annual event was

Downtown Athletic Club Building, West Street, New York, 2000

broadcast from the bar room on the third floor. The club survived into the 1990s, when commercial gyms and athletic clubs with modern equipment were blossoming in every neighborhood of New York, making the old private clubs obsolete. On the verge of bankruptcy, it negotiated the sale of its upstairs rooms to an apartment developer who also was on the verge of bankruptcy. In a final ironic twist, after the club was damaged in the World Trade Center attacks it was forced to celebrate its great revenue-producing media event, the awarding of the Heisman Trophy, at the Yale Club in midtown.

The dissipative logic, shifting categories, and history of self-organization by outcasts that applied in the Downtown Athletic Club had applied earlier in small-scale crisis heterotopias such as the Dutch almshouses. The almshouses have survived for centuries thanks to a network of institutions, including the Church, that surrounds them and supports them, and have become potent tourist attractors in recent years. But not all heterotopias can survive by changing status in this way; the Walled City of Kowloon met a very different fate. Its survival depended on the laws of, and on compression by, the surrounding colonial enclave. When these circumstances changed and the walls came down, the compressed heterotopia, the city within the city, became a redundant symbol of a past regime and was demolished.

Starrett and Van Vleck, Duncan Hunter: Downtown Athletic Club section, 1932

We have examined two types of heterotopia so far. The Dutch almshouses represent the crisis heterotopias (H1), which can form cellular agglomerations in the Archi Città fabric (e.g., the Oxbridge colleges). Bentham's Panopticon prison and the Downtown Athletic Club represent compressed heterotopias of deviance (H2), temporarily accommodating outcasts from the Cine Città. The organization of each type of heterotopia reflects and inverts elements of the larger city, creating a specialized, miniaturized, compressed city within a city for its displaced occupants. In the next section, we will examine the heterotopia of illusion, a type rather neglected by Foucault. We have already seen how the mixed codes of crisis heterotopias created strange bedfellows in premodern hospitals, categories lumped according to no apparent logic; in contrast, the "compensatory" codes of heterotopias of deviance were intended to bring order, to set up logical, scientific standards that would always be the same. With all their rational efficiency and apparent fairness, however, these codes tend to be rigid and resistant to change, making arbitrary and inflexible separations between elements, types, and sites.

Heterotopias of illusion reverse this rigid logic. They do so not by returning to the logic of the crisis heterotopia but by being fast-changing and flexible, with a high potential for change and recombination. We will now examine their capacity for change and explore their apparently irrational, nonlinear, surreal, combinatorial logic.

attempt various virtual or real combinations within these heterotopic zones without disrupting the entire system. Designers in the postmodern city have therefore adapted the techniques of rhizomic assemblage and brought them to the mainstream; heterotopias of illusion have proliferated to facilitate and protect actors making this "disjunctive synthesis" described by Rajchman.

Yet it took designers some time to articulate the passionate and engaged idea of rhizomic assemblage as an urban-design strategy in three dimensions. To do so, they needed to distinguish their projects from the "cool," intellectual, collage-and-bricolage tradition with its memories of overall order prompted by minimal visual cues. The layered, heterotopic combination of linear scientific codes with the nonlinear self-organizing capacity of rhizomic assemblage has produced a disruption of the normative, continuous space implied by the Newtonian world-view, thus producing many strange, new, hybrid public spaces. Zaha Hadid's pioneering The Peak Project, her Hong Kong competition entry (1981), created just such a new hybrid space. Hadid located an extraordinary public entry in discrete public volumes floating in the empty middle of the section of the hotel, itself hovering far above the city.[80]

Daniel Libeskind: housing project, for the International Building Exhibition, Berlin, ca. 1988

Hadid's space as a rhizomic assemblage owes much to the pioneers of modernism, specifically to Le Corbusier, El Lissitzky, and the Russian Constructivists, who merged paths for individuals with articulated massing as assemblage. But it also moves beyond them in its layering techniques, developing the section within a layered, three-dimensional matrix and creating a new public space above the city. The normative codes of the Modernist hotel are here inverted and turned inside out, resulting in an unusual sandwich of programmatic spaces accommodated in floating slab blocks above and below the entry level, producing a spectacular entry sequence.[81]

Since 1981, many architects have explored rhizomic assemblage in the public space opened up by medium-sized public buildings. Like the earlier Archigram group, they have introduced media devices such as large public video screens, creating highly mediated environments. The sectional approach allows for the easy assemblage of nonlinear strings of code and program while maintaining "scientific" control sequences through the hidden matrix of geometric coordinating structures managed by engineering firms like Ove Arup or Buro Happold. Coop Himmelblau, in their prizewinning but unbuilt master plan for the French city of Melun-Senart (1986), proposed a multilevel city center accommodated within a three-dimensional matrix of free-floating bar buildings that would grow in density and complexity as the city developed over time. Michael Sorkin proposed an entire utopian new town designed on the same principles.[82]

A similar multilevel, sectional city center appeared in the public space of architect Daniel Libeskind's unbuilt housing project for the Internationale Bauausstellung (IBA, International Building Exhibition), which hovered over the Berlin Wall,[83] or in his project for Berlin's Alexanderplatz.[84] Studio Asymptote's

Joseph Fenton: Monolith Building diagram, Hybrid Buildings, Pamphlet Architecture 11, *1985*

SOM: John Hancock Tower, Chicago, 1968–70

OMA, Rem Koolhaas; Central Chinese Television Tower, Beijing, 2004

projects provide more examples, like their winning design for the Los Angeles West Coast Gateway competition of 1988. Here the entire building hovered over the sunken trough of the downtown highway, where traffic moves at 4 mph in rush hour. The project included giant fish-tanks at the western end of a long, thin, bar-shaped building, designed to act as a prism for drivers facing the sunset below and to rock to create waves. Separate bars accommodated the Museum of Immigration and museum facilities, shops, cafés, and the like. Escalators and slanting elevators led up to the bars, which hung off a huge frame system centered on the highway divider. Beneath the two bars, Studio Asymptote proposed a three-dimensional public space with screens showing the activities inside (research being done by immigrants, events, public notices, etc). Two small, mobile cinemas also occupied this sectional public space, moving on tracks and viewable by the general public on foot and, far below, in cars. Such participatory involvement of actors distinguishes rhizomic assemblage from the singular control of designers in Modernist scenographic collage or montage techniques.[85]

These disjunctive, rhizomic assemblages are the exact opposite of the "monolith" typology that Fenton describes as his third typology, even though they share the monolith's super scale, bricolage, and layering. In *Hybrid Buildings* (1985), Fenton describes a third method of combination, in which the form of the overall ensemble becomes important as a "monolith" while its interior is varied. The large-scale mask of the megaform dominates, compressing the diverse functions and multiple cells in strange mixtures within, creating a strange assemblage. Fenton describes how SOM's John Hancock Center tower in Chicago (1970) set the pattern for American hybrid, megaform, postmodern "megaliths" (continuing a Modernist tradition going back to Sert and Rogers's far smaller hybrid towers.) The Hancock Center's section includes a shopping mall in the base, office and residential foyers just above, then several floors of parking, then offices, and then a sky lobby for apartments, which continue almost to the top of the building. A radio studio and broadcast antenna cap the building just above a public restaurant and bar. At 1,000 feet the building was the tallest in the world until the completion of the World Trade Center in 1977.[86]

The wedge shape of the John Hancock "monolith" marks it as a late-Modernist work in which program is repressed in favor of a simple overall shape on the skyline. Fenton writes that the scale of the "monolith" enables people to live and work in the same building. This is indeed possible in the Hancock Tower, but one must change elevators in the sky lobby or groundfloor lobby to get from home to work.[87] Fenton gives as other examples of "monoliths" SOM's Olympic Tower in New York (1976), with its stack of shopping arcade, offices, and apartments and Roche and Dinkeloo's United Nations Plaza Building, which mixes hotel, offices, an athletic club with tennis courts, a bank, and a ground-floor lobby in its single form. The Midtown Special Zoning District in New York explicitly encouraged such hybrid buildings from the 1970s onwards; several can be found in a cluster around Fifth Avenue and 56th Street, where the mixed-use Trump Tower (Swanke Hayden Connell, 1983) set the trend.[90] Michigan Avenue in Chicago now has several such buildings, following the success of the John Hancock Center.[91] Developers proposed to rebuild downtown Los Angeles in this period with a series of such hybrid towers, some of which, like the Biltmore Hotel Tower (late 1980s), were realized.[92]

Koolhaas continued a version of this monolithic, Modernist tradition of top-down assemblage (incorporating bottom-up input from privileged actors) in his monumental megaform projects of the 1990s, where the exterior form dominates the interior arrangements. Interior ramps and complex urban programs disappear within a generic modern facade, as in the library for the University de Paris[93] with its interior spiral ramp, or the snaking ramp proposed for the interior of the Kahlsruhe media-center project's giant cube.[94] Koolhaas's Beijing Media Center (still under consideration as of 2004) continues this tradition at a gigantic scale, as does his Seattle Public Library (completed 2003).[95]

In my account of the Tele Città's armatures and enclaves I have already mentioned the rapid transformation of the Las Vegas Strip from its Modernist, auto-friendly heyday in the 1950s to a postmodernist jumble of urban images, presented as pedestrian-friendly environment, in the 1990s. Here the megaforms of the casinos have been thinly disguised by illusory pastiche and trompe l'oeil environments. The illusion could not be more blatant or obvious, but like Walt Disney's scenographic triumph with Main Street, Disneyland (1954), these faux urban environments mirror a deep-felt need for pleasure, the city, community, and history in the midst of accelerating global flows of capital and migration.

Las Vegas casinos from the 1990s have complex megaform sections, offering a layered, rhizomic assemblage compressing the city in order to create a heterotopia of illusion. The skyline is dominated by monolithic elements, including scaled-down reproductions of the New York City skyline in New York, New York casino (1997) and of the Eiffel Tower in Paris, Paris casino (1999). Modernist monofunctional elements may be distributed without any apparent logic within the complex section of the megaform. The "residential" sleeping area, for instance, may take the form of a slab-block typology that floats over the gambling hall on columns, as in the Venetian casino (2002). This casino even has freestanding "villas" set in gardens on the rooftop, displacing that old Modernist luxury standard, the penthouse. Guests at the Venetian reach these residential and villa areas by elevators from the periphery of the ground-floor gambling hall. This hall is styled as an indoor, covered Italian piazza with cafés and bars surrounding the central slot-machine area. A "Grand Canal" armature serves as the themed element of a shopping mall on the third floor, above the gambling hall and below the tower.[96]

In the Tele Città, media corporations (often owners of theme parks and casinos) have adopted the large-scale, megaform heterotopia of illusion as a mainstream, normative, organizational instrument. The media giant Sony, for

Grand Canal Shopping mall, the Venetian casino, Las Vegas

Ground- and first-floor plans, the Venetian casino, Las Vegas

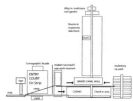

David Grahame Shane: section of the Venetian casino, Las Vegas

SOM: Time Warner Center, New York, 2004

instance, has built a huge media center, office complex, and hotel in Berlin (designed by the American architect Helmut Jahn) as part of the Potsdamerplatz development (2000). Noam Chomsky and Edward Herman, in *Manufacturing Consent: The Political Economy of the Mass Media* (1988),[97] have documented how these vast, global media conglomerates, now controlling satellites, television news stations, publishing houses, and more, are often owned by families descended from nineteenth-century and twentieth-century media barons: Murdoch, Gannett, Hearst, McGraw, Knight-Ridder, and so on.[98] The American media watchdog group FAIR (Fairness and Accuracy in Reporting) has documented the increasing concentration of media ownership, recently accelerated by the actions of the US Federal Communications Commission.[99] One media megacorporation, Sony, has embarked on a corporate strategy of building a global series of media centers comprising spectacle and sales rooms, with centers constructed so far in San Francisco, Berlin, and New York.[100] Another corporate media giant is currently constructing the Time Warner Center at 59th Street and Columbus Circle in New York. The Time Warner Center, presently the largest commercial project in America, is designed by SOM and David Childs. Here the hotel, apartments, television studios, and office components of both towers sit above a huge, curved, multistory shopping mall that includes a high-end gourmet food court, cinemas, and two large Jazz at Lincoln Center theaters with foyers overlooking Central Park. The developers have stuffed this vast assemblage of functions and actors into a monolithic form with twin towers. The $1.8-billion building was too expensive for any one bank to finance and was "condominiumized" into different compartments to spread the financial risk. Different developers, contractors and designers worked on different parts of the building within SOM and David Childs's virtual-design framework and building envelope.[101]

Like Bentham's Panopticon, this vast heterotopia of illusion represents a desperate attempt to miniaturize, mirror, and control the urban world, countering the speed of dispersal and globalization. It is a city within the city, a self-organizing system conforming to the codes of universal connectivity but disrupting the constant spread of the city powered by modern communications. Unlike the Panopticon, however, it is the multiple, fast-changing, "illusory" image-code that dominates in the shopping malls, cinemas, television studios, jazz theaters, gyms, food courts, and public rooms of this project. The very large hotel suites and apartment homes with 12-foot ceilings in the towers include every kind of luxury: multimedia rooms, libraries, gourmet kitchens, dens, gyms, office suites, and more. David Childs, the SOM partner in charge, emerged as the developer's representative in the rebuilding of the World Trade Center site after the tragedy of 9/11, modifying Libeskind's tower to propose the world's tallest building above an underground shopping mall, topped by a monumental public foyer, 70 stories of offices, and a public restaurant and viewing platform at 1,200 feet, with giant wind-turbine generators and a TV

Interior shopping arcade, Time Warner Center, New York, 2004

antenna above which would reach to 2,000 feet. A public theater or cultural building was originally to be folded into the foot of the building, though this component (to be designed by Frank Gehry) is now in a separate structure. The choice of SOM marks the ascendancy of heterotopias of illusion as the normative urban design typology for large-scale development in New York.[102]

Five-finger development plan, Copenhagen, 1940s

In contrast to the vast hybrid megamall and tower developments described above, I would like to end this section with the example of the community of Christiania, Copenhagen, a bottom-up heterotopia of illusion similar in some ways to the Walled City of Kowloon (both are on former military bases) but far lower density and more image savvy. Christiania provides an interesting test case because Copenhagen is a relatively small European capital city with a long tradition of democratic and participatory city planning where design standards have been held very high. In the nineteenth century, it grew in a ring-radial pattern around a compact medieval core (E1) and Enlightenment grid expansion (with the new royal palaces; E2). A recreational center was developed at the Tivoli Gardens outside the city walls (by the railway station) and played an important role in the early development of the modern European cinema (H3). Its extensive infrastructure of docks and railway is well preserved (A2, E2) and remained active until recently (the world's largest container-ship line is Danish-owned). In the postwar years, the city's famous "finger plan" guided growth in new towns and new developments along long, thin corridors associated with railways and highways (A2), with green space preserved between the fingers (E2) and thus always close to the new development. Much of the finger-plan housing was built on a low-rise, high-density model by public agencies or housing associations sponsored by the state (E2). Mall developers in Denmark must show regulators that their developments (H2) will not injure the trade of nearby towns and their stores (E1, E2).[103]

In the 1990s, the finger plan grew a sixth finger to the airport and a new bridge to Sweden that carries a new and high-speed train (A3, H3). The main railway station was redesigned to accommodate passengers to the airport, becoming another stop on the high-speed line to Sweden (H3). Much of Copenhagen's future housing growth has been predicted to occur along this corridor (E3) at the expense of dockland development. An enormous regional park with extensive recreational facilities (H3) replaces a former military firing range on the wetlands facing the old city (H2). Only recently has redevelopment started in the inner-city docklands, with new "wired" office blocks and "big box" retailing (H3).[104]

Central position of Christiania, Copenhagen, 2005

This well-ordered model of top-down, consultative, normative planning on the Cine Città model also contained an extraordinary example of a self-organizing system inside the specific boundaries of a heterotopia of illusion. Squatters established an illegal settlement in the abandoned Christianshavn military fort in Copenhagen in 1971 (]H2[). This settlement represents the great "unplanned" exception to the Danish town-planning success story. Much to the

Christiania

a) *Among Christiania's supporters are city planner Steen Eiler Rasmussen, lawyer Ole Krarup and writer Ebbe Kløvedal Reich, July 1974*
b) *Squatters moving into Christiania, 1971*
c) *Map of Christiania from free Christiania Guide*
d) *Laurie, A Time line of Christiania's struggles*

a

b

c

d

e

f

g

h

i

j

k

l

o

p

m

n

q

r

Christiania

e) *Christiania Gate,*
f) *Christiania self-built housing,*
(photographs from the Christiania Guide)
g) *Save Christiania Rally, 2004*
h) *Market place in Christiania*
(photographs from www.christiania.org)
i) *Painted house*
j) *Cabaret in Grey Hall, Christiania*
k) *Pedersen bike made in Chrstiania,*
(photographs from www.christiania.org)
l) *Protest graffiti in Copenhagen, 2004,*
m) *Signs at gate*
(photographs from Christiania Guide)
n) *Temporary protest banner on bridge in Copenhagen*
o, r) *Police take apart Pusher Street and one booth is moved to the National Museum, 16 March 2005*
(photographs courtesy of Nils Vest)

credit of the authorities, the squatters themselves, and the city-planning professions, a long-term debate has taken place about this heterotopic settlement that until very recently has resulted in multiple and complex forms of organization rather than in eviction.[105]

After squatters moved into the old base starting in 1971, they had to defend their illegal occupation against government forces. They created an entertainment area with restaurants, cafés, bars, and cabarets for theater groups and music festivals (H3 = I/D). In this battle, entertainment troupes and musicians proved essential to Christiania's survival. When the settlement was threatened, the artists appealed to the Danish's population's liberalism and sense of fair play through well-staged media protests. Christiania's exotically dressed (or undressed) cabaret artists were always sure to cause a sensation in the Scandinavian press as they faced the riot police and their batons and shields (H2 = D/I).

As a community outside the law, akin to the Walled City of Kowloon (H3), Christiania attracted renegades of many types, some of them criminals. However, the squatter community, in typical Danish fashion, required nonabusive behavior (H3 = I/D). The community enforced its own alcohol and soft-drug laws, banning

Protest movement in support of Christiania, 1976

hard drugs. It acted out psychodramas in the face of an invasion of hard-drug pushers on "Pusher Street" (A3). It built a decorated toilet for the motorcycle gangs in order to stop them urinating in public. Finally, it sought the help of the authorities to deal with the invasion of violent gangs and armed pushers of hard drugs who were exploiting the "free" situation (H2). At the same time, it vocally opposed uninvited incursions of the police into the community.

The Christiania squatters banned cars in favor of bicycles and pedestrians, as has also been done in the center of Copenhagen (A3). They also organized new industries, with cycle manufacturing and specialized cycle carts as an important business, thus supporting the mass cycling movement in Copenhagen. They also supported a female-run iron foundry making stoves and patio furniture, new carpentry and stone-cutting shops, antique stores, used-clothing stores, and the like in old military buildings (]H2[). Today, these stores also sell over the Internet (E3). The squatters organized a planning committee that prevented the building of large and extravagant houses, favoring communal habitations and cooperative arrangements in small, freestanding buildings (E3). They also self-administered their own everyday disputes and held all property in common. They restored and attempted to maintain many of the old military buildings, learning new crafts and applying for government preservation grants. With state support, they created their own schools, as did other communities outside Christiania (H3).

The Christiania squatters also pioneered the integration of many ecological reforms into the already progressive agricultural and industrial economy of Denmark. They grew organic farm products and vegetables for their restaurants (E3) and recycled their own waste products organically, using human waste for agricultural purposes as in present-day India or ancient China or Rome. They also created a new park for their community and the surrounding neighborhood in the old fortifications along the edge of Christianshavn, the portion of the city at the north end of Amager Island (E3).

Christiania, a heterotopic exception inside the predominantly social-democratic tradition of postwar Denmark, has always had a political dimension. It survived in part because of the liberalism of the planning profession, including Steen Eiler Rasmussen, who argued in the 1960s against suppression of the commune. Rasmussen, the author of *London, the Unique City* (1937) and *Towns and Town Building* (1949), wrote in a letter to the press that Denmark would lose its soul if it allowed this symbol of freedom to die. Christiania functioned as an important social safety valve for people inside a well-ordered democratic state. The newly elected conservative government of Denmark of the early 2000s, however, has vowed to sell the land of Christiania to developers, reversing the code of accommodation established by earlier governments. The pioneering hippy settlement sits in an area close to the dockland office corridor, on valuable central-city real estate beside a new university campus (H3) located on a decommissioned naval base (]H2[). As of 2004, occupants have been offered the opportunity to buy their own homes (subverting Christiania's communal ethic) and face the loss of some areas to redevelopment under proposed legislation. The new government has also proposed reducing the state planning office's role and privatizing public housing (E3), mimicking the British Thatcherite agenda of the 1980s.

Christiania is an example of a heterotopia of illusion organized from the bottom up that has, so far, managed its relationship with the surrounding disciplinary regimes (i.e., the government and planning profession) in a spirit of optimism and hope. Nor is Christiania unique in its determination to survive despite official disapproval; many cities have areas of "squatter" housing, shanty towns, favelas, or barrios that survive despite official prohibitions.

In the next section I review how heterotopias interact with the cities that surround them, mirroring, working with, and modifying the normative models in which they are embedded.

Heterotopias

a) *Aerial view, Forbidden palace, Beijing*
b) *Roman colosseum converted into a medieval town, Arles, France,*
c) *Ocean liner, 1950s*
d) *Mining camp Belgian Congo, ca. 1900*
e) *Ford factory, River Rouge, Detroit, 1920s*
f) *Mike Webb:* Sin Center *project, Leicester Square, London, 1962*
g) *Coop Himmelb(l)au:* model of Gasometer B Conversion *project, Vienna, 1995–2001*
h) *Bernard Tschumi: conversion of factory to art center, Le Fresnoy, France, 1991–97*
i) *Boyarsky-Murphy: conversion of Wren church tower to apartments, London, 2004–05*

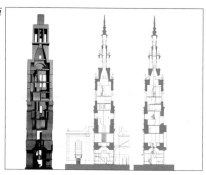

dispersal along corridors of acceleration. Eventually this binary system of organization proves incapable of managing the flows of the system and a second period of instability ensues—as it has for most cities in the last 50 years.

Out of this second period of transition, a multicentered network system emerges to handle the apparently chaotic flows of diverse participants in an increasingly global network (I call this arrangement the *net city*). Growth appears to take place at random over the network, with no clear hierarchy or top-down patterning. Relationships can shift and change among actors, resulting in rapid change and instability.

The rest of this section expands on this brief sketch of the evolution of urban systems, incorporating Lynch's theory of urban actors, three normative models, and the enclaves, armatures, and heterotopias we have examined in previous sections.

Urban actors have recurrently combined and recombined certain devices in modeling their own operations. The enclave, armature, and heterotopia are among these devices in all city models and transitional periods. That is, actors in the three normative models have used them both as steady-state organizational aids and during the two traumatic transitions (Archi Città to Cine Città, Cine Città to Tele Città). These two transitions are particularly associated with heterotopias of deviance and illusion, respectively.

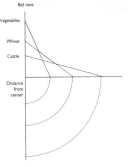

I. Steady State: The Archi Città: Gleick's First Phase

Gleick's sequence begins with a "steady state" of self-organization and growth around a single center. In urban terms, this is the city model of Von Thünen's Central Place theory (discussed in Chapter 1). It is the European Archi Città, which grows in annular rings, like Paris, demolishing its walls at intervals to provide more room for growth, as a lobster sheds its shell. This city can be denoted E/A + H1, where H1 = (D + I). In various cultural models this city's sub-elements are arranged around central enclaves that include Aztec temple enclosures, Greek and Roman agoras or forums, and the squares associated with Islamic mosques and medieval European cathedrals. We have already seen (Chapter 3) different urban patterns in the residential, multi-use fabric of such cities, ranging from the grids and courtyard houses of China, Greece, and Rome to the nonperspectival, syntagmatic housing fabrics of medieval Islamic and western European cities with their systems of cul-de-sacs. We have also noted the development of the row house in Europe by the Vikings.

Paul Krugman: diagram of Von Thünen's; Central Place theory, The Self-Organizing Economy, *1996*

In our study of the shifting enclave–armature relationship we concentrated on the town square and its approach street. We also distinguished several subphases within the "steady state" growth phase of nested enclaves and connecting armatures. From a Eurocentric point of view, these steady-state phases comprise the preclassical period (Egypt, Middle East, China, Japan, India and Central America, Aztec Empire, etc.), classical period (Greek, Rome, etc.), the Viking and Gothic periods, and the Islamic invasion. This history continues with the western European medieval period (with its new towns and trade around the Mediterranean), the Renaissance city-states of Italy, and the development of perspective, which led to the recasting of the enclave and armature relationship in the continental European baroque period. Here we noted the emergence of the network city model developed for tourists in Rome—multiple centers with stretched armatures between—anticipating the breakup of the single-center system in Europe in the Enlightenment (discussed at the end of Chapter 3). H1 heterotopias are built into the fabric of this urban system at the scale of the single urban cell. Small-scale H1 heterotopias act to contain change, sickness, or any kind of turbulence within the fabric of the city; exceptional large-scale structures—e.g., castles and walls (H2) or cathedrals and mosques (H3)—also act as stabilizers in the system, containing utopian aspirations of actors for control or freedom.

This "steady state" system of city organization began with networks of small urban settlements. As we saw in Chapter 1, Kostof noted that there were few cities of over 10,000 people in the ancient and medieval worlds. Settlements formed a hierarchy from tiny hamlets to villages, towns, and cities. Such a hierarchical network structure has its limits; it breaks apart when a scale of operation is reached that is beyond the control of a single center, given available communication rates. When this occurs, the original E1 enclave does not simply disappear as a new system develops but continues to exist, competing with other organizational forms. For example, the hinterland connections of the larger centers remain intact: a network of smaller subsidiary towns, villages, and hamlets persists as one stratum in a layered set of networks, one level of function in the developing, accidental city assemblage.

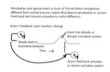

David Grahame Shane: diagram of perturbation of steady state

As I noted in the brief history of the relations between armature and enclaves given in Chapter 3, in the transitional state of the French and American revolutions revolutionary actors recoded the symbolic display system of the multicentered baroque armature and enclave system for the secular values of the emerging nation-state. This recoding created a new urban system with the grid as an underlay, as in L'Enfant's plan of Washington or Napoleon's plan for the western Paris extension.

II. The Steady State Disturbed: Heterotopia Type 2: Gleick's Second Phase

In the second of Gleick's phases (as applied to city theory), heterotopias of deviance or discipline (H2) move into dominance over heterotopias of crisis (H1). There are crucial differences between heterotopias of crisis and heterotopias of deviance or discipline. Both act to maintain order in the overall system by containing change, but the former (H1) is located anywhere inside the fabric of the city, while the latter (H2) is either moved outside the city or placed in a central position at the city's core. Foucault pointed to this geographical shift in his "heterotopology," instancing the cemetery that migrated from the churchyard to a peripheral, suburban location and became a garden or park in the process. Further, the Industrial Revolution results in larger organizational capacity, larger urban fragments, and a scale-jump in the size of heterotopias (H1 to H2), which, like society in general, become more specialized, sorting and segregating people, goods, ideas, and information with more speed, accuracy, and precision.

Foucault chose Bentham's Panopticon to symbolize the heterotopia of deviance and discipline (H2). This choice is significant, for in the Panopticon cells surround the hidden "eye of power" in the central tower, exactly reflecting the annular organization of Von Thünen's Central Place theory. Foucault wrote that despite Galileo's best efforts, space resisted homogenization, remaining "thoroughly fantasmatic" for many generations. The old, feudal hierarchical power structures and mental ordering devices survived; this social and conceptual organizational "tree" apparatus did not disappear overnight but remained as a central-place model within the new system, impeding expansion and limiting movement across the center. In Europe, the ring-radial hierarchy of the Panopticon and garden city models dominated, albeit with technologically enhanced and extended armatures. As Batty and Longley note in *Fractal Cities* (1996), the potent tree structure of this hierarchical system allowed for repetition of the same basic pattern (the ring-radial arrangement) at several levels from the top down, while also suggesting room for local variations.[107]

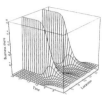

Paul Krugman: diagram of Alan Turing's, ring-pulse development model, The Self-Organizing Economy, 1996

Foucault stresses the transformational power of H2 heterotopias of deviance such as Bentham's Panopticon, where professionals applied "compensatory" discipline to those who could not conform to the behavioral norms of modern society. On the periphery of the old attractor, actors found a new space and freedom to make alternative spatial arrangements, developing new morphologies and typologies, recombining armatures and enclaves to house their activities. Later versions of the Panopticon feature armatures: long, top-lit galleries inside multistoried cell blocks radiating from the warden's central station, a ring-radial plan that could also be applied to hospitals, insane asylums, museums, universities, and cities. Here people could be sorted and held under the watchful eye of the central controller, the centralized coordination point whose logic ran counter to the prevailing "extensive," uniform space that prevailed outside the enclave's walls. Inside the walls there was a surfeit of order and discipline; outside, individuals faced the chaos of the city and were expected to choose the "freedom" of the open, infinite space of the reformed industrial city, represented by Cerdá's grid or the Garden Cities of Tomorrow (1904) network diagram.

The breakdown of the steady-state system with its slow, incremental growth and spatial emphasis on incremental "emplacement" is marked by proliferation of H2 heterotopias of deviance on the edge of the old city. As in Howard's diagram, many functions previously held inside the city fabric in H1 heterotopias of crisis move with the expansion of the city to the periphery. Hospitals, prisons, slaughterhouses, factories, insane asylums, colleges, orphanages, and boarding schools appear as freestanding, urban fragments in the green belts surrounding satellite and mother cities. Eventually, these models are applied to the center of the city itself. The H2 heterotopia becomes dominant in association with the armatures of flow that facilitated the emergence of the industrial city. This is Cerdá's age of boulevards, railways, and accelerated communications systems.

The European port cities, with their global networks of trade and colonies, acted as the most powerful H2 heterotopias, transforming the feudal city. In ports and colonies, actors developed new modes of organization to handle and accelerate the sorting of complex flows from around the globe. Armatures provided essential linear conduits for this process. Ships and other vehicles traveling along the corridors of stretched armatures were mobile heterotopic elements in the system (recall that for Foucault, ships are the heterotopia "par excellence"). First docks, later railway stations and goods yards provided the interface between the old system of centering and the new systems of flows with their large-scale, global geometries.

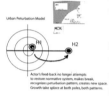

Urban Perturbation Model

H1 Central Place system holds disturbance within city until it threatens to disrupt normative system.
H2 Creates new attractor outside city with economic advantages, cheap land, low taxes etc.
Disturbing urban activity is shifted to new site outside normative system.

David Grahame Shane: Migration of Heterotopia 2 to edge of city

In Chapter 1 we saw how Krugman described the emergence of two subcenters in close proximity to the first center of Von Thünen's Central Place theory, located on opposite sides of that center. One of these subcenters would prosper while the other fell into the "shadow" of the original and of its farside twin. This twin-subcenter configuration is a familiar pattern; paired cities have often emerged in proximity to an attractor on either side of town, but small variations give certain points an initial advantage, leading to asymmetrical and uneven development that becomes amplified over time, resulting in the typical twin-city phenomenon (two healthy twins with a third center struggling for survival). Rather than being eradicated by the City as a Machine, these small variations are amplified by urban actors seeking an advantage, however slight, in their struggle to make a living or find pleasure in the city.

Turing's model of the bifurcation of the single-center model through a period of turbulence to form a double center took these slight perturbations into account to explain how a double-center system emerged. For Turing this was the first stage in the development of a multicenter system based on feedback and built-in amplification systems in the ring (single-center) city. In fact, this twin system involved the initial failure of a multicenter system. This failure resulted in part from resistance to change by entrenched urban actors who were supported by an existing social and urban hierarchy, represented in our dictionary definitions of the city extending down to the hamlet.

Small differences in topography and perturbations in climate contribute also to these functional and locational differentiations, helping one of the subcenters to become dominant. In London, for instance, prevailing winds and the presence of noxious industries meant that the west of the city became the high-income area of consumption and government while the east became the working-class area of production. Heterotopias of illusion (H3)—theaters, shops, arcades, galleries, and eventually department stores and cinemas—congregated in the

something of a blockage, converted to administrative and cultural purposes (with as much of the medieval "slums" as possible demolished by new road cuts).

State streets like Napoleon's Rue de Rivoli in Paris (1808), Nash's Regent Street in London (1810), and Schinkel's Unter den Linden in Berlin (1820s) acted as specialized armatures for ceremonial events, new public spaces leading to new suburbs. Later, boulevards and railways handled the commercial flows of the city. The Archi Città still existed inside the new Cine Città network as an attractor, a distinct enclave and blockage to the free flow of people, goods and information, housing undesirable elements of the population in its slums and rookeries. As we saw in our overview of London's A2 armatures in Chapter 3, this situation led to increasingly complex vertical sectional developments for transportation infrastructures and ultimately to the desire to spread these infrastructures along the width of enormous boulevards stretching as linear cities across the city's hinterland or territorial network. Over time, these once exceptional arrangements became normative modes of urban development, as in the streetcar suburbs of early-modern industrial cities (exemplified by the A2-type Ocean Parkway armature in New York, designed by Frederick Law Olmsted and Calvert Vaux in the 1870s, whose roadway, park, and railway systems provided the skeleton for a finger of new development penetrating rural Brooklyn to the Atlantic seashore).[109]

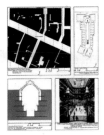

Cleveland Arcade, Cleveland, OH, 1888–90 (courtesy University of Toronto)

Armatures dominate the Cine Città as symbolic intermediaries between urban actors, functioning as linear organizing devices connecting locations in a universal system of spatial coordinates. Enclaves, as places of storage, monofunctional systems, and places of rest, are subsidiary to armatures, as are heterotopias (which still house people, activities, and things excluded from the logical structure of the dominant order). We might express this relationship as Cine Città equals A2 (armature) dominating or "over" E2 (enclave) plus H2 (heterotopia): Cine Città = A2/E2 + H2, where H2 = D/I (the heterotopia of deviance or discipline).

While armatures dominated, compressed heterotopic enclaves at nodes of the communication and transportation systems played an important role in this sorting, sequencing and ordering activity in the industrial city. Here actors developed self-organizing skills and feedback systems for the handling and temporary storage in heterotopic nodes of the goods, information, and people that daily flow into the city from its surrounding territory and global networks. In the nineteenth century, for example, industrial city clerks and secretaries proliferated, maintaining the ledgers and bank balances of organizations, helping monitor their performance and efficiency with useful statistical information. Written records, filing systems, reference libraries, and research offices were a part of this professional maintenance system.

Actors participating in the feedback loops that maintained the overall balance of the system developed their own architectures, building typologies, and urban morphologies to house their own functional requirements. Specialized industrial building typologies such as the factory, department store, shopping arcade, casino, stock market, public library, university, parliament house, and so on emerged inside modernizing nation-states of the nineteenth century. The skyscraper office building symbolized the importance attached to these feedback mechanisms within the City as a Machine.

By the beginning of the twentieth century a globally networked hierarchy of industrial cities had been established, with London and New York as primary centers of control and command, secondary cities like Paris or Chicago, and tertiary cities with specialized functions. As Kostof noted, these specialized landscapes sometimes were places of production (port cities, factory towns, mill towns, etc.) and at other times were places of leisure (spa towns, resort towns, seaside towns, leisure centers, national parks in America, etc).[110]

First-generation reformers like Cerdá and early city planners imagined a Cartesian system where all space was in theory the same, and any one point in the grid therefore potentially as good as any other. The City as a Machine model incorporated this concept of universal space along with Newton's laws of action and reaction, inertia, force, and gravitational attraction. In such "scientific" thinking, armatures corresponded to the flow of energy between attractors, an attractor's size being approximately proportional to its capacity to attract. A system of state-sponsored street armatures, such as those comprising the Vienna Ring-strasse praised by Otto Wagner in *Modern Architecture* (1896) and attacked by Camillo Sitte in *Town Planning on Artistic Principles* (1889), represented the new public space of flow.

SOM: Freedom Tower on the New York skyline, 2004 (courtesy LMDC website, 2004)

The second generation of modern "scientific urbanism" inherited all the morphologies and typologies of the first, but sought to break the connection between the stretched armature and the city. The CIAM designers specifically detached the housing fabric of the city to form blocks separate from the channels of high-speed transport. They isolated the new public space of the city in new enclaves or precincts that replaced the old town squares. All the functions of the city were segregated in special monofunctional enclaves and special transportation armatures.

Le Corbusier and many other Modernists inherited the central emphasis of their cities from old Beaux Arts hierarchies. As late as 1932, Le Corbusier's Ville Radieuse still had a single town center with skyscrapers gathered at its symbolic center of administration and control (a great central armature led to this complex) and an industrial complex forming its opposite pole. In his plan for rebuilding St. Dié (1945), Le Corbusier reverted to exactly this same axial armature formula to connect the castle-cathedral on one side of the river and the railway station-industrial belt on the other. (He replaced the old main street of the town with a highway axis and then pedestrian axis on a civic, raised platform above a gigantic parking garage.)

In the City as a Machine, enclaves survived as self-organizing, specialized, monofunctional E2 places protected by their occupants, owners, or operators.

Old agricultural-field divisions often provided the framework, setting boundaries for residential, industrial, or commercial development. Agrarian villages with high streets might be incorporated into the sprawling metropolis, becoming local subcenters as in London (e.g., Hampstead) or New York (e.g., Greenwich Village). As the edge of the city expanded into previously agricultural territory, functions were pavilionized in specialized buildings, each isolated from the other (see Chapter 2). Extrapolating this trend, the reforming Modernists of the CIAM movement foresaw a city of large, isolated towers and slab blocks interconnected by highways. In reality, however, postwar pavilionization took a very different form.

The dumbbell mall, which we discussed in Chapter 3, reflected the basic armature-based bipolarity of the City as a Machine in miniature, providing in turn a model for the H2 development of suburban subcenters. Around these subcenters were grouped the residential enclaves of single-family homes, isolated, individual pavilions sprawling over the landscape at low densities. At the center the skyscraper, as also noted earlier, was organized around a vertical armature, compressing an enormous number of cells into a small H2 footprint. The skyscraper should be ranked alongside Bentham's Panopticon as a symbol of the modern city as sorting machine.

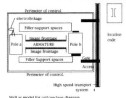

David Grahame Shane: enclave and armature–diagram of dumbbell mall

In the network city, as it turned out, supplementary systems of communication—not the megaform physical interconnections anticipated by CIAM—helped coordinate actors in the city, spanning great distances across colonial networks. These systems were necessary to link rich and poor, metropolis and colony, center and edge, city and country, consumption and production. They had been present, though less technically powerful, in the Archi Città, as verbal lines of communication. In the City as a Machine, telegraphs, telephones, and typewriters mechanized communications, requiring and imposing their own symbolic conventions and codes. First photography, then the cinema produced mechanical images of the world, providing more opportunities for actors to construct visual codes and conventions. Accelerated and mechanized communication armatures inevitably bypassed some enclaves, namely those areas without enough income to afford the initial expense of the new technologies. (This phenomenon continues today, as the poor are left with inferior access, or no access, to the Internet.)

Heterotopias of illusion played a secondary role in the Cine Città—secondary, that is, to the all-important armatures of technicized movement and communication—but were important as an alternative, noncoercive way to order society through the promulgation of norms associated with leisure and pleasure. As mentioned earlier in this chapter, perspective, photography, and the cinema implied the mechanization of vision, mirroring, and introspection. Modern media had the power to suggest new identities, new styles of living, and new fashions to consumers anxious about the terms of their complex and fluid urban existence. Walter Benjamin connected the anxiety caused by the chaotic boom-and-bust patterns modern living with our desire for compensatory outward signs of financial and social success. He identified arcades, department stores, boulevards, and world's fairs as display spaces for the emerging urban bourgeoisie. Foucault, using categories different from Benjamin's but compatible with them, identified the world's fair (along with the modern theater and cinema) as a heterotopia of illusion.

Again we should note the presence of transitional heterotopias in the Cine Città. Heterotopias of crisis (H1) survived residually in the city fabric well into the Industrial Revolution. "Cottage industries," for example, in which factory work was done by families in the home, started the Industrial Revolution and continued to compete successfully with machines far into the nineteenth century. Indeed, they can still be found in developing countries (e.g., in the garment industry). It also should be noted that a heterotopia of illusion—the cinema, a place of collective entertainment—gives this città its name. The linear order of production structures the organization of the city; the cinema indicates the corresponding importance of consumption (accelerated by communications) and the new, irrational rules of nonperspectival montage that the cinema itself (and related technologies) make possible.

IV. Disturbing the Binary Dynamic: Heterotopia 3: Gleick's Fourth Phase

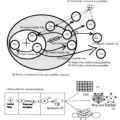

David Grahame Shane: media and the proliferation of heterotopia 3

Krugman, starting from the "twin city" configuration described above, went on to explain the emergence of multiple centers using mathematical formulas developed by Turing, one of the inventors of the computer. Turing hypothesized that the pattern of growth around a city's perimeter was controlled by the spacing and timing of pulses of growth radiating from the original nucleus of the old city. Satellite cities would have their own dynamic; some would flourish and some would fade. This has certainly been the case in London, where some new towns (i.e., to the northwest, like Milton Keynes) have flourished while others (i.e., to the northeast) have struggled. Small differences in topography, location, and climate can contribute to the success or failure of a satellite town, given the binary relationships of the City as a Machine.

Compensatory attempts to construct a level playing field for new towns, making them all equal and the same (e.g., in postwar Sweden) led the Lund School of urban geographers to stress the need for differentiation. Proponents of the Lund School argued for the agglomeration of specialist services in dense, compact nodes to facilitate and accelerate development, stressing that despite accelerating networks of communication the need for "milieux," where people could meet face to face and simply talk, would increase. These milieux would, however, have good transportation links and high-speed media connections to facilitate feedback into the network.

The key work of milieux, according to the Lund School, is data processing and pattern recognition, that is, interpreting flows and finding relationships ("sites") within these flows. Heterotopias of illusion facilitate this process through their emphasis on the virtual and conceptual mirror–spaces that allow reflection and the modeling of emerging patterns. Heterotopias of illusion are places where actors can experiment without impacting the whole system; they provide a sense of release and freedom. They are set apart by their speed and flexibility, already evident in the stage sets of the Renaissance and baroque theater and further enhanced by mechanization in the industrial era. This acceleration has itself accelerated with the onset of the digital era and miniaturization of communication devices such as televisions, telephones, and personal computers.

While the modeling of emerging patterns can in theory take place anywhere, as in "data havens" or "computer farms" (i.e., banks of storage computers in offshore or hinterland locations), the skilled operatives needed for this process often prefer to live in cities or sprawling urban areas. Large global corporations who need such operatives create heterotopic concentrations of milieux as attractors that run counter to the dispersive tendencies of both the Cine Città and Tele Città. These informational milieux reinforce old centers and secondary centers as well as multiple "edge-cities" and satellite towns. Giant theme parks and megamalls form the tip of this cyberneticized iceberg, impacting the network city at mega scale, middle scale, and micro-urban scale. Las Vegas's casinos have been highly commercial, highly successful examples of these H3 heterotopic devices, both in the 1960s Modernist phase studied by the Venturi, Scott Brown, and Izenour team and in their postmodern form as pedestrian-friendly, pseudo-urban, scenographic-village environments. Such mixed-use, multifunctional, heterotopic armatures and enclaves in central- and resort-city milieux disrupt the City as a Machine segregation into four specialized functions (as described by CIAM's 1933 Modernist manifesto, the Athens Charter; see Chapter 1). They create new attractors that are not easily replicated in all locations.

View of Main Street, Celebration, FL, 2000

The breakdown of the "binary" system, with its pulses of growth at two poles, has been marked by the growth of H3 heterotopias of illusion at multiple strategic points in the global urban network. These heterotopias appear at the center (e.g., festival markets), on the edge (e.g., megamalls like the Galleria, Houston), and within the basic cell of the system, the individual house (e.g., MacMansions, West 8 on Borneo Island, Amsterdam), in order to process and store the enormous flow of information and images that enable the dispersed city to function efficiently.

V. Multicentered Network Cities: The Tele Città: Gleick's Fifth Phase

Gleick's fifth phase and final phase of self-organizational growth is the "chaotic system," which switches between multiple models, nodes and systems of growth, stasis and shrinkage.

Here the lessons of H3 heterotopias, especially the flexibility enabled by the ongoing communications revolution, allow both increased urban density and continued dispersal at a low density. Actors recondition parts of the Archi Città and Cine Città as they are incorporated into an emergent global network city. This network city allows both bottom-up feedback from individuals who want to customize their performance space and environment, creating their own personal narratives, and the economies of the top-down distribution of mass-market items that are now fundamental to life. This double structure is enabled by the ongoing information revolution that distributes information widely throughout the system, allowing the apparently random combination of urban elements at any point (modified of course by local conditions). Fractal patterns that designers used to associate with standardization (as in Ebenezer Howards's top-down, hierarchical garden city diagram) can now be broken apart; each element can be customized from off-the-shelf elements, giving morphological and typological studies a new importance and flexibility as sources for hybrids.

Two contradictory spatial conditions—openness and density—are highlighted in this process of personalized narrative and customized morphogenesis in the network city. Both conditions appeared previously in the Cine Città, but they are no longer limited by informational restraints to their old spatial locations. They can appear anywhere.

View of New York, New Visions Meeting, New York, 2002

Openness may appear in the center of the city as a result of civic irresponsibility and economic conditions (as in Detroit, USA), of war (as in Beirut or Sarajevo), or natural disasters (hurricanes, floods, tornadoes, etc.). It may be occasioned by some heartrending tragedy requiring a memorial performance space where urban actors can recast their city, whether from the bottom up, the top down, or in an imperfect dialogic process involving many voices. (A much-flawed version of this process occurred in New York in the wake of 9/11, namely, the 5000-person consultative process sponsored by Imagine New York in the Jacob Javits Center in the summer of 2002.)

Openness, which depends on the ability of managers to hear and process multiple voices in making decisions, has also allowed the further dispersal of the city. This openness depends on expanded communications systems that allow the inhabitation of remote regions beyond the limits of the old regional city and support a mobile, nomadic lifestyle for rich and poor alike.

The second condition is a new compression and enclosure at previously unheard of densities. This is made possible by the increased computational power of informational systems, which enable actors to design and manage these complex situations on a massive scale. Vast computational power enables actors to handle the multiple personal narratives of individual actors as threads in a massive informational weave, creating a web of individualized flows that merges in and out of larger, massive, fractal patterns in the city (e.g., commuting to work or play).

Density and compactness enables megaform nodes within the network to act as heterotopic attractors, contrasting with the dispersal and diffusion otherwise facilitated by the Tele Città network. The privatization of previously public activities and a devotion to mobility, travel, and open (or at least cavernous) spaces creates an enormous nomadic population that flows from one such attractor to another, depending on the season, employment patterns, and income. Since distances can be enormous and populations can be dispersed and displaced, media images—which can catch up with anyone anywhere, anytime—become important in defining an attractor. Attractors must perforce become "cybrids," hybrid places with a cybernetic or media presence. The creators and managers of heterotopias of illusion (H3) thus dominate this city, exploiting armatures and enclaves for their own scenographic purposes. We might express this relationship as Tele Città equals heterotopia of illusion (H3) dominating or "over" both A (armature) and E (enclave); thus, Tele Città = H3/(A3 + E3).

Heterotopias of illusion play a primary role in the Tele Città, providing a noncoercive way of ordering society through norms associated with leisure and pleasure. These norms are flexible and capable of being generated from the bottom up in self-organizing systems in the new, wired media as well as from the top down in traditional hierarchies. The mechanization of vision implied by perspective, photography, the cinema, and later media has the power to suggest new identities, new styles of living, and new fashions to consumers. Marshall McLuhan has examined the impact of mass media on the American suburbs in *The Mechanical Bride* (1951), especially the effect of advertising aimed at the female consumer, housewife, and mother trapped in isolated pavilions amid housing developments distant from the urban nucleus. After the success of Disneyland in 1955, American mall developers quickly learned the power of advertising and the importance of theming their developments to attract customers.

Night view of Times Square and 42nd Street, New York, 2000

In Chapter 1, I described the emergence of the scenographic armature in Serlio's *Five Books of Architecture* (1541), as a setting for specific urban actors, related closely to Lynch's three normative models. In Chapter 2 we saw how such armatures also played an earlier role in the period of the emergence of urban design in New York and the design of Battery Park City. In Chapter 3 we noted the reconfiguration of the armature and enclave to accommodate H3 heterotopias of illusion. In New York highly mediated, themed armatures were imported into traditional entertainment enclaves (e.g., 42nd Street), often accompanied by purging of their red-light heterotopic allure (H2). On 42nd Street, in particular, this reconfiguration of the heterotopia of illusion (H3) was accompanied by the installation of a series of million-square-foot offices—largely for media companies, their lawyers, and their accountants—in bulky towers above the street's neon glitter. With the ascendancy of the H3 heterotopia of illusion, suburban malls and multiplex cinemas could not remain competitive unless updated with New Urbanist street scenographies designed to combat the convenience of the elaborate media centers inside MacMansions or beginning to appear in American cars and mobile homes.

The drive toward concentration still remains in the Tele Città; however, concentration no longer occurs at the binary poles of the modern city, but at multiple heterotopic subcenters. As we have seen, it took time for urban designers to catch up with the impact of the media on the city, to develop new public spaces in the city section that could carry media images and communication systems, and to absorb the notion of rhizomic assemblage. An early and influential avant-garde image of the exploded megaform heterotopia of illusion was Zaha Hadid's Peak Project project for Hong Kong (competition 1981, design submitted 1983; never built). Developments such as the Time Warner Center in New York, designed by SOM, have taken ideas from avant-garde work, especially regarding the heterotopic organization of mixed uses in the base of the towers and mixed use of the towers as hotels, apartments, and offices.

These once exceptional arrangements are becoming normative modes of urban development in the informational network city. This shift is exemplified by the H2-to-H3 conversion of the Mizner Park mall in Boca Raton, Florida, to an open square, and by the New Urbanist conversion of the Winter Park mall in Orlando, Florida to an isolated main-street scenography in the midst of parking lots. Smart-growth policies merely trim the edges of the urban megamachine with village-like scenographic elements without interfering with the fundamentals of the City as a Machine methodology outlined in Chapter 1. Ecological reformers such as Doug Kelbaugh, author of the utopian *Pedestrian Pocket* (1989), have had to struggle hard against the grain of an American society used to cheap gasoline and open landscapes ready for development.

Mizner Park Regional Mall conversion, Boca Raton, FL, 1992

The network city might, as we have noted earlier, take different forms depending on land costs, available energy sources, political controls, cultural preferences, and the transportation and communication technologies of the period. US patterns of sprawl have differed from Latin American, with suburbs and strips predominating in the former and barrios and favelas in the latter. In Europe, there have been different patterns of suburban growth in southeast England, Holland, Belgium, France, Spain, the Veneto region of Italy, and the Swiss valleys. Asian network cities, because of climatic considerations, are inhabited quite differently still, despite all their gloss of New Urbanism or Eurocentric design.

As in the City as a Machine, urban actors are taking lessons learned from once exceptional situations in heterotopias—in this case, H3 heterotopias of illusion—and applying them to the city as a whole. H3 heterotopias, with their multiple virtual combinations of armatures and enclaves for sorting flows of imagery, information, goods, materials, and people, are providing equipment crucial to the stabilization and success of actors in this phase of the urban-network system. Instability and flow are constant in this city, requiring a relaxed, flexible emphasis on timing, sorting, and ordering of relationships to form "sites."

In the Tele Città informational flows dominate the city. Every cell can, in theory, be wired into the larger informational network (though some are more equal than others), providing an organizational capacity beyond earlier models.

This mode of organization allows for top-down informational distribution in the traditional "propaganda" mode of earlier cities; it also allows for a new responsiveness to bottom-up (one-to-many or person-to-person) feedback and organization via the Internet, consumer surveys, and the like. Every cell in this network becomes a fractal image of the city, a miniature, multicellular, heterotopic element that allows for work space, recreation, living arrangements with fast connections to global and local communication and transportation networks. The heterotopia becomes the rule rather than the exception.

VI. The Emergence of Heterotopic Nodes in the Tele Città

We are still in the throes of shifting from a primarily Cine Città world to a primarily Tele Città world, so it is difficult—as usual—to predict the future. It has, however, become clear that heterotopic developments are one of the norms of the network city. They allow for a great flexibility in the retrofitting of previous, specialized built structures for new uses. In the Tele Città, old heterotopias survive in new situations or roles and heterotopias continue to play their transitional role in reworking the Archi Città and Cine Città for use in the Tele Città. In the early 1990s Renzo Piano, for instance, remodeled the old Fiat factory in Turin, with its rooftop race trial track praised by Le Corbusier in *Towards a New Architecture* (1927), as an H3 mixed-use building containing conference center, hotel, offices, and exhibition hall. Bernard Tschumi created a new media center using the rooftop of a factory shed at Fresnoy in France (1991–97), partially wrapping the old building with a new skin and inhabiting the space in between the two roofs. Old power stations (e.g., the Bankside power station in London, remodeled in the late 1990s as the Tate Modern art museum), military barracks, and even railway stations (e.g., Paris's Gare d'Orsay (H2), converted to the Musée d'Orsay (H3) in the early 1980s) have all been taken over by arts organizations.

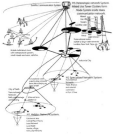

David Grahame Shane: Networks and heterotopic nodes

I have also highlighted the role of the festival mall and theme park as heterotopias of illusion and predecessors of the larger transformation of society into one based on commodified leisure and pleasure. This transformation has incorporated our bodies into a larger system of consumption and production in a number of ways anticipated in Foucault's study of heterotopias, through modified daily practices of exercise, eating, hygiene, leisure, and sexuality. In the Tele Città, older forms of city organization are constantly being brought into play as organizational or image-making devices at the service of this commodification.

Part of the festival markets' success was based on food, as in the early case of Ghiradelli Square in San Francisco in the 1970s with its chocolate factory, or Faneuil Hall in Boston in the 1980s with its upscale produce markets, or Covent Garden in central London with its tradition of restaurants serving nearby theaters. Food, cultural tourism, and street entertainment have been important components of these historic revivals, addressing our bodily and sensory desires directly.

Major players in the mall market have sought to replicate these environments. Disney's Main Street, USA in Disneyland was one of the inspirations for this downtown tourist revival. Desirable heterotopic environments can also be manufactured using sampling techniques, taking facades from many places in a city (as demonstrated by Jon Jerde at City Walk Los Angeles).

In addition we have seen the use of the skyscraper as a multifunctional organizational device employing compression on a vertical armature. The skyscraper is now often coupled with the enclosed shopping-mall armature format, as at SOM's 1968 John Hancock Center in Chicago. SOM was also the lead architect of the megaform Time Warner Center in New York in the early 2000s, designing the exterior shell into which an enormously complex and diverse set of programs was crammed in a chaotic corporate assemblage. Like Koolhaas's Beijing China Central Television Center (CCTV), these megaform buildings look like throwbacks to a past era of triumphant Modernism—until their underpinnings of the network city are examined. Then they are clearly seen to belong to a wired urban future and to represent the cutting edge of the network city. They offer a complex, hybrid model of one aspect of our urban future.

Feedback and self-organization are fundamental to this reconcentration and restructuring of the city. Information is widely distributed through the communication systems; intelligence becomes distributed and decentralized. In this sense we can talk of this situation as an Ecological City as well as a network city, because the initially linear self-organization of the City as a Machine (with its systems of closed feedback loops) has been pried apart and become a complex, nonlinear matrix of possibilities and probabilities mobilized by catalytic actors both from the bottom up and the top down.

The "second nature" of communication and transport systems coordinates the manufacture of the parts needed for the global network city and processes the supplies as required, delivering them to sites at almost any point of the globe (in good weather). This Ecological City, as presently designed, includes industrialized farming and agricultural methods using petrochemicals as fertilizers; its agribusiness techniques now extend on a global scale. This Ecological City can also contain urban agriculture and subsistence farming in cities with favelas (I have seen goats kept on *ranchero* roofs in Caracas). It also has the possibility of realizing Frank Lloyd Wright's dream of a net city of homesteaders on 4-acre lots growing some of their own food, as in Broadacre City. Here openness takes the form of vast new tracts of territory made accessible by the ongoing communications revolution. This allows the exploration of ideas like Landscape Urbanism, in which the city appears as a flexible system of growth and change which can easily merge back into the landscape, appearing as a performance by actors on common ground only when needed, a temporary, dissipative efflorescence like a 1960s pop festival.

In terms of Gleick's model of shifting organizational growth patterns, the Ecological City represents a shift from a period of instability and uncertainty in the application of the Modernist model with its two alternating patterns. The switch from the orderly, linear logic of the City as a Machine to the nonlinear logic of the Tele Città creates its own patterns, which are just beginning to emerge. It is clear that the powerful, bipolar model reached a limit. Like its unipolar predecessor it could not handle the flows of information and multiple voices that were unleashed by its own success in transforming the world (especially by establishing a global system through colonial trade). Gleick's fifth stage, the "chaotic" growth model, has neither a single-centered nor a binary pattern. These earlier two patterns remain available, but growth now takes place in a system that is not only multicentered but multimodal and multivocal as well. Multiple forms of growth are theoretically possible at any point and many new hybrids are to be expected.

Mike Webb: Sin Centre *project Leicester Square, London, 1962, an early heterotopia 3*

*London
heterotopic nodes*

a) *View down to
Trafalgar Square,
1996–2003*
b) *Foster and
Partners: view from
Trafalgar Square to
the National Gallery,
2004*
c 1) *Street
entertainment, South
Bank, 2004.*
c 2) *Thames beach
access, South Bank,
2004*
d) *The Marks Barfield
Architects, London
Eye 2000*
e) *City of London
skyline from Tate
Modern (Herzog and
de Meuron), 2004*
f) *Layered London,
analysis, drawn by
Rodrigo Gardia
Dall'Orso, 2004*
g) *Foster Associates
Swiss Re Tower, Hayes
Wharf Mall,
1997–2004*
h) *Millennium Bridge
(1996–2002) and St.
Paul's, Cathedral*
i) *Greater London
Authority
headquarters
building, 1998–2002*

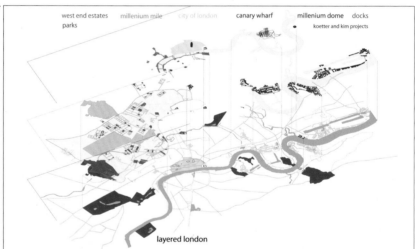

west end estates   millenium mile   city of london   canary wharf   millenium dome   docks
parks   koetter and kim projects

layered london

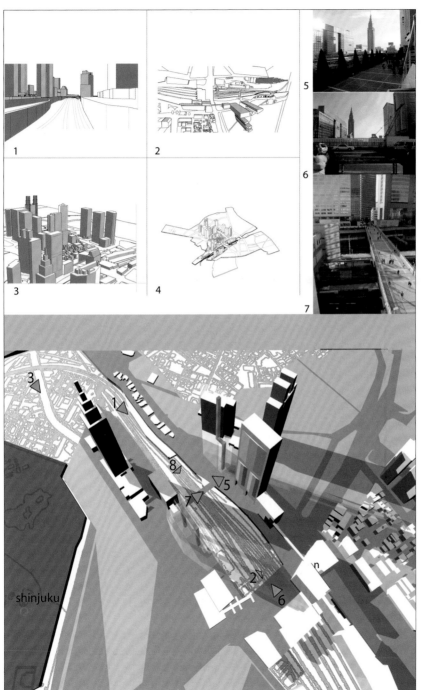

*Tokyo
heterotopic node*

1) *Train approach to Shinjuku station, 2004
From a computer animation drawn by Rodrigo Gardia Dall'Orso 2004*
2) *View toward the royal palace and park, downtown Tokyo*
3) *Kenzo Tange: Shinjuku master plan area with tall towers and grid, 1980s*
4) *Shinjuku node and surrounding administrative boundary, 2004*
5) *Southern terrace, with Empire State Tower beyond, 2004 (photographs courtesy of Utsumi)*
6) *Southern terrace at bridge junction, 2004*
7) *View to bridge from Times Square department store, 2004*
8) *Layered drawing of Shinjuku, by Rodrigo Gardia Dall' Orso, 2004*

a

b

c
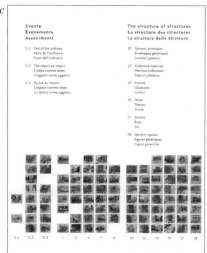

Events Événements Avvenimenti	The structure of structures La structure des structures La struttura delle strutture
0.1 Out of the ordinary Hors de l'ordinaire Fuori dell'ordinario	10 Generic envelopes Enveloppes génériques Involucri generici
0.2 The object as object L'objet comme objet L'oggetto come oggetto	12 Collective matrices Matrices collectives Matrici collettive
0.3 Space as object L'espace comme objet Lo spazio come oggetto	14 Frames Ossatures Cornici
	15 Grids Trames Trame
	17 Streets Rues Vie
	18 Generic figures Figures génériques Figure generiche

0.1 0.2 0.3   1   2   4   7   9   10   12   14   15   17   18

d

World Business

Volkswagen's Lopez faces indictment

O&Y's American arm emerges with a bang

Conclusion

Heterotopias, the Net City, and Recombinant Urbanism

Over the years, many students have asked me why I place so much emphasis on heterotopias. If heterotopias are exceptional, aren't they less important?

It is precisely the exceptional nature of the heterotopia that makes it so fascinating a window through which to see the city, and which first led me to redefine Foucault's concept so that it could apply to the contemporary city. Heterotopias of illusion are becoming a new norm in postmodern cities, and this is a result of fundamental shifts in the structure of society. I will conclude this book by fleshing out this claim and present three major global cities (and one small terrace in Montreal) as examples of rhizomic assemblage for consideration by city theorists, urban designers, and architects.

The belief that one person can control a whole city or urban situation marks a crucial difference between Modernist designers (who affirmed it) and postmodernist designers (who don't). My account of the 1970s and 1980s (Chapter 2) stressed the attempts of the structuralist and Rationalist designers to construct a language of urban architecture that included all the traditional elements of the city as a Newtonian clock coordinating the universe by simple laws—all organized around an unanswered question of control. The post-Structuralist and Deconstructivist designers of the 1980s and 1990s pointed out this central omission and articulated the consequences for the whole city territory, from edges to center.

The chief consequence of this revelation was that there was no longer a place for a master plan or a master planner. The complexity of the city's various autonomous systems, each with its own logic, meant that nobody could coordinate everything. As a result, a preoccupation with the periphery, landscape, edge-cities, systems of flow, and the reverse city territory dominated professional discourse in the 1990s.

With hindsight, we can see the post-structuralists and Deconstructivists were right to describe the city as a chaotic situation of competing systems. We can also see that this chaotic situation has an emergent logic of its own, produced noncentrally by actors designing systems across vast territories without regard for each other's decisions, each adding their own system as a new layer to existing topography, historic structures, and landscapes. The result is a tangle of actors and systems in a spaghetti system of flows and private motives, interacting with each other through complex feedback mechanisms wherever their paths cross. Each actor follows their own logic, creating a life-world that is a mixture of the usual urban concerns: land and property, trade and market share, social and political position. Each actor forms their own hybrid priorities and sets goals in the face of competing actors, contesting for territory.

A city of multiple actors connected by a spaghetti tangle of relationships

Melvin Charney: Un Dictionnaire… Illuminations, 1970–1996 at the Canadian Centre for Architecture, Montréal. Shown here from Un Dictionnaire "Meta-Events," from Series 20, Buildings and Cities
a) *Plates 1, 2, 5, 6, 8 from Series 20, 1970–96 (courtesy of the artist)*
b) *View of installation of Un Dictionnaire in Brussels, 1997*
c) *Organizational matrix for cataloguing Un Dictionnaire*
d) *Plate 4, from Series 20, 1970–1996*

produces patches of only local order, and no obvious mechanism of overall coordination. One urban actor might control a particular spatial environment while another manipulates flows between patches; and they might (or might not) talk to each other.

City planners try to imagine conversations between urban actors from a top-down perspective and to create structures to serve actors' needs. However, local and global actors on the ground meanwhile create independent lines of communication using their own logics, forging relational ecologies of fragments and enclaves unimagined by large-scale planners with their mathematical models of traffic flows and demographics. Local ecologies of actors' relationships can link patches into a larger system—a network, constellation, or archipelago. Today such patchwork systems are highly dependent on fossil fuels and centralized electrical generation to power their transportation and information (including communications) systems. Contemporary urban actors have used rapid communications systems to superimpose the network city on older city systems over the city territory. This superimposed network city may be relatively inconspicuous, dissolving into the landscape thanks to high-speed transportation and communications networks. The result is a scattering of semi-autonomous cells across the landscape, each with its own logic and interested actors, who can use mobile modules (cars, phones, etc.) to move between patches of order while remaining in contact with each other.

Among these patches of order are highly structured nodes at various scales that serve multiple actors and provide meeting places and spaces of negotiation. Since no single person or actor is in command at this level either, relationships between actors can quickly shift. Rapid relational shifts typify a heterotopia of "illusion." Further, these heterotopic nodes of negotiation are also contested spaces in which different models of relationships between actors may compete. Individual choices matter in these spaces, influencing the emergence of new solutions (or, possibly, problems) from the bottom up. For example, individual actors can influence design outcomes and modify products through their personal choices and adaptations of standardized products; alert urban actors and corporations are always scanning their markets for new developments. For some corporations, the co-optation of change and experiment for profit is essential for survival. On one hand, this co-optation uses heterotopias of illusion to accelerate change, which may be good; on the other, such actors may, by exploiting incipient change for corporate profit, weaken or nullify it.

In our highly mediated situation, *all* enclaves have a heterotopia-of-illusion aspect—a dream of freedom or infinite choice partly embodied in a real place as an attractor controlled by local actors. The characteristics of the heterotopia—its multicellular structure, its flexibility, and its ability to combine diverse elements and desires—make it an ideal instrument for actors seeking a sense of freedom. Unlike the rigid heterotopias of deviance or discipline that ushered in the Industrial Revolution, heterotopias of illusion are especially flexible and tuned to the virtual dimension. This plays into the hands of urban actors interested in media representations and telemarketing. The contemporary activities of urban tourist boards, theme-park owners, and mall owners testify to the effectiveness of these mass-marketing strategies for heterotopias of consumption and illusion.

Single-function enclaves are thus no longer the norm, as multifunctional enclaves proliferate over the postmodern city territory. We have caught up with Foucault's insight in the 1960s, and are aware that heterogeneous mixtures are now the *norm* in everyday life. This raises interesting questions about the rehabilitation of Foucault's heterotopias of deviance (my heterotopia type two), as well; the category that includes work camps, military camps, old-style prisons, hospitals, insane asylums, factories, and the like, which contributed essentially to the production of the modern world. Many recent design competitions have concerned the rehabilitation of such institutions and their associated towns ("shrinking cities" like Detroit, the "rust-belt" towns of Mid-America, industrial towns in Britain or Japan, even in the Ruhr Valley in Germany.

The proliferation of heterotopias of illusion posed a logical problem for modern planners accustomed to segregating and sorting single functions following the strategies of Le Corbusier or the CIAM group of the 1930s. Places where codes were engineered to produce a temporary illusion of stability, retro-scenographies, did not easily fit into the Modernist categories except as places of decadence and depravity to be eradicated. Malls and theme parks were also seen as aberrations, and positive studies of Las Vegas in the 1970s met with a barrage of criticism. Even Lynch, who was critical of Modernism, retained the Modernist planners' overview, drawing beautiful sketches of views from 30,000 feet and helping by his diagrams to eradicate Boston's red-light district in Scollay Square.

The New York City Urban Design Group of the 1960s elegantly closed this gap through their reinvention of the special district as a tool to accommodate multiple actors, providing a contested space within specific limits and a set perimeter and allowing for the proliferation of small, heterotopic enclaves of illusion. Here planned incentives could encourage retrostyling, reintroduce the street corridor, or preserve a historic district or community territory, responding to the demands of local actors. New Urbanists perfected this systemic approach and applied it on a vast scale to the American suburbs, where large-scale, corporate, standardized, planned unit developments had become the norm. The dark side of this collagist approach is evident in the postcolonial "Third World" cities that become unplanned attractors where, patch by patch, urban immigrants built their own houses without any overall controls or master plan.

Collage City provided a framework for designing cities where there is no one voice or actor in control of the overall plan. Rowe and Koetter faced the consequences of the abandonment of the master-planning idea. They recognized the inward focus of urban actors' enclave-planning and tried to identify elements and fragments of order in the new, chaotic situation. And they explored the political dimension of this dilemma, opting for a kind of enlightened prince or patron to coordinate the fragments created by private parties in the interest of building an open society and city.

Critics of *Collage City* pointed to the unsatisfactory nature of this political solution, yet without articulating more-democratic alternatives for how a city without a master plan might be made to operate. The problem is not trivial. As I noted in my "Seven Ages of Postmodern Design" section (Chapter 2), urban actors must make complex choices about design strategies; these range from the montage techniques of scenographic sequencing proposed by advocates of "townscape" (e.g., Gordon Cullen) to the Deconstructivists, with their focus on the empty center and the potential of new urban public spaces to participate in layered, sectional urban collages that reverse traditional codes and hierarchies. The Deconstructivists' emphasis on the periphery did articulate fully the surprising juxtapositions that result when no one is in charge, while their sectional emphasis allowed for surprising new recombinations in the city center.

Rhizomic assemblage as a design methodology and political strategy also recognizes the polyphonic situation where no one voice dominates. It accommodates the autonomy of urban actors each following their own logics, but also allows for the relationships that will inevitably develop between such actors. It provides designers with a new freedom to break old molds and make new combinations, both in section and over vast spaces of the city territory. This method of design, like heterotopias of illusion as a method for organizing real places in the city, is well suited to the management of the surprising juxtapositions that occur when no one person is in charge of a master plan for the entire city.

It is therefore not so surprising that urban actors, whether in the high-density metropolitan nodes of the global system or on the unplanned periphery in the barrios and shanty towns, are opting for rhizomic design solutions in heterotopias of illusion (H3). Urban actors seek spatial flexibility of use, multitasking, the potential to mix home and work, the potential to mix work and leisure. At the end of this section I provide double-page illustrations of several such networks and heterotopic nodes in London, New York, and Tokyo.

I particularly wish to emphasize the reconstitution of a landscape network in London and New York using the waterfronts, docks, and river fronts of both cities. Urban actors have rewired both cities for high-speed communications, refreshing old networks and converting formerly industrial sections into postindustrial hubs (e.g., Covent Garden in London or the SoHo loft district in New York). At the same time, these new communications systems have enabled urban actors in both cities to vastly expand the *virtual* city territory, reinforcing London's position in southeast England and New York's position in the east coast megapolitan corridor.

Urban Landscape theorists such as Secchi and Viganò at the University of Venice and James Corner at the University of Pennsylvania have emphasized the "reverse city" quality of the landscape which forms a "fifth facade " (Viganò) in

24 Lynch, *Good City Form*, 331, 337.

25 Krugman, *Self-Organizing Economy*, 26–28.

26 Ibid., 39–46 and Lynch, *Good City Form*, 334.

27 Krugman, Self-Organizing Economy, 46, 95–96. For a fuller exposition see Masahisa Fujita, Paul Krugman, and Anthony J. Venables, *The Spatial Economy: Cities, Regions and International Trade* (Cambridge, MA: MIT Press, 2000), 181–205.

28 Reyner Banham, Peter Hall, Cedric Price, and Peter Barker, *New Society*, March 20, 1969. Reprinted in J. Hughes and S. Sadler, eds., *Non-Plan* (Oxford: Architectural Press, 2000).

29 Roy Landau, *New Directions in British Architecture* (London: Studio Vista, 1978).

30 Peter Cook, ed., *Archigram* (London: Studio Vista, 1972), 48–49.

31 Lynch, *Good City Form*, 72, 364.

32 Lynch, "Quality in City Design" (1966), in *City Sense and City Design: Writings and Projects of Kevin Lynch*, Tridib Banerjee and Michael Southworth, eds. (Cambridge, MA: MIT Press, 1990), 430.

33 Lynch, *Good City Form*, 277.

34 Ibid., 144.

35 Ibid., 153, 160.

36 Ibid., 116–117.

37 Ibid., 288.

38 Ibid., 278.

39 Ibid., 277.

40 Ibid., 279.

41 Ibid., 285.

42 N. J. Habraken, *The Structure of the Ordinary: Form and Control in the Built Environment*, Jonathan Teicher, ed. (Cambridge, MA: MIT Press, 1998).

43 Juval Portugali, *Self-Organization and the City* (New York: Springer, 2000), 175–200.

44 Lynch, *Good City Form*, 285.

45 Ibid., 293–317.

46 David Gosling and Maria Christina Gosling, *The Evolution of American Urban Design: A Chronological Anthology* (Chichester, UK: Wiley-Academy, 2003), 71, 74. Also David N. Lewis, *The Pedestrian in the City* (Princeton, NJ: Van Nostrand Reinholt, 1965) and *Urban Design Associates, The Urban Design Handbook: Techniques and Working Methods* (New York: Norton, 2003).

47 Emily Eakin, "Architecture's Irascible Reformer," *New York Times*, July 12, 2003, B9.

48 Lynch, *Good City Form*, 345–372, 373–55.

49 University of Southern California Department of Architecture, "History," http://www.usc.edu/dept/architecture/context/history.html (accessed November 19, 2003).

50 Lynch, *Good City Form*, 345.

51 Lynch, *Good City Form*, 419–439.

52 Ibid., 335 and René Thom, *Structural Stability and Morphogenesis*, (New York: Benjamin Addison Wesley, 1975.)

53 Lynch, *Good City Form*, 353.

54 Ibid., 355–357.

55 Ibid., 286–87.

56 See Anne Buttimer, ed., *Creativity and Context*, Lund Studies in Geography #50 (Royal University of Lund, Department of Geography, 1983). I am grateful to Vassilis Vakis for drawing my attention to this issue.

57 *City Sense and City Design*, 287.

58 Ibid., 103–134.

59 Lynch, *Image of the City*, (Cambridge Mass: MIT Press and London, England, 1961), 16–32.

60 Lynch, *Site Planning* (Cambridge, MA: MIT Press, 1962), 47.

61 Lynch, *Good City Form*, 148–149.

62 *City Sense and City Design*, 665–674 and Lynch, *Site Planning*, 118.

63 Gosling and Gosling, American Urban Design, 55.

64 Kenneth Halpern, *Downtown USA: Urban Design in Nine American Cities* (New York: Whitney Library of Design, 1978), 183–199. See also Gosling and Gosling, *American Urban Design*, 124–125.

65 Lynch, *Good City Form*, 291.

66 Ibid., 454–455.

67 Ibid., 373–404.

68 Ibid., 289–290.

69 Ibid., 285.

70 Françoise Choay, "Urbanism and Semiology," in *Meaning in Architecture*, Charles Jencks and George Baird, eds. (London: Studio Vista, 1969).

71 Lynch, *Good City Form*, 73.

72 Ibid., 73.

73 Ibid., 74.

74 Ibid., 79.

75 Noam Chomsky, *Media Control: The Spectacular Achievements of Propaganda* (New York: Seven Stories Press, 1991, 1997), 15–16.

76 Lynch, *Good City Form*, 81 (bottom of Fig. 43).

77 Ibid., 62, 64.

78 Cook, *Archigram*, 48–49.

79 Le Corbusier, *The Athens Charter*, trans. T. Eardley (New York: Grossman Publishers, 1973; original French edition, 1943), 96.

80 See S. Johnson, *Emergence: The Connected Lives of Ants, Brains, Cities and Software* (New York: Scribner, 2001), 87–88.

81 A. Pope, *Ladders* (New York: Princeton Architectural Press, 1996), 165, 188.

82 L. Hilbersheimer, *The Nature of Cities: Origin, Growth and Decline; Pattern and Form; Planning Problems* (Chicago: Paul Theobold, 1955), 82–84.

83 Lynch, *Good City Form*, 81.

84 Camilo J. Vergara, *The New American Ghetto* (New Brunswick, NJ: Rutgers University Press, 1995), 215–225, and *American Ruins* (New York: Monacelli Press, 1999), 48–67.

85 Andres Duany and Elizabeth Plater-Zyberk, *Towns and Town-Making Principles* (New York: Harvard Graduate School of Design, 1991), 24–25.

86 Lynch, "City and Regional Planning", in *City Sense and City Design*, 557–561

87 Lynch, *Good City Form*, 89.

88 Ibid., 90–94.

89 Ibid., 116.

90 Ibid., 96.

91 Krugman, *Self-Organizing Economy*, 58.

92 Fritjof Capra, *The Web of Life: A New Scientific Understanding of Living Systems* (New York: Anchor, 1996), 5.

93 *The Random House Dictionary of the English Language* (New York: Random House, 1987).

94 Capra, *Web of Life*, 27, 18, 33.

95 Werner Heisenberg, *Physics and Philosophy* (New York: Harper & Row, 1962), 107.

96 Capra, *Web of Life*, 32.

97 Ibid., 6.

98 Robin Evans, *The Projective Cast: Architecture and Its Three Geometries* (Cambridge, MA: MIT Press, 1995).

99 *City Sense and City Design*, 835–840, and Kevin Lynch and Michael Southworth, eds., *Wasting Away: An Exploration of Waste: What It Is, How It Happens, Why We Fear It, How to Do It Well* (San Francisco: Sierra Club Books, 1990).

100 Lynch, *Good City Form*, 89–98

101 Ibid., 91.

102 Ibid., 94–95.

103 Ibid., Chapter 6.

104 Ibid., 291.

105 Ibid., 290–291.

106 Lynch, "Urban Design", *City Sense and City Design*, 511–534.

107 Stephen Graham and Simon Marvin, *Splintering Urbanism* (London: Routledge, 2001), 51.

108 US Dept. of Commerce, "Falling Through the Net: Toward Digital Inclusion," http://www.ntia.doc.gov/ntiahome/fttn00/contents00.html (accessed November 19, 2003).

109 Saskia Sassen, *The Global City* (Princeton, NJ: Princeton University Press, 1991).

110 "Quality in City Design" (1966) in *City Sense and City Design*, 430.

111 Lynch, "City Design and City Appearance" (1968), ibid., 483.

112 J. L. Sert, *Can Our Cities Survive?* (Cambridge, UK: Harvard University Press, 1942).

113 Gosling and Gosling, *American Urban Design*, 66, 112.

114 Lynch, "Urban Design," in *Encyclopaedia Britannica*, 15th edition, 1974. Included in Lunch, "Urban Design", *City Sense and City Design*, 529.

115 Lynch, *Good City Form*, 511.

116 Eric Darton, *Divided We Stand: A Biography of New York's World Trade Center* (New York: Basic Books, 1999).

117 *600 contreprojets pour les Halles: Consultation internationale pour l'aménagement du quartier des Halles* (Paris, Editions Moniteur, 1981).

118 Edith Iglaur, *Seven Stones: A Portrait of Arthur Ericson, Architect* (Seattle: University of Washington Press, 1981), 105–112.

119 Lynch, *Good City Form*, 758–759.

120 Ibid., 653.

121 Ibid., 652.

122 Ibid., 509.

123 Ibid., 674–678.

124 Ibid., 290–291.

125 Peter Calthorpe and William Fulton, *The Regional City* (Island Press, Washington DC, 2001), 139.

126 Lynch, *Good City Form*, 90.

127 *City Sense and City Design*, 316–337, 268–269.

128 Monica Turner, Robert Gardner, and Robert O'Neil, *Landscape Ecology in Theory and Practice: Pattern and Process* (New York: Springer, 2001).

129 Grahame Shane, "The Emergence of Landscape Urbanism," *Harvard Design Magazine*, Fall 2003/Winter 2004 and
http://www.gsd.harvard.edu/research/publications/hdm/back/19_onlands.html (accessed 17 January 17, 2004).

130 John Kaliski, "The Present City and the Practice of City Design," in John Chase, Margaret Crawford, and John Kaliski, eds., *Everyday Urbanism* (New York: Princeton Architectural Press, 1999), 88–109.

131 Ibid., 105.

132 Ibid., 106.

133 Ibid.

134 Cedric Price, *Opera* Samantha Hardingham, ed. (London: Wiley-Academy, 2003), 92–93,

135 International Society of City and Regional Planners (ISoCaRP) Conference, *Honey, I Shrunk the Space*, 2001. See "Honey, I Shrunk the Space: Planning in the Information Age: The 37th Annual IsoCaRP Congress,"
http://www.isocarp.org/pub/events/congress/2001/top/index.htm(accessed January 17, 2004)

136 ISoCaRP (accessed January 17, 2004).

137 Ibid.

138 Ibid.

139 MVRDV, *Costa Iberica: Upbeat to the Leisure City* (Barcelona: Actar, 2002).

140 Lynch, *Good City Form*, 309.

141 Ibid., 309.

142 Ibid., 311.

143 Ibid., 310.

144 Michel Foucault, "Of Other Spaces: Utopias and Heterotopias" (1964), in *Architecture Culture 1943–68: A Documentary Anthology*, Joan Ockman, ed. (Cambridge, MA: MIT Press, 1998), 419.

Chapter 2

1 Christian Norberg-Schulz, *Existence, Space, and Architecture* (New York: Praeger, 1971), 38.

2 Peter Madsen, Introduction to *The Urban Life-World: Formation, Perception, and Representation*, Peter Madsen and Richard Plunz, eds. (London: Routledge, 2002), 9–23. Also Dalibor Vesely and Moshen Mostafavi, *Architecture and Continuity* (London: Architectural Association, 1982). Re. vernacular, see Paul Oliver, ed., *Shelter and Society* (London: Studio Vista, 1969).

3 Edmund Husserl, *The Crisis of European Sciences and Transcendental Philosophy: An Introduction to Phenomenological Philosophy*, trans. David Carr. (Evanston, IL: Northwestern University Press, 1970).

4 Françoise Choay, *The Rule and the Model: On the Theory of Architecture and Urbanism* (Cambridge, MA: MIT Press, 1997), 234; Ildefons Cerdá, *The Five Bases*

of the General Theory of Urbanization, Arturo Soria y Puig, ed. (Madrid: Electa, 1999).

5 Henry A. Millon, ed., *The Renaissance from Brunelleschi to Michelangelo: The Representation of Architecture* (New York: Rizzoli, 1997), 211.

6 Choay, *The Rule and the Model*, 271–85; "layered structure," 155.

7 Re. Utopia see ibid., 137–72.

8 Ibid., 150–152.

9 Ibid., 154.

10 Ibid., 138.

11 Manfredo Tafuri, *Architecture and Utopia: Design and Capitalist Development* (Cambridge, MA: MIT Press, 1976); Manfredo Tafuri and Francesco Dal Co, *Modern Architecture* (New York: Abrams, 1982), 153–157.

12 Re. Panopticon, see Michel Foucault, *Discipline and Punish: The Birth of the Prison* (New York: Penguin, 1978), 95–228 and R. Evans, *The Fabrication of Virtue: English Prison Architecture, 1750–1840* (Cambridge, UK: Cambridge University Press, 1982), 195–236.

13 Dora Wiebenson and Pieter Uyttenhove, "Au Fond de la Cité Industrielle, Givors," in *Les Nouvelles Conditions du Projet Urbain*, Alain Charre, ed. (New York: Braziller, 1969); also *Critiques et Méthodes* Megalopole 22 (Sprimont: Pierre Mardaga, 2001), 17–26.

14 Choay, *The Rule and he Model*, 233–256.

15 Andre Corboz (essay) and Dennis Keeley (photographs), *Looking for a City in America* (Santa Monica: Getty Center for the History of Art and the Humanities, 1991 [1987 in France]), 56.

16 Cerdá, *Theory of Urbanization*, 139–99, 307–314.

17 Ibid., 87–88.

18 Ibid., 280–28s7.

19 Robert Fishman, *Bourgeois Utopias: The Rise and Fall of Suburbia* (New York: Basic Books, 1987), 67–72.

20 Jean Gottmann, *Megalopolis* (New York: Twentieth Century Fund, 1961), 735–738.

21 R. E. Pahl, *Urbs in Rure: The Metropolitan Fringe in Hertfordshire*, LSE Geographical Paper #2 (London: London School of Economics, 1965).

22 Fishman, *Bourgeois Utopias*, 182–207.

23 Joel Garreau, *Edge City: Life on the New Frontier* (New York, Doubleday, 1991), 6–7.

24 Reyner Banham, *Los Angeles: The Architecture of the Four Ecologies* (London: Allen Lane, 1971); Robert Venturi, Denise Scott Brown, and Steven Izenour, *Learning from Las Vegas* (MIT Press, Cambridge, MA and London, England, 1972). See also Stephen Kieran and James Timberlake, "Paradise Regained," *Architecture*, December 1991, 48–51.

25 Saskia Sassen, *The Global City: New York, London, Tokyo* (Princeton, NJ: Princeton University Press, 1991); *Global Networks, Linked Cities*, Saskia Sassen, ed. (New York: Routledge, 2002).

26 Corboz, *Looking for a City in America*, 57–59.

27 Celeste Olalquiaga, *Megalopolis: Contemporary Cultural Sensibilities* (London: University of Minnesota Press, 1992).

28 Anthony Vidler, *The Architectural Uncanny* (Cambridge, MA: MIT Press, 1992),

177–188; Francis Yates, *The Art of Memory* (London: Routledge and Kegan Paul, 1966); and Francis Yates, "Architecture and the Art of Memory," *Architectural Association Quarterly*, Vol. 12, No. 4, 1980, 4–14.

29 Rem Koolhaas and Bruce Mau, *SMLXL* (New York, Monacelli Press, 1995), 1,264.

30 Mario Gandelsonas, *X-Urbanism: Architecture and the American City* (New York: Princeton Architectural Press, 1999), 30–43.

31 Lars Lerup, *After the City* (Cambridge, MA: MIT Press, 2000).

32 Victor Gruen and Larry Smith, *Shopping Towns USA* (New York: Reinhold Publishing, 1960); Barry Maitland, *Shopping Malls: Planning and Design* (New York: Nichols, 1985).

33 Victor Gruen, *The Heart of Our Cities* (New York: Simon and Schuster, 1964), 190–191.

34 E. W. Soja, *Postmodern Geographies: The Reassertion of Space in Critical Social Theory* (London: Verso, 1989); E. W. Soja, *Postmetropolis: Critical Studies of Cities and Regions* (Oxford: Blackwell, 2000), 207; Haya El Nasser, "Big Burbs Rival Central Cities," *USA Today*, June 22, 2001, 11A.

35 Jean Gottmann, "Megapolitan Systems Around the World," *Eckistics*, No. 243, February, 1976, 109–112, reprinted in *The Urban Writings of Jean Gottmann: Since Megalopolis*, Jean Gottmann and Robert A. Harper, eds. (Baltimore, MD: John Hopkins, 1990), 162–171.

36 *A Hundred years of Tokyo City Planning*, Tokyo Metropolitan Government, Municipal Library #28 (Tokyo: Tokyo Metropolitan Government, 1994), 56, 74.

37 Xavier de Geyter Architects, *After Sprawl* (Rotterdam, Netherlands: Nai Publishers/DeSingel, 2002).

38 Soja, *Postmetropolis*, 236.

39 Dennis R. Judd and Susan S. Fainstein, eds., *The Tourist City* (New Haven, CT: Yale University Press, 1999), 1–34; John Hannigan, *The Fantasy City: Pleasure and Profit in the Postmodern Metropolis* (London: Routledge, 1998); Berci Florian, "The City as a Brand: Orchestrating the Unique Experience," in *City Branding: Image Building and Building Images*, Veronique Patteeuw, ed. (Rotterdam, Netherlands: NAI Publishers, 2002), 20–31.

40 Rem Koolhaas and Bruce Mau, "Generic Urbanism," in *SMLXL*, 1248–64. Re. New Urbanism scale-jump, see Andres Duany and Elizabeth Plater-Zyberk, *Towns and Townmaking Principles* (New York: Rizzoli, 1991), 25–26.

41 W. B. Yeats, "The Second Coming," in *The Collected Poems of W. B. Yeats* (New York: Macmillan, 1974), 184. (I thank Larry Gilman for this reference.)

42 Lynch, *Good City Form*, 290.

43 Christopher Alexander, Sara Ishikawa, and Murray Silverstein, *A Pattern Language: Towns, Buildings, Construction* (New York: Oxford University Press, 1977).

44 William Cronon, *Nature's Metropolis: Chicago and the Great West* (New York: Norton, 1991).

45 Siegfried Giedion, *Mechanization Takes Command, A Contribution to Anonymous History* (New York: Oxford University Press, 1948).

46 Le Corbusier, *Towards a New Architecture*, trans. Frederick Etchells (New York: Payson & Clarke, 1927).

47 Le Corbusier, *The Athens Charter*, trans. T. Eardley (New York: Grossman Publishers, 1973), original French edition, 1943; D. G. Shane, "The Street in the Twentieth Century: Three Conferences: London (1910), Athens (1933), Hoddesdon

6 Terry R. Slater, "Starting Again: Recollections of an Urban Morphologist," in *The Built Form of Western Cities*, Terry R. Slater, ed. (Leicester, UK: Leicester University Press, 1990), 22–36. See also links from the Urban Morphology Research Group home page at http://www.bham.ac.uk/geography/umrg (accessed December 22, 2003).

7 Moudon, 301–307; Jean Castex, Patrick Celeste, and Phillipe Panerai, *Lecture d'une Ville: Versailles "Built Landscape"* (Paris: Editions Moniteur, 1980).

8 Moudon, *"Built Landscape"*, 290–293; quotation, 290. P. L. Cervellati e R. Scanvini eds. *Bologna: politica e metodologia del restauro nei centri storici* (Bologna, Italy: Societa editrice Il Mulino, 1973), 66 and 137–145.

9 Paola Viganò, *La Città Elementare* (Milan and Geneva: Skira, 1999) and *Territories of a New Modernity*, Paola Viganò, ed. (Naples, Italy: Electa, 2001).

10 Viganò, *La Città Elementare*, 28.

11 Ibid., 66–72.

12 Rosalind E. Krauss, "Sculpture in the Expanded Field," in *The Anti-Aesthetic: Essays on Postmodern Culture*, Hal Foster ed. (Port Townsend, WA: Bay Press, 1983), 31–42.

13 Viganò, La Città Elementare, 106–115 and 127–137.

14 Ibid., 72–77 and 151–178.

15 Ibid., 88.

16 Ibid., 188.

17 Ibid., 189.

18 Ibid.

19 Ibid., 148.

20 Richard T. T. Forman and Michel Godron, *Landscape Ecology* (New York: John Wiley, 1986), 34.

21 Xaveer de Geyter Architects, *After Sprawl* (Rotterdam: Nai Publishers/DeSingel, 2002); Stephano Munarin and Maria Chiara Tosi, *Tracce di Città: Esplorazioni di un territorio abitato: l'Area Veneta* (Milan, Italy: Franco Angeli, 2001); Bruno de Meulder and Michiel Dehaene, *Atlas 1: Fascikel Zuidelijk-West-Vlaanderen, Anno 02*, (Zuidelijk West-Vlaanderen, 2002).

22 Franz Oswald and Peter Baccini, Netzstadt: Designing the Urban (Switzerland: Basel; Birkhauser, 2003), 130–53.

23 Viganò, *La Città Elementare*, 77–78.

24 Ibid., 171–178.

25 Stephano Bianca, *Urban Form in the Islamic World* (New York: Thames and Hudson, 2000), 153.

26 Viganò, *La Città Elementare*, 140–143.

27 Stephen Graham and Simon Marvin, *Splintering Urbanism* (London: Routledge, 2001), 167, Fig. 4.6.

28 Simon Sadler, *The Situationist City* (Cambridge, MA: MIT Press, 1998), 60.

29 Viganò, *La Città Elementare*: "bricolage," 33–36, 137–144; "layering," 21–33 and 187–190.

30 Ibid., 139–148.

31 William Rubin, *Picasso and Braque: Pioneering Cubism* (New York: Museum of Modern Art, 1989).

32 Peter Geoffrey Hall, *Cities in Civilization: Culture, Innovation, and Urban Order* (London: Weidenfeld & Nicolson, 1998), Fig 21, 284.

33 Paul Citroen, "Metropolis" (1921), in *La Ville, Art and Architecture en Europe, 1870–1993* (Paris: Centre Georges Pompidou, 1994), 258.

34 R. Etienne, *Pompeii: The Day a City Died* (New York: H. N. Abrams, 1992).

35 Bianca, *Islamic World,* 54–57.

36 Mario Morini, *Atlante di Storia dell'Urbanistica (dalla Preistoria all' Inizio del Secolo XX)* (Milan, Italy: Hoepli, 1963), 77 (Lucca) and 87 (Split). Re. mall conversion, see John A. Dutton, *New American Urbanism,* 113–115.

37 John Bradley, "The role of town-plan analysis in the study of the medieval Irish town," in Slater, Built Form o Western Cities, 39–59.

38 Yves Cohat, *The Vikings, Lords of the Sea* (New York: Abrams, 1992).

39 OMA, Rem Koolhaas and Bruce Mau, *SMLXL* (New York: The Montacelli Press, 1995), 972–989; "Euro Landscape," in Peter Wilson and Katarina Bolles, *Bolles+Wilson* (Basel, Switzerland: Birkhauser, 1997), 60–67.

40 Richard Ingersoll, "Jumpcut Urbanism," in *Casabella, Milan,* Vol. 597–598, January–February 1993, 52–57.

41 Sadler, *Situationist City,* 60.

42 Etienne, *Pompeii,* 44–49 and 86–105.

43 Richard Sennett, *Flesh and Stone: The Body and the City in Western Civilization* (London: Norton, 1994), 212–51.

44 A. J. Christopher, *The Atlas of Apartheid* (London and New York: Routledge and Witwatersrand University Press, 1994), 103–140.

45 Slater, in *The Built Form of Western Cities,* 68–82.

46 John Summerson, *Georgian London* (New York: Scribner & Son, 1946), 163–176.

47 Harold James Dyos, *Victorian Suburb: A Study of the Growth of Camberwell* (Leicester, UK: Leicester University Press, 1961).

48 John Summerson, *Inigo Jones* (Hammondsworth, UK: Penguin, 1966), 83–96.

49 F. W. H Sheppard ed. *Survey of London XXXVI: Parish of St. Paul, Covent Garden* (London: Athlone Press, 1970).

50 Manuel Delanda, *A Thousand years of Nonlinear History* (New York: Zone Books, 1997), 74.

51 Robert E. Park and Ernest W. Burgess, "The Growth of the City: An Introduction to a Research Project" (1925), reprinted in Richard T. Gates and Frederic Stout, eds., *The City Reader* (London: Routledge, 1996), 95–96.

52 Ibid., 94.

53 Ibid., 95.

54 Ibid., 95.

55 M. L. Clausen, "Northgate Regional Shopping Center—Paradigm From the Provinces," in *Journal of American Society of Architectural Historians (JASAH).,* Vol. XLIII, May 1984, 144–161.

56 Victor Gruen, *The Heart of Our Cities; The Urban Crisis: Diagnosis and Cure* (New York: Simon and Schuster, 1964), 177–198.

57 Ibid., 272–286.

58 Bruce C. Webb, "Gulfgate: The Generation Gap," in *Cite,* No. 31, 1994. For Gulfway, see "Historic Houston Freeway Planning Maps," http://www.texasfreeway. com/houston/historic/freeway_planning_maps/houston_historic_maps.shtml (accessed December 22, 2003).

59 Stephen Fox, *The A.I.A. Houston Architectural Guide,* Nancy Hadley, ed. (Austin, TX: Herring Press, 1990), 233ff.

60 Galleria 1 design first published in *Architectural Record*, March 1967, and again on completion of project in 1969. For critique, see Architectural Design, November 1973, 695.

61 *A Hundred Years of Tokyo City Planning* (Tokyo: Tokyo Metropolitan Government, 1994), 74.

62 Roman Cybriwsky, *Tokyo* (New York: Wiley, 1998), 162.

63 Re. Houston, see Peter Odell, *Oil and World Power* (London: Penguin, 1970). Re. Tokyo, see David Smith and Michael Timberlake, "Hierarchies of Dominance Among World Cities: A Network Approach," in *Global Networks: Linked Cities*, Saskia Sassen, ed. (London: Routledge, 2002), 124.

64 "Animated Architecture," special edition of *Architectural Design*, November, 1982.

65 Jonathan Barnett, *An Introduction to Urban Design* (New York: Harper & Row, 1981), 44–4s6.

66 Ibid., 44–51. See also Halpern, *Downtown USA*, 195. Bruce Erlich and Peter Dreier, "The New Boston Discovers the Old; Tourism and the Struggle for a Liveable City," in *The Tourist City*, Dennis R. Judd and Susan S. Feinstein, eds. (Newhaven and London: Yale University Press, 1999), 155–178.

67 For Fanueil Hall, South Street Seaport, etc. see General Growth Properties, Inc. at http://www.generalgrowth.com/Index.asp (accessed December 27, 2004) and for the Forum des Halles, see http://www.forum-des-halles.com/prod/index.jsp?pays=2 (accessed December 27, 2004).

68 Re. Celebration, see Dutton, New American Urbanism, 127–128.

69 Andres Duany and Elizabeth Plater-Zyberk, *Towns and Town-Making Principles* (New York: Rizzoli, 1991), 25–26. Re. Kentlands, see Peter Katz, *The New Urbanism: Towards An Architecture of Community* (New York: McGraw Hill, 1994), 30–45.

70 Evan McKenzie, *Privatopia; Homeowner Associations and the Rise of Residential Private Government* (New Haven and London: Yale University Press, 1994), Edward J. Blakley and Mary Gail Snyder, *Fortress America; Gated Communities in the United States* (Washington, DC and Cambridge, MA: Brookings Institute Press and Lincoln Land Institute, 1997), Setha Low, *Behind the Gates; Life, Security, and the Pursuit of Happiness in Fortress America* (New York and London: Routledge, 2003), 175–95.

71 Loïc Wacquant, "The Ghetto, the State, and the New Capitalist Economy," in *Metropolis: Center and Symbol of Our Times*, Peter Kasinitz, ed. (New York: New York University Press, 1995), 413–449.

72 Mark Abrahamson, *Urban Enclaves: Identity and Place in America* (New York: St. Martin's Press, 1996), 137–145.

73 E. W. Soja, *Post-Modern Geographies: The Reassertion of Space in Critical Social Theory* (London: Verso, 1989); John Hull Mollenkopf, *The New York City Region in the 1980s: A Social, Economic and Political Atlas* (New York: Simon and Schuster, 1993).

74 N. John Habraken, *The Structure of the Ordinary* (Cambridge, MA: MIT Press, 1998), 304–305.

75 Juval Portugali, *Self-Organization and the City* (New York: Springer, 2000), 81–85.

76 *Venturi, Rauch and Scott Brown: Buildings and Projects*, Stanislaus Von Moos, ed. (New York: Rizzoli, 1987), 239, 280–281.

77 Jan Gehl and Lars Gemzøe, *New City Spaces* (Copenhagen: Danish Architectural

Press, 2001).

78 Norman Foster, "London the World City?" (1999), in *On Foster . . . Foster On*, David Jenkins, ed. (Munich, Germany: Prestel, 2000), 701–705.

79 Francisco Arsenio Server, *Redesigning City Squares and Plazas* (New York: Hearst, 1997), 8–17.

80 Jan Gehl and Lars Gemzøe, *Public Spaces, Public Life: Copenhagen 1996* (Copenhagen: The Danish Architectural Press and the Royal Danish School of Architecture Publishers, 1997), 40–43.

81 "Parks, Plazas, and Central Squares," Project for Public Spaces, at http://www.pps.org/project_lists/ParksPlazasCentralSquares/PlazasEtc.html (accessed December 22, 2003).

82 "Greenmarket at Union Square," Union Square Journal, http://www.unionsquarejournal.com/greenmarket.htm; "World Trade Center Catastrophe," NY ArtLab Online Gallery of Fine Art, http://www.nyartlab.com/bombing/09-15/index.html ; "September 11, 2001 Tragedy Memorial Website," Artistcrafts.com, http://www.artistcrafts.com/tragedy/washsqgall.htm (all accessed December 22, 2003).

83 Lynch, *A Theory of Good City Form* (Cambridge, MA: MIT Press, 1981), 310.

84 Morini, *Atlante di Storia Dell'Urbanistica* 47–51.

85 Ibid., 103–105.

86 See W. L. MacDonald, *The Architecture of the Roman Empire II: An Urban Appraisal* (London: Yale University Press, 1986). Re. Krier connection, see W. L. MacDonald, "Palmyra: On Columns, Streets and Roman Urban Design," in *Daidelus*, No. 24, June 1987.

87 MacDonald, *Architecture of the Roman Empire* 5.

88 Ibid., 15.

89 Ibid., 10.

90 Ibid., 15–17.

91 Ibid., 179–183,

92 Ibid., 30–31, 41–42.

93 Kostof, *The City Shaped*, 1991, 46–51.

94 Bianca, *Islamic World,* 55–57.

95 Ibid., 122–124.

96 Slater, "Starting Again", in *Built Form of Western Cities*, 22–36.

97 Jean-Pierre Leguay, *La Rue au Moyen Age* (Rennes, France: Ouest-France, 1984).

98 Re. Camden Town and high street, see John Summerson, *Georgian London* (London: Pleiades Books, 1945 [first pub. Penguin 1962]), 282.

99 Hermione Hobhouse, *A History of Regent Street* (London: Macdonald and Jane's, 1975).

100 For London, New York, and Tokyo in historical perspective, see Michael Peter Smith, *Transnational Urbanism: Locating Globalization* (Oxford, UK and Malden, MA: Blackwell, 2001), 48–71.

101 Louis Aragon, *Paris Peasant* (London: Cape, 1961 [first pub. 1926]); Johann Frederich Geist, *Arcades: The History of a Building Type* (Cambridge, MA: MIT Press, 1983), 445–536; Werner Szambien, *De la rue des Colonnes à la rue de Rivoli: Délégation à l'action artistique de la ville de Paris* (Paris: Ville de Paris, 1992).

102 Federico Bucci, *Albert Kahn* (New York: Princeton Architectural Press, 1993); Le

Photocredits

The author and the publisher gratefully acknowledge the following for permission to reproduce material in the book. While every effort has been made to contact copyright holders for their permission to reprint material in this book the publishers would be grateful to hear from any copyright holder who is not acknowledged here and will undertake to rectify any errors or omissions in future editions.

Acknowledgements

No book like *Recombinant Urbanism* is the work of a solitary, isolated author. I owe an enormous intellectual debt to a vast network of friends, fellow students, teachers, and colleagues. Three important teachers stand out from the early days of this network. The first is Philip Whiting, my high-school history master at St. Paul's School, London, and a pioneer local historian of the Annales School (also an expert numismatist and scholar of Byzantium). Whiting released me from the normal British Oxbridge academic path at the tender age of 17 and then helped me find the best architecture school for my further studies. The second is Alvin Boyarsky, who I met in my first year at the Architectural Association as a visiting lecturer in 1963 and whose International Summer Sessions (1969–72) became an essential part of my education. The third is Colin Rowe, an intellectual giant whose generous support of my graduate studies at Cornell in the early 1970s gave me much-needed space to grow, as well as introducing me to a neoclassical tradition of regenerative urban innovation that forms one basis of my idea of "recombinant urbanism."

I have also benefited from talking over many years to a group of distinguished teachers from the Architectural Association. These include Dalibor Veseley, Bob Maxwell, Robin Middleton, Ken Frampton, Dennis Crompton, and the late Sam Stevens and Warren Chalk. My A.A. classmate, the late Robin Evans, was also a great resource and friend.

Since it is impossible to list everyone else whom I would like to thank, I will instead note intellectual milieux that have been particularly important for me. Besides the Architectural Association, Cornell, and the International Summer Sessions mentioned above, Peter Eisenman's Institute for Architectural and Urban Studies formed an important intellectual center in New York in the late 1970s. In the 1980s and 1990s, the Municipal Arts Society of New York, the Architectural League, the Storefront for Art and Architecture, the Skyscraper Museum, and the Van Alen Institute all became places of interest to me.

In addition to my New York base I am fortunate to have a global network of colleagues stretching from Melbourne, Australia, to Tokyo, Japan, and from Aarhus, Denmark, to Istanbul, Turkey. I am especially grateful to friends on the faculties of the graduate urban design programs at the University of Tokyo, the University of Venice, Leuven University in Belgium, and the Bartlett School of Architecture, University College, London. Lecturing in these distinguished urban-design programs around the turn of the century enabled me to develop my ideas further in a friendly seminar setting.

Recombinant Urbanism began as an attempt to record a lecture series entitled "Urban Design Since 1945" that I have taught at various schools. I started this interdisciplinary course at the invitation of Chairman David Leatherbarrow of the University of Pennsylvania in 1988, drawing together students of architecture, urban design, city planning, and landscape. I taught it at Penn for many years, also presenting it at the New Jersey Institute of Technology at the invitation of Dean Urs Gauchat. I began to teach the course in 1991 for Professor Richard Plunz of the Urban Design Program at Columbia University, the following year for the late Dean John Hedjuk at Cooper Union, and finally in 2002 for Professor Michael Sorkin's Graduate Urban Design Program at City College, New York. Over the last two years Dean Anthony Vidler at Cooper Union has been very supportive of my efforts to publish. I owe a debt of gratitude to all these institutions: their deans, chairmen, urban-design faculty, and especially their students, who enabled me to conduct my research in a sympathetic setting.

The translation from lecture notes to book proved to not be a simple task. Every time I completed the Introduction, I realized I had not defined an important concept or aspect of urban design. As result, I began the Introduction three times and eventually saw I had three separate chapters. Early in this struggle I had editorial support from Catherine Crompton and two wonderful research assistants, Renia Markoianniki and Osamu Hoshino, who introduced me to Japanese urbanism. Two friends—Richard Ingersoll, who had been the editor of *Design Book Review*, and Zenip Celnik, the distinguished urban historian and editor of the *Journal of the Society of Architectural Historians*—read my early manuscript. They helped me realize that I was writing a text with its own independent logic, and that logic demanded a fourth chapter. The book then took on a life of its own, apart from the lectures.

Two other friends—Michael Sorkin and my colleague from Columbia, Brian McGrath—read the resulting document two years later. Their enthusiastic encouragement gave me the strength to continue. Thanks to Zenip Celnik's recommendation I received a grant from the Columbia University City Seminar Fund that enabled me to work for 18 months with an excellent freelance editor, Larry Gilman. In addition I am grateful to Richard Solomons and the Graham Foundation of Chicago for financial assistance in the production of this book. The Graham Foundation's timely grant enabled me to hire very capable assistants who had begun as volunteers: Adam Lubinsky and Monica Tiulescu (permissions and photo acquisitions), Rodrigo Gardia Dall'Orso (city drawings), and Irene Vallye (graphic design).

I am especially grateful to Nicholas Boyarsky for introducing me to the editorial team at Wiley-Academy in London. It was like a homecoming to return to Academy and *Architectural Design* magazine, where editor Monica Pidgeon had given me my first journalistic assignment in the early 1970s. I thank my current editor Helen Castle, assistant editor Famida Rasheed, and project editor Mariangela Palazzi-Williams, all of whom have helped my progress through the production process, improving the book by their efforts at every stage.

Finally I owe an enormous debt to my family, without whose support I could never have completed this book. My parents, wife, and children have all endured my long absences and periods of abstraction, burnt toast and missed appointments. I am deeply grateful to them all, but especially to my wife, Regina Wickham, and to our children, Ben, Rachael, and Michael, who rallied around to help me prepare material for the publishers, turning our dining room into a temporary production facility.